The Chicago Way

By

Don Herion

The Chicago Way

∞

By
Don Herion

Copyright © 2010 by Don Herion.

ISBN: Hardcover   978-1-4500-1639-1
         Softcover   978-1-4500-1638-4

All rights reserved. No part of this book may be reproduced or transmitted in any form or by any means, electronic or mechanical, including photocopying, recording, or by any information storage and retrieval system, without permission in writing from the copyright owner.

This book was printed in the United States of America.

To order additional copies of this book, contact:
Xlibris Corporation
1-888-795-4274
www.Xlibris.com
Orders@Xlibris.com

DEDICATION

To my wife Gen, and our six children, Patrick, Nancy, Don, Tom, Jayne and Mary Ann. Writing on a computer is really nice if you know how to use it properly. It was necessary for me to get assistance from them all to learn about margins, indents, toolbars, scanning and a hundred other things. Their assistance on some of my undercover investigations was invaluable. On occasion I had to do some things that were quite legal but some people would call it vigilantism, "if that's a word?" But I managed to get the job done and the bad guys went to jail.

#1 REVIEW:

Don Herion has given me the OK to reveal this: he has been one of my primary sources for Organized Crime intelligence during 30 years of reporting on the Outfit in Chicago. Don's wealth of knowledge and breadth of experience always add up to one thing: credibility. If Herion says it, then it happened that way. He knows the ins and outs of the outfit better than any Grand Avenue racketeer…and he knows the over and under of Chicago better than any Rush St. bookie.
Don Herion knows THE CHICAGO WAY…because he's lived it.
–Chuck Goudie
–Investigative Reporter
ABC-7 News

#2 REVIEW:

Don Herion is the top expert on the Chicago Outfit's gambling operations and has made over 4,000 raids in his career and locked up hundreds of mobsters. His first book, Pay, Quit, or Die described how the outfit operated in the Chicago area. The Chicago Way follows more stories about Organized Crime including numerous gangland murders. This is really The Chicago Way.

–John Drummond
–Inducted into journalism
Hall of Fame 1997.

#3 REVIEW:

I am not a literary expert by any means, my name is Bob and I'm a barber. I wish to remain anonymous for obvious reasons. I know Don Herion and I have his book, Pay, Quit, or Die. I found the book to be a great read about the Chicago Outfit and how they operate. The book is in my shop and a lot of my customers pick it up and read it when I'm trying to cut their hair. Most of them have glasses on and can't read without them, so they tell me to cut around them because they want to keep reading the book. Herion has written another book called **THE CHICAGO WAY**, this one describes great stories and tells about 150 gangland murders in Chicago. I think I'll keep this one in the back room.

–Bob the Barber
–N/W Side

INTRODUCTION

He never intended on writing a book, let alone two books it kind of just happened. One day he started writing about a few incidents he was involved in when he was on the Chicago Police Department in uniform and in plain clothes. The first six years on the job was spent in uniform and the last forty were in plain clothes. Eight of those years were with the Cook County Sheriff where he was the Director of a vice unit busting up illegal mob operations.

Pay, Quit or Die was the name of his first book which was about 63 stories involving the Chicago outfit and how they operate. 559 pages describing mob operations in the Chicago area and how they conducted their illegal enterprises like gambling, loan-sharking and narcotics. Some of the raids against these operations had to be accomplished by vigilante methods.

His next book, "The Chicago Way," has the same meaning as "Pay Quit, or Die." It describes how Detective Sergeant Don Herion spent 40 of his 46 years in law enforcement fighting the Chicago outfit using whatever means it took to get the job done.

The mobs income from gambling was their main source of revenue which financed other illegal operations like juice loans, narcotics, prostitution and porno shops.

1.

By the time he retired he effected more then 4,000 raids, arrested hundreds of mobsters and disrupted the outfits illegal operations. Herion explains a few facts about working as a cop. Most people are of the opinion that informants area always calling the police and reporting illegal mob operations. "Forget about it." I only wish that were true, but the sad truth of the matter is if you work on organized crime you had better get out in the street and rattle some people who are connected to the mob.

After you harass and lock up a few associates of the outfit and threaten to terminate their little operation, whatever it may be, like taking a few horse bets or dealing in football parlay cards they will want you to get off their backs. Some of them will cooperate with you and some won't. he had a great deal of success getting information from small time gamblers who actually trusted him with their lives.

But make no mistake; working on the outfit calls for working ungodly hours, you have to work when they work, weekends, holidays or whatever it takes to get the job done. Mob guys meet in bars, restaurants, car washes, shopping malls, golf courses, health clubs and toll ways. Whatever it takes you have to cover them, if you want to get the job done. Don Herion did whatever it took, he got the job done. "The Chicago Way" describes over 160 gangland murders, who, why, how and where they were whacked.

ACKNOWLEDGMENTS

I would like to thank my wife Gen for putting up with me while I was fumbling around on a computer trying put together some stories about being a cop for 46 years. This was my second book about the Chicago Outfit and some of my adventures as a cop in uniform when I was "Joe the new guy." "Pay, Quit, or Die," was the first.

I must admit being an Austin high school graduate who barely passed English showed up while I was scrambling around on my computer. I drove a lot of people goofy that were trying to explain the way to do margins, scan photos, send e-mails, undo and redo, delete and numerous other basic things. I can only hope that I followed their advice correctly, my saviors are listed below.

My son's Don, Tom and Pat, were very patient with my screw-ups and didn't holler at me when I fowled up. My daughters Nancy, Jayne and Mary who were helpful with proper English, involving nouns, adverbs and adjectives, correct place for a comma or whatever.

Former Chicago vice detective Virgil Mikus could have written his own book. A great deal of technical help also came from Mike Boehmer, Jesse Guiterrez and John Kaprales. Of course I have to thank all the cops I worked with over the years tormenting the outfit's illegal operations. Carlo Cangelosi, Bob Peters, John Spellman, Frank Kelly, E. Kolerich, R. Kirby, Ray DelPilar, Jim

Brennan, T. Beck, Bill Mundee and Phil DiPasquale. I.R.S. agents Tom Moriarity and Bill Desmond. There are others to numerous to mention because of a bad memory.

Contents

1. Introduction..9
2. Acknowledgments..11
3. The Chicago Way...15
4. Traffic Tickets – What a Pain..19
5. Our Lady of the Angels Disaster...25
6. Election Day and Cops..33
7. Vinnie...36
8. Suicide is Final...39
9. The Dead Get Robbed Too...42
10. You're Under Arrest, Now What?..45
11. Arrest Procedure..52
12. Surviving Prison...54
13. Prison Violations..58
14. Disciplinary Rules of Indiana State Prison...............................59
15. Louis Tragas – One of a Kind...62
16. Martin Luther King Jr. Assassinated – Chicago Burns...........71
17. The Bell Brand Ranch Scam – Chambers, Arizona................78
18. Horse Race Wire Service...87
19. Jiggers, the Cops!...91
20. Angel-Kaplan *Sports News Inc.*..97

21.	The Friendly Card Game	104
22.	Richard "Dick" Cain	108
23.	Sam Giancana and the Rosemont Hotel	113
24.	Mafia Initiation Rites	119
25.	Ken "Tokyo Joe" Eto	124
26.	Casinos	131
27.	The Japanese Mafia – Yakuza	137
28.	Roger "The Dodger" Riccio	143
29.	Gregory "Emmett" Paloian – The Paper Eater	155
30.	Undercover Methods	163
31.	Video Poker Machines	176
32.	The Chicago Dungeon	186
33.	The Corporation	194
34.	Mario "Motts" Tonelli – American Hero	203
35.	Ronald W. Jarrett – Kill and Be Killed	213
36.	The Gambler	219
37.	Anthony "Tony the Hatch" Chiaramonti	226
38.	Joseph "Jerry" Scalise	230
39.	**Public Enemies** – Technical Advisor	235
40.	The Execution of Mike Norton	248
41.	Some of the Alleged Mob Guys We Busted As Well As Their Associates	253
42.	Gangland Murders: 1961-1992	261
43.	The Fat Lady is Singing	322
44.	Index	329

The Chicago Way

The cover of this book tells one of two things, maybe someone has a flat tire or maybe there is a dead body in the trunk. In this case, we have a body in the trunk. The victim was a man by the name of Leo Foreman, male, white, forty-two years old, an ex-convict, a real estate agent, and of course, a juice loan collector for Sam "Mad Sam" DeStefano.

Sam DeStefano was a member of Sam "Momo" Giancana's West Side Forty-two Gang, a gang which was made up of an assortment of thieves, killers, and bootleggers. By the 1960s, DeStefano moved up in the Chicago Outfit from petty hoodlum to a major force in Chicago's loan-sharking and drug-trafficking rackets. His brother Mario joined him in the juice loan business in which violence is used to force payments from debtors.

DeStefano became known as a vicious executioner; he was known to use his favorite tool, an ice pick. DeStefano used ice picks to stab his victims in the throat, testicles, and torso to squeeze payments out of them or as foreplay to murder. Sam lived near North Avenue and Sayre in a nice brick house; he was married and had three children. Sam's basement was soundproof for good reason because that was where Sam kept all his torture tools. One victim of Sam's was Arthur Adler, a local restaurant owner who made the mistake of being late making his payments. Sam had Adler brought to his basement where

Sam began using Adler as a pincushion with his ice pick; Adler had a heart attack and died while Sam was sticking him. Adler's body was dumped in a nearby sewer near North Sayre Avenue where he stayed until the spring thaw. The Department of Sanitation got a call in the spring about a backed-up sewer, and that's where Adler's punctured corpse was found.

When Sam's boss, Sam Giancana, ordered the hit of DeStefano's younger brother Michael, Sam made the hit without blinking an eye. When he was questioned about Michael's murder in 1955, DeStefano refused to answer any questions; instead he giggled uncontrollably. The more the investigators questioned Sam, the more he laughed. Sam, with the help of his other brother Mario, killed Michael who was a drug addict. The fact that Michael was a dope fiend bothered DeStefano. Therefore, he and Mario took great pains to cleanse their brother's corpse of drugs before dumping the body in the trunk of a car.

Leo Foreman of 4817 North Neva Avenue, was reported to be president of the LeFore Insurance Company at 7050 West Belmont Avenue. Police records showed that Foreman had been arrested twenty times since August 1939. The charges included passing worthless checks, forgery, confidence game, and embezzlement. In 1955, he was sentenced to a year and a day in Joliet prison. His last arrest was for impersonating a bail bondsman; he had been a bondsman in the past and used other aliases, including Leo Wilson and Leo Seymour Foreman.

Sam DeStefano was a prime suspect in Foreman's murder because Foreman was employed by Sam as a juice loan collector. One day in November 1963, DeStefano paid Foreman a visit in Foreman's real estate office, and Sam started an argument. The quarrel ended with Foreman throwing Sam out of the office. Foreman was later lured to the Cicero home of Sam's brother Mario by Tony Spilotro and Chuckie Crimaldi. Foreman went on the false pretense that Sam wanted to kiss and make up about their earlier argument. Once in the house, Leo was coaxed into the basement where he was grabbed and tied up by Spilotro, Mario DeStefano, and Crimaldi. The three of them proceeded to beat up Foreman to get him ready for Mad Sam DeStefano's arrival. Foreman was beaten with a hammer on the knees and about the head, ribs, and crotch.

When Sam arrived, he applied his normal technique with his ice pick, stabbing Leo twenty times. When Foreman had been sufficiently wounded, a pajama-clad DeStefano began giggling like a madman, telling Foreman, "I told you I would get you." Foreman pleaded for his life as DeStefano shot him in both buttocks. DeStefano's crew watched Foreman bleed and whimper for a while before torturing him to death with a butcher knife. DeStefano and his crew then took turns cutting chunks of flesh from Foreman's arms. Foreman's body was found in the trunk of the car he had rented in February 1963 from Courtesy Motor company in the name of the LeFore company. He had rented it for two years and it was equipped with a telephone. The vehicle had been parked at 5204 West Gladys Avenue, Chicago, Illinois. The body was dressed in underclothing with the undershirt pulled over the head. Only one leg of the trousers remained on the body. After a closer observation of the trunk, the police did not find any blood, which indicated that Foreman had been killed elsewhere; no other clothing was found.

Foreman's murder would come back to haunt Mad Sam in later years. In 1972, the FBI convinced Chuck Crimaldi to be a government witness. The DeStefano brothers Sam and Mario and Tony Spilotro were indicted for the murder of Leo Foreman on the evidence given by Crimaldi. The three of them were incarcerated pending the trial, which was set for May 1973. At the pretrial, Sam DeStefano made a circus of the proceedings, acting as his own attorney. Sam began to alienate the judge and jury. Making the trial such a high-profile media event was an obvious mistake. It would be very hard to influence the judge and jury with bribes or other forms of corruption if the trial was front-page news. So Mario and Spilotro devised a plan to keep Sam quiet for good.

Mario, Sam, and Tony Spilotro had been charged with the November 19, 1963, murder of loan shark Leo Foreman. Mario was eventually convicted in the Foreman murder and sentenced to twenty to forty years in prison. Spilotro was acquitted. While out on bail during the trial, Sam was murdered in his garage. Police considered Mario and Spilotro to be suspects in Sam's murder, but the two men were never charged. On July 9, 1975, Mario's sentence was overturned by the Illinois Appellate Court. While awaiting retrial, Mario DeStefano died on August 12, 1975, of a heart attack.

George "Bugs" Moran (middle no-tie) survived St. Valentines Day Massacre February 14th 1929, because he was late arriving for meeting at location of execution.

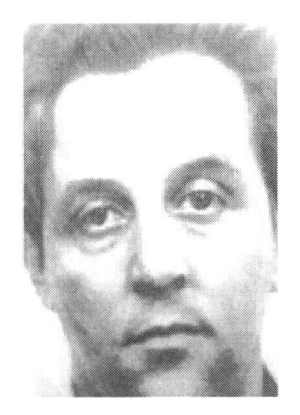

(from Left to Right) Leo Foreman, Sam DeStefano, and Tony Spilotro.

Traffic Tickets—What a Pain

Every police officer is issued a traffic summons book when he is assigned to a district. The supervisors have what we used to call a quota on tickets issued. When an officer is assigned to the traffic division, he is expected to write at least eight moving violations a shift. But that is all he has to do; he doesn't handle any crime scenes or domestic disturbances or whatever else comes along. On occasion, he has to handle a traffic accident, but that's about all. Don't get me wrong. I hated to write tickets, especially moving violations like red lights, speeding, or no left turn. Parking tickets were also a pain in the ass; all they accomplish is that the poor soul that gets the ticket now hates you.

I guess that they are a necessity though, and maybe in some way they help keep drivers from getting too crazy behind the wheel of their car or truck. Personally, I would rather be out in the street locking up bad guys and harassing gang bangers. Some of these traffic guys really like working traffic, giving out their quota of summons, and putting a few drunk drivers in jail before they kill somebody or themselves.

People that get stopped by the police for a traffic violation really come up with some original excuses. I remember an elderly lady that we stopped for driving the wrong way on a one-way street. This violation is usually an open-and-shut case. When I asked her for her driver's license and explained why we had stopped her, she called me a liar and asked why wasn't I out chasing down dope dealers or communists instead of bothering a woman alone in a car trying to get home.

No matter what I said to her, she had a look of hate in her eyes; and if she had a gun, she would have shot me dead. When I began opening the summons book to write her the ticket, she pulled an acting job on me that was a beauty. The first thing she did was to roll her eyes up in her head and then grab her heart like she was going to have a heart attack right there. Well, needless to say, she hit the right button and her act worked. Even though I knew she was probably faking it, I didn't want to take a chance of her dropping dead in front of me. I asked her if she needed an ambulance or wanted to be taken to the nearest hospital. She said that she only lived two blocks from there and that her heart pills were in her bathroom. She explained that if she got them, she was sure to be OK. Well, at this point, I was pretty aggravated and couldn't imagine myself giving this wacky broad mouth-to-mouth resuscitation if she was telling the truth. Of course, I told her that we would be glad to drive her home if she couldn't drive. She said no, that she felt better, and she thought that she could drive home OK.

I said, "OK, lady, under the circumstances, I won't give you a ticket this time but that you had better be more alert in the future." I just knew that I made this old broad's day when she thought she really bullshitted me about the heart attack. To top it off, when she was driving away, she winked at me and said, "Thanks, Officer, have a nice day."

The best part of all is when I got back in the squad car, my partner Bob was just shaking his head and laughing. It seems that he had stopped this old witch in the past for doing the same thing and she pulled the heart attack routine on him too. He admitted that he didn't want to take a chance and have the old broad drop dead on him either and gave her a pass. The thing that got him was when her eyes went up in her head and all he could see was the whites of her eyes. Later on, we talked to a few of the other guys that were working in that part of the district, and they all had stopped her for doing the same thing, driving the wrong way on a one-way street. They all witnessed her heart attack routine, and none of them gave her a ticket. I thought, your day will come, you old bitty. Not only will I give her a ticket, but I'll also tow her car.

I'm reminded of another traffic story that was really good. This man and woman were traveling at a very high rate of speed north on Lake Shore Drive, about thirty miles per hour over the limit. It was foggy out, and the street was very slick from a misty rain that had been falling. The purple Mercedes they were in was brand new, and the sales sticker was still on the window. The man was driving with one hand on the wheel, but the other hand was waving around in the car and even turned into a fist on occasion. The female could also be seen pointing a finger at the man. She even slapped the man on the back of his head.

These actions could be seen as their car was being pulled over to the side of the road. When the car stopped, the man driving the car immediately got out and rushed up to the officer getting out of the squad car. The man had his hands in front of him, palm to palm. He pleaded with the officer to please arrest him and put the cuffs on him because he knew that he was speeding and should be put in jail. The man explained that his wife was driving him crazy and was upset because he forbade her to smoke in their new car. It seemed that she was a chain-smoker and the car they just traded in smelled and had burn holes all over the seat from her dropping ashes.

The man kept pleading with the officer to arrest him so he could get away from his bitchy wife for a few hours. At this point, the officer spoke to the wife and explained that her husband was very upset and that he might have to arrest him for speeding and tow the car as well. This information seemed to calm her down. She started copping a plea about the way she had acted and swore that she would never try to smoke in the car again. She asked if he would have mercy on her husband.

The officer then returned to the husband and told him that he was not going to get a ticket, be arrested, or handcuffed. He would have to go home with his wife and that would be punishment enough for one day. The man then told the officer, "This is not America anymore. I can't even get arrested for breaking the law." He said he was moving to Australia as soon as he could.

It's amazing to me how much people hate to get a traffic ticket; they would rather have you beat the hell out of them, I think. The Chicago Police Department had a bad reputation years ago. It was rumored that whenever you would get stopped by the police for a traffic violation, you could pay off the cop and he would let you go. All you had to do was have some money clipped to your driver's license, and when the cop asked to see your license, he would remove the money and give your license back to you with a warning to be more careful in the future. If that type of thing happened on occasion, I never witnessed it. There are probably some cops out there that would risk losing their job and maybe even go to jail for a few bucks, but the old saying is "Don't do the crime if you can't do the time."

Once while working on street tracking and trailing some outfit guy, I violated more traffic laws in one day than the average citizen did in his lifetime. Tailing a bad guy is an art all by itself. I had five undercover cars with car-to-car radios all set up to follow this one juice guy who was going to meet his boss, Rocky Infelise. We set up on this goof at 5:00 AM just to make sure that we wouldn't miss him. He left his house about 7:45 AM and got in his car and just sat there for ten minutes, looking up and down the street. Next, a woman in jogging clothes came out of the house and began running down the street. In a few minutes, the same woman ran up to the juice guy's car and talked to him for a minute. She proceeded to sit on her porch while the bad guy left. His wife or girlfriend was watching for any cars that might start following him. If she spotted any squad cars in the area, she would call him on a mobile telephone and warn him of the heat.

It was lucky that we had a lot of experience with these mutts in the past, and we were ready for any trickery that he might pull on us. I had one vehicle that had what we call the eye on the bad guy's car, and he kept us informed of when the bad guy left his house. He was under orders that when the subject left his house, he was not to follow him under any circumstances. His job was to tell us when he got in his car and which direction he was headed. Being a weekday around 8:00 AM, there was a lot of traffic on the street with a lot of people going to work. It was going to be a bitch to stay with this guy. The key to this type of police work is not to be seen by the subject; of course, if he notices you, the show is over and all you did was cause a lot of heat and waste your time. Naturally, this guy is going to drive down alleys and pull in gas stations where you have to set up on his car all over again. Basically, you don't know which way he is going to leave the gas station. This mutt loved to pull into a left-turn lane with his signal on and then make a U-turn and go back in the same direction he came from. Well, believe me, I had to drive in an erratic manner at times just to keep this guy in view. I, was always concerned about the police stopping me or one of the other guys that had the lead tail on the subject because that would blow the tail for the day.

It just so happened that I had the eye on the subject who was speeding down Western Avenue. I had a couple of cars between him and me. I knew that he didn't make me out, and we were getting close to him meeting with Rocky. Sure as shit, the next thing I saw in my rearview was blue lights. I hoped that he was after somebody else. Forget about it, the next thing was the siren and the loudspeaker blaring for me to pull over. I tried waving the squad car up so that I could show him my star, but the cop wouldn't go for that. He was on the radio probably reporting that he was in a chase and that I wouldn't stop. I guess that I couldn't really blame him because he was just doing his job. How the hell was he supposed to know that I was a cop tailing somebody?

When I decided to pull over, I got out of the car with my star in my hand. I told him that I was in the middle of an investigation and that the car I was driving was an unmarked squad car. I had notified my other partners that I had been stopped by the police and to try and pick up the subject who was way ahead of me by this time.

Being a little upset at the time, I told the traffic officer that I was leaving and to stick his ticket book up his ass. With that, I jumped back in my squad and took off after the rest of my crew, hoping that they picked the subject up somewhere ahead of me. As luck would have it, there was a construction zone up ahead and our juice man got stuck in the middle of it, so we were able to continue our surveillance. We tailed our guy to a restaurant in Cicero across from the racetrack. As things turned out, we missed Infelise, but we grabbed our juice man when he met another mutt from Taylor Street. They both had juice records and over $40,000 in cash.

I started to think of the traffic cop that stopped me. When I thought about all the violations I committed during this surveillance, I just shook my head. As close as I could recall, I went through three red lights, I was speeding, made four illegal U-turns, and drove the wrong way on a one-way street. Needless to say, a truck going through one of the red lights almost hit me. However, I didn't lose the dope I was following, and he never made the tail. Now how stupid is that? I could have hit somebody or maybe gotten hit myself, and I would have been in the wrong. But at the time, it seems common sense leaves your head and all that matters is getting the job done no matter what.

In almost every squad, there is one man who develops a reputation as a traffic cop who turns in large numbers of movers, but his zeal is not an embarrassment or an annoyance to less-productive partners. His actions are usually attributed to a lack of interest or courage for "real police work," and he is allowed to go his own way. Patrolmen have little regard for this kind of work because movers are so easy to get and frequently the people they stop may argue or fight. But each man is expected to write some every month. The easiest place to find traffic violators is at an intersection. Usually he selects a corner with a traffic light or a stop sign. Impatient drivers often choose to run lights or slow down at a stop sign but never stop. There is always one word on each patrolman's mind, *activity* for the sergeant. How can a man who has handled fourteen assignments from the radio dispatcher listen patiently to complaints, drive his squad through clogged and steamy streets, and say he has no activity? The sergeant judges his men by their productivity, which includes traffic tickets issued on their tour of duty as well as the jobs they handled. It is possible that a patrolman gets tied up on some assignments and doesn't have the time to write any tickets. At the end of each tour, the sergeant signs off his men, examines their patrol logs, and enters into his notebook the activity each man produced during the tour. There are separate categories for parking tickets, moving violations, and juveniles who violate the city's curfew ordinance. If he stops a pedestrian or a motor vehicle, he is supposed to file a report, giving details of why he stopped them.

The lieutenant is interested in how his sergeant is handling his men, the captain is interested in how the lieutenant is handling his sergeants, and of course, the superintendent's office is interested in how the captain is handling his watch. I guess the fact of the matter is, tickets are a fact of life on the police department and that will never change.

Our Lady of the Angels Disaster

When I reported to work on December 1, 1958, for the four-to-twelve shift, the weather was clear, but cold. It was less than twenty degrees outside. I didn't have any idea of what I was in for that day. It turned out to be the worst day of my life. It was the day that ninety-two schoolchildren died in a fire at Our Lady of the Angels Catholic grade school. Three nuns also perished trying to help the children that were trapped in the smoke and flames that terrible day. The fire started at about 2:45 PM and spread throughout the school so rapidly that a lot of the victims were still in their classrooms. Some of the students even leaped out of windows to escape the smoke and flames only to be badly injured.

As soon as my partner Bob Peters and I reported for roll call, we were sent directly to the scene of the fire at 909 North Avers Avenue. The school was still burning, and we were told to help in any way that we could. When we got in the area of the school, it was complete chaos; fire trucks, ambulances, paddy wagons, and squad cars were all over. Traffic was at a complete standstill, except for the ambulances and wagons that were taking burn victims to the hospital or morgue. Parents of schoolchildren that had not come home from school were trying to get in the building to try and find them. Some parents who did find their children burned or injured took them to the hospital themselves because most of the emergency vehicles were filled.

The mayor of Chicago, Richard J. Daley, was also on the scene of the disaster to offer any assistance and to make sure that everything that could be done was done. My partner and I were told to report to Father Joe and to assist him. Father Joe was Reverend Joseph Ognibene. He was thirty-two years old and had been ordained May 1, 1952. He had rescued several children from the fire and had been burned in the process.

When Father Joe asked us if we would take him to the Cook County Morgue, he appeared to be near collapse. He told us that he was to report to Monsignor Pellicore to assist in the identification of the victims of the fire. We could tell by the look on his face that he dreaded this assignment as much as we did. He asked us if we could stay with him through the identification process and help him comfort the grieving parents and relatives of the victims.

Father Joe told us that Our Lady of the Angels had been his first parish assignment after he was ordained. As we got closer to the morgue, Father Joe told us about all the happy times he had at the school. But now, all he could think about was the horror he had witnessed and the little victims that had been killed. It was only going to get worse as we were about to enter a world that would leave us with greater nightmares. When we arrived at the morgue, a policeman was standing guard at the basement door He was stationed there to prevent parents and relatives of the victims from entering a large room where bodies were on stretchers covered with white sheets. There were priests, nuns, as well as doctors, nurses, detectives, and morgue attendants. The unmistakable stench of death was everywhere.

Father Joe had known many of the students, and the monsignor asked him if he would try and identify some of the kids before the parents and relatives were let in. Bob and I accompanied Father Joe and two nuns from the parish as they checked the bodies one by one. The white sheets that were covering them were pulled back so that they could try and recognize someone. The process took a very long time as the bodies were almost totally black from soot and burns. When it was over and they had viewed all the remains, only ten of the victims could be identified. A nurse saw Father Joe rubbing his left arm, and when she asked him to roll up his sleeve, she found that his arm was covered with blood and blisters. He was taken across the street to the Cook County Hospital emergency room where he was treated for his wounds.

When we returned to the morgue, Father Joe was told that his brother, who was also a priest, was looking for him and wanted him to call home and talk to his mother to tell her that he was alive. It appeared that the news had reported he had been killed in the fire. Some reporters and photographers were taking pictures of the bodies that were on the floor. Coroner McCarron was present and directing his people as to what to do. At one point, a photographer asked McCarron if he would pose for a picture with one of the victims. He readily walked over to a body and lifted the sheet halfway off the victim. He asked the photographer if this pose was OK as he stared at the body of a small child who was the color of charcoal. I didn't like McCarron doing that; it just seemed to be out of line, but I guess he had to cooperate with the press. McCarron was an elected county official, a wealthy trucking executive from Oak Park who had a reputation as a slick politician and well schooled in the art of politics. He had no background for the coroner's office and no training as a medical examiner.

On occasion, he would view a homicide victim, but he was unprepared for the difficult task ahead of him. When McCarron approached Monsignor Pellicore who told him that they had prepared for a hundred bodies and were ready to let the parents come downstairs all at once, the monsignor thought for a moment. It would be unwise to do that, he told McCarron, because he knew Italian families and to let them down all at once would cause a riot. McCarron agreed and told the monsignor, "All right, whatever you think is best."

I overheard some of the parents of the victims saying that this was an act of God to pay back some of the Mafia people in the neighborhood who had children that went to the school. They said that the Mafia was evil and God would punish anyone associated with them.

The nuns and nurses who tried to console grieving parents broke down and cried as did newsmen and policemen. The officials decided to allow only men in the basement to view the victims; nothing would have prepared them for what they were about to encounter.

They were first taken into an anteroom where they were asked to identify a wristwatch, necklace, ring, or a piece of underwear. Then they were escorted into the holding area where there were rows of white sheets. The sheets were pulled back to reveal a body. Screams could be heard when they confirmed the findings. One father wasn't sure if the body he was looking at was his nine-year-old daughter; he had to call his wife at home to see if the girl had worn a red ruby ring that day. She did.

An ID bracelet made of sterling silver that was found on his right wrist identified a nine-year-old boy. When the fire was first discovered, he had escaped the school but ran back inside in search of his younger sister; he didn't know that she had been safely evacuated.

Morgue attendants had laid the recognizable bodies in one row. Bodies that appeared to be beyond recognition were laid out in another row. Pieces of clothing and jewelry were removed from each victim and given a corresponding number. The approximate age of a boy or girl was recorded as well as what they were wearing. The identification process went on all night and into the next morning. It was a morbid sight watching a steady stream of hearses pull up to the back door of the morgue to pick up the dead bodies and take them to local funeral homes. Bob and I were relieved from duty in the morning, and on the way back to the district, we didn't say anything to each other. When I got home, my wife asked me a few questions about the fire. I just looked at her and shook my head. She reminded me that I didn't talk for four days after the fire. In December 1961, an anonymous letter was sent to the Cicero Fire Department that identified a thirteen-year-old boy who was setting fires in apartment buildings. This information was given to police lieutenant Victor Witt and youth officer Ron Richards for investigation. Their investigation revealed that this boy had been seen at several fires that were suspected arsons in Cicero. Upon interrogating him, he confessed to setting the fires. Further investigation of the boy revealed that at one time, he had attended Our Lady of the Angels School in the late '50s. The boy and his mother lived on Springfield Avenue several blocks from the school. Upon checking the attendance records of December 1, 1958, they showed that the boy was ten years old and was in the fifth grade assigned to room 206.

The Cicero police notified Chicago police sergeant Drew Brown of the Bomb and Arson Unit, and he took over the investigation of the boy. Further investigation of the boy revealed that he did admit that he set the fire. He had asked his teacher if he could be excused to go to the washroom. After he went to the washroom, he went into the chapel, which was in the basement, to see if anyone was around.

Finding it empty, he walked back to a round cardboard can filled with papers underneath the stairs. He said that he lit three matches and threw them into the can and watched the flames for an instant. He then returned to his room. The boy's statement covered eight typewritten pages, which was signed by four witnesses. The boy's stepfather and mother were given a copy of the statement. They were quite upset. The parents were informed that despite the boy's confession, he could not be charged with a crime because the law stipulates that a juvenile under the age of thirteen was "incapable of committing a crime" and could not be held criminally liable until he reached the age of thirteen. The boy was ten years old at the time of the school fire; therefore he was immune from prosecution.

Cook County state attorney Daniel P. Ward decided to file a delinquency petition in family court, charging the boy with the three fires he was alleged to have set in Cicero, Illinois. He also indicated that he was going to file a second petition charging the boy with the Our Lady of the Angels fire, even though he knew the Illinois Criminal Code forbade the conviction of any person under the age of thirteen at the time of the committed offense. By charging the boy, officials were hopeful that a judicial ruling could find the boy responsible for the school fire, the cause of which was still listed as "undetermined," and thereby lay the mystery to rest.

Meanwhile, Judge Cilella ordered him to be examined by a court-appointed psychiatrist who, along with three consulting psychiatrists, agreed that the boy was aware and had full knowledge of the nature of the proceedings initiated against him and was capable of cooperating with his attorneys. He was not mentally defective or psychotic.

When the case was heard in family court, the young suspect, on the advice of his attorneys, entered pleas of not guilty to all counts and denied that he had ever started any fires. John Reid, who took the confession from the boy, was called as a witness and told the court that he was convinced the boy was telling the truth when he described how he had set fire to Our Lady of the Angels School. A defense attorney, John Cogan, objected to Reid's statements, stating that the confession obtained by Reid was involuntary and under color of coercion. Other witnesses from the Chicago fire and police departments introduced evidence in court and testified that in their opinion, the school fire started exactly where the boy said he had set the fire.

At the final court session, the boy was called to the witness stand; and under questioning by Cogan, he recanted his confession that he had set fire to the school. He said that he signed the confession after Reid told him that if he did so, he could go home. He said he was frightened and tired

On March 13, 1962, Judge Cilella rendered his decision. He concluded that "upon the evidence before it, the court did not have an abiding conviction that the boy set the Our Lady of the Angels fire. Such being the case, the court will not burden this child with the judicial determination that he is responsible for that tragedy." For setting the fires in Cicero, Judge Cilella ordered the boy sent to the Star Commonwealth boy's center in Michigan. There the boy received psychiatric treatment to help cure him of his fetish for starting fires. He remained at the center until his release in 1965, when he entered military service and was sent to Vietnam.

OBITUARIES

REV. JOSEPH OGNIBENE, 77

Saved pupils in Our Lady of Angels fire

By Angela Rozas
Tribune staff reporter

The Catholic priest who helped to rescue many children in the 1958 fire at Our Lady of the Angels School didn't like to talk about the experience.

Humble and emotionally scarred by the fire that claimed the lives of 92 children and three nuns, Rev. Joseph Ognibene downplayed his role in the rescue.

"You would never know that he was a hero, the way that he talked and how he did his work," his brother Gene Ognibene said.

"He just said it was a part of his job. He was very concerned always about the people who lost their lives. Those were children he baptized."

Father Ognibene, 77, died of cancer Friday, Dec. 19, in St. Colette Church parish in Rolling Meadows.

At age 32, "Father Joe" was an associate pastor at Our Lady of the Angels.

He ran into the school after seeing smoke, according to a book about the fire, "To Sleep with the Angels," published in 1996.

He helped to lead children to safety, either by directing them down stairs or carrying them.

Accounts of the fire describe how he and Sam Tortorice, a neighbor, swung students trapped in one classroom out of the window to an adjoining classroom.

After the fire, Father Ognibene was asked to identify victims at the morgue and later spent a lot of time in hospitals with the injured, victims recalled.

"I would wake up in the middle of the night, and he'd be standing in the doorway, looking over me," said Luciana Mordini Kuziw, who was 11 when she was injured in the fire. "He was an amazing man, always there for us and for the other families."

Father Ognibene grew up in Portage Park, the second of five children.

He was ordained in 1952, Gene Ognibene said.

After leaving Our Lady of the Angels in 1961, he served as associate pastor at several churches, including Our Lady Help of Christians, St. Ferdinand Church, St. Francis of Rome Church.

In 1973 he became pastor of St. Beatrice Church in Schiller Park in 1973.

In 1983, he was named pastor of Our Lady Mother of the Church, where he led a massive renovation and was known for his outreach to invalids, said Rev. Dan Fallon, the church's current pastor.

The fire left its mark, though, as Father Ognibene didn't allow many candles in the church, he said.

Father Ognibene retired to Rolling Meadows in 1996.

He is also survived by a sister, Agnes Love. Visitation is scheduled from 2 to 9 p.m. Monday in Our Lady Mother of the Church, 8747 W. Lawrence Ave. Mass will be said at 10 a.m. Tuesday in the church.

Sheet-covered bodies awaited identification at the Cook County Morgue (above)

Election Day and Cops

Before I went on the job, I really never thought much about election day in Chicago. I would vote at the polling place in my precinct, and that would be that. I did recall seeing a Chicago policeman at the polling place, but I thought maybe he was voting or visiting someone. Well, I was in for a surprise. I was informed the day before the election that I had been detailed to a polling place on the east end of the district. The hours were from 6:00 AM to 6:00 PM, I was to report at 5:30 AM. It seems that on election day about four thousand uniformed police officers were assigned to polling places throughout Chicago. The reason for this was to prevent electioneering and the chance that some ghost votes may appear. I was also told that I was to prevent any of the judges or precinct captains from assisting voters in the voting booths unless the voter requested assistance.

My sergeant told me that I would be relieved for two hours during the day by a relief officer so that I would also have an opportunity to vote. The polling place I was assigned to was in the basement of a house. I knew that was not good because they do not have voting machines in basements, only ballot boxes. Paper ballots are a pain in the neck because they have to be counted individually, which takes a long time. There were three Democratic judges and three Republican judges seated at a table with voter registration books in front of them. All of the judges were female and appeared to be from sixty-five to eighty years old and looked like they took their job very seriously.

I noticed that they all had different colored hair – purple, blonde, black, brown, blue, and white. Their job was to check the voters who came in to vote by cross-checking their names and addresses to make sure that they really did exist and were not ghost voters. A small card table had been set up with cookies, candy, and coffee for the voters and workers; a folding chair was set up for me. The old couple that lived in the house leased it out for the day to the local Democratic precinct captain. It would have been better if they didn't have their underwear hanging all over the basement. Outside of the house, there were numerous political signs with photographs of the candidates who were running for a variety of public offices. The signs were affixed to trees and tied to fences as well as being stuck in the ground. The precinct captains and their assistants would greet each and every voter who approached the polling place and shake hands with them as well as hand them brochures of their favorite candidates. On some occasions I swore that I saw a few dollars passed out to some of the voters, but I couldn't be sure. The rules were that there would not be any electioneering within one hundred feet of a polling place. I did my best to enforce that rule, but on occasion, I must admit that a precinct captain managed to cross that boundary line when I wasn't looking.

Because this polling place was in a basement, there wasn't much ventilation, as I recall; and with the six female judges smoking along with me, there was a continuous smog and a lot of coughing going on, so I spent most of my time by the back door. I also noticed that some of the judges seemed to have bad eyes and had a problem reading addresses. So that caused a lot of bickering among the judges. I just wondered what was going to happen when it came time to count the paper ballots. Finally the polls closed at 6:00 PM sharp, and the final votes had to be counted by hand. At this point my job was to sit there and make sure no one stuffed the ballot boxes and to keep the peace while the judges tallied the votes. Well, after the judges tabulated the votes four times and they didn't come out right, I was about half nuts, and everybody was blaming everybody else for the difference in the voters and the votes.

This was turning into a real debacle, and at 11:00 PM, I offered my services to help the judges count the votes one more time, which of course was against all the rules. To my surprise, none of the judges complained and seemed to be happy to have me volunteer my services because at this point nobody gave a damn, and they all wanted to go home.

Well, working together the votes were finally tabulated correctly. The totals were called into a central location downtown, and the box was sealed and transported to election headquarters. It was now 1:00 AM, and I had just gotten through an aggravating experience about politics and Chicago, the city that works. It should also be noted that back then, there wasn't any overtime pay or overtime hours that would be accredited to you if you worked over eight hours. The police department donated your time, and that was that. This was one of the times that the job sucks.

Vinnie

After a couple of months on Ryan's Raiders, I was sent back to my district, a lot wiser and definitely with more street smarts. One thing for sure, I was getting to like being a cop more and more. It seemed, no matter what, every day was different; and at any moment, something could happen to somebody, to you, or to something. When you were out in the street in uniform or whether you were on a three-wheeler, walking a beat or in a squad car, it was always a good idea to remain alert for your own safety.

Like the day I was relieving on a squad car on the south end of the district. My partner was a guy by the name of Lenny; he was about five feet ten, 220 pounds, forty-five years old, and had twelve years on the job. He acted like he was about sixty and was not an aggressive policeman. Anyway, it was a hot August day as I recall. Back then the only air-conditioning in a squad car was when the windows were open. We got a call of an opened fire hydrant, and water was all over the street because the sewers had been blocked. Kids in the neighborhood were having a good time frolicking under the man-made shower. This happened to be in an Italian section of the district and was not an unusual occurrence on hot days. They are opened by turning a hexagonal nut in the top of the hydrant with a special wrench. It seemed that someone in the neighborhood had tied planks to the hydrant, and when they opened it, the water sprayed all over the street like a gigantic shower. When fully open, each hydrant will gush about a thousand gallons per minute. With the use of simple tools – a board or discarded tire – it is possible to convert the flow into a geyser, a fountain, or other streams to meet the needs of children. They do not care that the hydrants belong to the city and that opening them, except in case of fire, is forbidden by city ordinance. The problem with something like this was that the water pressure in the immediate vicinity would get very low, and if a fire started, maybe there wouldn't be enough water pressure to fight the fire. When the hydrants in the area are fully opened, the water pressure to homes, factories, and hospitals disappears. Well, being Joe the new guy again, Len told me that it would be good experience for me to turn off the hydrant. So he gave me a large wrench that he had in the trunk of the squad. I tried to get one of the teens to turn the hydrant off, but they refused so I was stuck. I managed to turn it off, but of course, I got a little wet doing it – my shoes and socks were soaked as well. I must admit that I wondered why the police had to handle a job like this when it should be handled by the fire department. Needless to say, we didn't make any friends with the kids in the area or a couple of older guys that were also under the water. Before we left, we told them not to turn it on again because of the problem it caused with the water pressure in the neighborhood. Their answer was "No problem, officer, have a nice day." We left the area, but guess what, in about ten minutes we got another call of the same hydrant being turned on again and that a neighbor reported that it had been turned on by a guy in a blue dago T-shirt and white shorts. We went back and turned it off again, and of course, I got wet again, and got mad again. We didn't see the guy in the dago T-shirt and white shorts though; obviously, he saw us coming and went into hiding. This time we warned everybody that if we had to come back again, somebody was going to the shithouse. This time we drove out of the area, and I asked Lenny if he could double back through an alley, and lo and behold, Mr. T-shirt was busy turning on that damn hydrant again. We then watched him put the wrench he used into a black Ford parked around the corner. Mr. T-shirt, Vinnie Greco, twenty-one years of age, was shocked when he saw us walk up to him and told him that he was under arrest for turning on the hydrant. Vinnie of course denied doing such a vile thing. I asked him how his clothes got so wet; Vinnie claimed that he perspired a lot in the summertime. I told Vinnie that he had better turn off that damn hydrant with his favorite wrench, and remove the boards and tire as well before I cuffed him and put him in a paddy wagon that had just picked up a dead body from the river. Of course, Vinnie was more than happy to cooperate with us and swore he would never ever turn on a hydrant again; he even wanted to donate his wrench to us to prove it.

Vinnie was locked up and put in a cell for a few hours before he could make bail. I appeared in court with Vinnie a week later and presented my case to the judge. After the judge heard my side of the story, he asked me on what day did this happen. When I told him, he said, "Oh, yea, I remember that day, it was really hot, wasn't it?" I said, "Yes, it was, Your Honor, but under the circumstances, the hydrant being on caused a hazard in the neighborhood because of the water pressure being way down." The judge looked at me and said that under the circumstances Vinnie was just trying to get some relief for the kids in the neighborhood by turning on the hydrant. Discharged. Another lesson learned, I never arrested anyone again for turning on a fire hydrant.

I remembered an instructor at the academy telling us to be tactful in dealing with "open" hydrants. "The people are hot and angry. Nobody has given them a pool, and then you come along and turn off the one they are making. If we aren't careful, we could wind up wearing our wrench," he said. Moreover, every time an officer closes a hydrant, he gets wet. The water has spilled over the curb, and sometimes he must step into the water to get close enough to close the nut. His shoes and socks get wet, which really gets him pissed off, but he turns the hydrant off.

When he is patrolling the streets and finds an open hydrant that is causing the intersection to flood and there isn't a complainant, he contemplates closing it. He usually approaches slowly while making his decision. The children become aware of his presence but do not acknowledge it until he actually stops his car or drives on past, causing them to break into happy smiles. But if he stops, the children will rush up to him and plead with him not to close it down. If he refuses to leave it open, they plead for a chance to turn it off for him. He is also reluctant to give them the wrench to turn it off, which will save him from getting wet, but there have been occasions in the past where some children have ran away with the wrench and an embarrassed policeman was seen chasing him. Like the judge said, "Oh, yes, I remember it was a hot day." Discharged.

Suicide is Final

My partner Bob and I had just returned to the district from the criminal court building at 2600 S. California Avenue. We were lucky to get permission to use the squad car to go to court because we had to carry a couple of large boxes of evidence to be used in a burglary case we had. Naturally, the case was continued for the third time because the defense attorney needed to study the case further. We had gone off the air when we went to court; now we notified the squad operator that we were back in the district and ready to take calls. We hadn't eaten lunch yet, so we decided to get an Italian beef sandwich at Marge's beef stand at 1400 N. Cicero Avenue.

Of course, we had to eat in the squad car because we were tied to the radio and were afraid that we might blow a call. Sure as hell, we were half through eating when we got a call of a suicide in progress on the west end of the district in a house on Ohio Street. Some guy allegedly had cut his wrists and was sitting by his rear basement door bleeding to death. That was the end of lunch, but we forgot one basic rule, never put your coffee on the dash without a cover because when we start to drive, you're going to get wet. My fault, Bob looked like he had wet his pants and was not happy, and threatened to get even someday.

When we arrived at the location, we found a white guy, about forty years old, sitting on the floor near his rear basement door. He was only wearing a pair of pants, no shirt, socks, or shoes. He was bleeding from his wrists, and it appeared that he had slashed them with a razor or knife. He didn't look good and was very pale. We called for a wagon right away and told the squad operator it was an emergency. We put a tourniquet on both arms in an attempt to stop the bleeding. It didn't look like he had too much blood left in him. He was conscious, so we were able to ask him his name and if he lived there and what had caused him to try to kill himself. He said that everybody was against him. He had lost his job, his life savings, his car, and didn't have a reason to live anymore. I asked him how he had lost all of his possessions. And then he said the magic word. "Well, I was making a few bets and got carried away." He said that he couldn't pay the bookmakers, so they loaned him some money, which turned out to be a juice loan, which he couldn't pay either. I asked him who the bookmakers and juice men were. He just stared at me like I was some kind of nut. Then he came out with the goofiest answer I ever heard, especially under the circumstances. He said, "I couldn't tell you that. If I did and they found out about it, I would wind up in a trunk or sewer." Now here is a nut that wants to die and is nearly dead from loss of blood, but refuses to tell us who the bad guys are. How the hell do you figure this shit out?

Now at the same time we're talking to him, he was trying to take the tourniquets off his arms so that the rest of the blood he had in his veins could drain out. Finally, the wagon showed up, and he was taken to St. Anne's Hospital where they gave him blood transfusions to try and keep him alive. But it was too late; the guy got his wish, he died.

We went through an address book we found in his pants pocket and found some interesting phone numbers, like "Book," with the phone number, and "loan," with a phone number also. We gave this information to the detectives in the station for further investigation. I also kept a copy of the numbers myself. You never can tell in this business, if you know what I mean. Our next assignment that day was a school crossing at North Avenue and Laramie; it's all part of the job. When we were crossing some of the kids, some of them were giggling and pointing at Bob's wet pants. All he could say was "Your time will come, pal."

Frankie "The Enforcer" Nitti – committed suicide for fear of going to jail – Chicago 1943

The Dead Get Robbed Too

Having just been assigned to work a steady car, Bob Peters and I were raring to go and get after all the bad guys. Just knowing what your assignment was going to be every day was a plus; besides, it eliminated a lot of those details that I had been making a career of up to this point. Besides that, you felt like the real police instead of being assigned to a walking post or a three-wheeler or even one of many details that were around.

We started out first day on the day watch, 0800 to 1600 hours, which was not the busiest time of day. But hell, who's complaining? There are bad guys who come out during the day too.

Like I said, nothing surprises me on this job anymore. Because the first job that we caught was at a funeral home on West Division Street. On our arrival, a man who was extremely excited greeted us. He identified himself as the director of the funeral home, and he was talking about somebody who was trying to steal a body. He kept saying, "Follow me, follow me, or it will be too late." We looked at each other and just shook our heads. We followed the director to a rear parlor. It was the weirdest sight I ever saw. There was a fellow in a suit who must have been an employee of the funeral home, sitting on top of this closed casket, kicking his feet at another guy who was yelling at him to get off his mother, who was apparently in the casket. He kept yelling and swearing that she couldn't breathe and that he was killing her. We managed to subdue the guy and asked him just what the hell he was trying to do. He told us that his mother wasn't dead and that his brothers were trying to get rid of her because he was her favorite son and they were jealous of him.

This guy had obviously been drinking a little and smelled like a brewery. He also seemed a little nutty. The funeral director told us that he happened to walk into the parlor to see if any flowers had arrived for the wake and saw this guy trying to take his mother out of the casket. He had her halfway out when they stopped them. He told his associate to call the police. He said that it was a good thing that we arrived when we did or this nutcase – who was about six feet two inches tall and weighed about 220 pounds – would probably have accomplished his mission. The funeral director told us that the son told him that he had borrowed a station wagon from a friend and was going to put her in it and take her home. It was a good thing that we had the guy cuffed because he was starting to act up again and cussed us out and said that he and his mother had their rights. After talking to him for about ten minutes, he began to calm down and started to cry. We tried to explain to the poor guy that his mother was really dead and that he couldn't take her out of the casket and put her in the station wagon. Also, that we were sure that she was in heaven with the angels.

We told him that we would open the casket for him so that he could see for himself. He then calmly said, "Oh, thank you, officers, I would just like to hold her hand one more time and talk to her in private and say some prayers for her." We made him promise that he wouldn't try to take her out of the casket if we met his wishes. He agreed. And we told him that we would take his handcuffs off but that we would be at the back of the room. By this time, the funeral director had contacted one of the other sons, who was handling his mother's funeral arrangements; and the son requested to talk to the police. I talked to the son about the situation with his brother, and he told me that his brother was a drunk and also used drugs on occasion. He told me that the brother had never visited his mother or called her on the phone, and when his mother had been dying in the hospital for two weeks, he never bothered to visit her or call to ask how the mother was doing. He said that his mother had a very expensive wedding ring on and a diamond bracelet that she had requested to be buried with her.

He said that maybe his drunken brother was trying to steal his mother's jewelry and all his actions were just an act to cover his real intentions. I thanked the brother and told my partner, Bob, what I had just been informed; and we went back to the drunk, who was bending over the open casket as if he was praying and holding her hand. He then looked up at us and said, "Thank you, officers, for your kindness and patience." Then he made the sign of the cross and said goodbye to his mother. When he got away from the casket, I looked at his mother's hands and wrists, and sure as hell, if his mother had any jewelry on before her grieving son held her hand, it was all gone now. That did it; we were really pissed off now. We had trusted the bastard, and he stole his own mother's jewelry right in front of us. We put the handcuffs back on him and searched him. And sure as hell, he had taken his mother's wedding ring, diamond bracelet, and gold wristwatch. We brought him into the station and explained the situation to the desk sergeant, who told us to lock him up for disorderly conduct and return the jewelry to the funeral director, who could put it back on the deceased woman or give the jewelry to the other son. Bob and I both knew that there were a lot of wackos in the big city, and we had just met another one.

You're Under Arrest, Now What?

OK, you're innocent. But then everybody claims that. It wasn't me, you say, who was walking down the street drinking that beer, relieving yourself against the wall, scalping those tickets to the Chicago Cubs play-off game, or maybe smoking that joint in Lincoln Park. That is for the courts to decide. The fact remains that you have been busted. A police officer has just put you under arrest, and you are about to enter the unnerving behemoth known to cops and robbers alike as "the system."

Now use your head. You must have learned something from watching all those cop shows on TV like *Hill Street Blues, San Francisco Beat, Dragnet,* or *Kojak*. Oh yeah, you remember, Miranda rights, everybody has them. You have the right to remain silent, anything you say can be used against you in a court of law, and they have to give you one phone call. But what if you get a recording or a wrong number? Just what does happen after they put handcuffs on you?

It is not such an idle question. If you are arrested, you are far more likely to go through the system even on a minor charge. You may be jailed until you are brought before a judge to be charged at arraignment. By law, this process is not supposed to take more than twenty-four hours. But depending on circumstances involving your arrest, some people have been held in cells for more than forty-eight hours, waiting to see a judge for crimes such as fare-beating, sleeping on park benches, and drinking beer in public. Getting a handle on how the criminal justice works is not such a bad idea.

This is what you can expect if you are arrested in Chicago; it's not like the movies. For one thing, the police don't always say, "You're under arrest." But it should not be hard to tell. You're officially arrested as soon as a police officer put hands or handcuffs on you. In addition, police officers do not always recite the Miranda rights.

"They didn't read me anything," recalled Willie Long who claimed he was an artist who was arrested for painting graffiti on a garage door after midnight in an alley. Another good citizen who was arrested for urinating in a grocery store bakery section also claimed that the police never read him his Miranda rights. "He further stated that he had been arrested several other times in the past and has never heard the Miranda warning from the mouth of a police officer, ever."

Whether or not you hear about your right to remain silent depends on whether or not the police want a confession. If they want to use your testimony against you, they must read and explain to you your Miranda rights. If a cop witnesses a crime, he can arrest you and decide not to ask you any questions. If he chooses not to ask questions, then he doesn't need to inform the arrestee of their Miranda rights. But judges and prosecutors want to see people Mirandized if an arrest is made. OK, with or without Miranda, what else happens when you are arrested?

First, you will be searched. The police will be looking for any type of weapon or contraband, like drugs. They will tell you to put your hands up against the wall and spread your legs, pat you down, and warn you to tell them if you have any sharp objects, like needles in your pockets. At this point, if you cross your hands one over the other, it will be more comfortable when they cuff you. Above all, stay calm. It is illegal to resist arrest, even if the arrest is uncalled for. It is bad form to aggravate the arresting officers. Call them officer, sir, or ma'am.

The artist Willie Long was handcuffed and was put into a police paddy wagon for a trip to the district station. The wagon men were informed of the charges against Mr. Long. Sometimes your trip to the station may not be so quick. Mr. Long was put in the wagon that contained ten other people that were also under arrest and handcuffed. The wagon's seats were metal and uncomfortable; some of the other arrestees were sitting on the floor. One of the prisoners claimed that he was having a heart attack, so the wagon had to go to a hospital emergency room to have him checked out. The other prisoners just sat in the wagon. There was no ventilation, no toilet, and it smelled of urine. Grown men were crying because their cuffs were too tight. One guy tried to kick out the back window.

There are twenty-five district stations in Chicago; most of them are new. What happens there is the same. You are booked. And the police make a crucial decision: whether to let you go home with a nontraffic summons and a court date or to send you to the lockup to appear in court the next day. If you are sent to the lockup, you are searched again, sometimes strip-searched. Anything that can be used as a weapon, like a scarf or a pen, and other personal items including prescription drugs are seized. You will be asked to sign a voucher: read it. Make sure that everything taken from you is listed.

A police officer takes down your name, address, date of birth, where you work, etc. This is to verify that you are who you say you are. Cooperation at this point is important; providing full information speeds the process and may help you obtain your release with a nontraffic summons and a court appearance. A driver's license will help verify your identity. If you don't drive, get an Illinois State identification card.

You are then fingerprinted; your prints as well as your palm print will be processed to check for matches from old arrests or outstanding warrants. This may take hours depending on the system. If this is your first arrest, it may take longer because the computer system is searching for a nonexistent criminal history. Years ago, a prisoner was fingerprinted in the district station. Hopefully, the lockup keeper took a good clear set of your prints using ink; they would then be sent downtown to the records section by regular police mail. This took many hours, and hopefully, the person that checked your prints didn't put them on the bottom of a pile of other prints. The prisoner wouldn't be released until the prints cleared. Today's method of processing prints should be much faster, that is, if the prisoner is cooperative.

About this time, you may be allowed to use the phone to call an attorney, family member, or friend who can call an attorney. You may be in a cell by yourself, or you may be in a holding cell with other prisoners. Some of the other prisoners may be charged with a felony such as possession of narcotics or burglary, etc. The police may interview some of the other prisoners charged with a more serious crime. Sometimes the prisoner will request to talk to the detectives in private.

At this point, it bears repeating, "You have the right to remain silent." Defense attorneys recommend that you use it. Why? One reason is because the police are allowed to lie to get a confession, as long as their tactics are not considered coercive. Police love to get confessions. If you are arrested with someone else, they'll say the other guy ratted you out, so you should come clean. Even if it's not true, it is considered good police work. For example, a teenager suspected of raping a Grant Park jogger confessed after a detective told him "We know you were in Grant Park and we have fingerprints from the woman's pants, and if they match yours, you're going away for rape. But if you cooperate, maybe we can help you in court and tell the prosecutor you were cooperative." The detective admitted later that he might have exaggerated about the prints.

If you are accused of a crime and you think you can talk yourself out of trouble, you usually talk yourself into more trouble. By telling the police that you were at the bank, but did not rob it, puts you at the scene of the crime. Saying that you drove the getaway car, but did not kill the guard, is a confession to felony murder. Rather than participating in a crime that led to a murder. They'll try to be paternal, especially to young men who don't have father figures." More than likely, you will be given the good cop/bad cop routine.

No one is automatically entitled to a nontraffic summons, which is considered an arrest, but you will be set free to appear at a later date in court. Over the years, the police routinely issue them for some nonviolent misdemeanors. Depending on what you have been charged with will determine what court branch you will be sent to.

Legally you are supposed to be arraigned within twenty-four hours. The time between arrest and arraignment is dropping, which is an improvement for the arrestees. The whole prearraignment process is often a harrowing one. On occasion, some people have been in for two or three days. These people are presumed innocent and haven't been convicted of any crime in the eyes of the law at this point.

Although nontraffic summons would appear to be a humane alternative, there is a big problem: almost half the people who get them never show up for their court date. Some legal experts worry that processing these low-level crimes clogs a system already bursting at the seams. They also worry that the arrest policy gives the police broad discretion and question whether a white teenager caught drinking beer might get a warning whereas a black teenager might be arrested.

The same legal experts say sending people through the system is part of the new policing strategy: take care of the little things, and the big things will take care of themselves. Furthermore, it gives the police more time to see if suspects are wanted in connection with any old crimes. Police officials point to the Robert Wise case. In August, Wise was arrested for robbing a high school teacher at the Oak Street beach and killing a druggist on the North Side. The police found his prints near the druggist's body; luckily, his prints were on file when he had been arrested a few months earlier for being drunk and disorderly.

Next, is your court appearance. The court is usually in a building that is also a police district and detective area combined. You will be taken to a holding pen along with other prisoners who are also awaiting arraignment. If your cell mates make you nervous, try to sit near the front of the cell in view of the guards. Females will, of course, be in their own cell. Deputy sheriffs will then search you once more for weapons or drugs. If they find any that the police missed, "a rare occurrence," they call the police and you are arrested again. You will be asked if you have any contagious diseases such as TB. If the police had taken away vital prescription medication when you were arrested, you can request to go to a hospital. People who have recently been through the system say that the police sometimes try to discourage prisoners from seeking medical help, telling them that it will lengthen their time in custody.

You now wait for your fingerprints to come back from the identification section where your prints are processed. If you have strong community ties that will make you unlikely to flee, if you have such ties – a fixed address, job, family, someone to vouch for you – agency workers will recommend that the judge release you on your own recognizance. If you do not, they will recommend that the judge set bail or hold you without bail.

Finally, your prints come back and you're clean. Hopefully, the paperwork is put in its correct order – arrest sheet, complaint form, rap sheet, and any outstanding warrants that may be pending against you. When the court is ready to hear your case, you are then brought to a cell near the courtroom. There are two courtrooms: Branch 23 misdemeanor court and Branch 50 felony court. When your name and case number is called, a sheriff's deputy takes you into the courtroom to face the judge. You will be asked if you have an attorney; if you do not, a public defender will be appointed for you. The case is delayed until you and the public defender have a chance to go over your case.

The scene consists of the judge sitting on a chair higher than the prosecutor or public defender and a court reporter located in the middle of the courtroom. The courtroom has a tile ceiling, the walls and benches are beige bricks, and the floor is carpeted. A clerk who calls out the name and docket number of the next case is situated next to the judge. Police officers and attorneys sit in the first two rows of the court.

Arraignments follow a pattern. The assistant state attorney reads the charges, also known as the complaint, against you. Depending on the charge, he may ask the judge to hold you on a high bail. Your lawyer, court appointed or not, tries to make the charge sound less serious and asks the judge to release you or lower your bail. The judge may ask you a few questions before rendering his decision: high bail, low bail, or no bail. It helps to have family or friends come to court; it may impress the judge as to your community ties and influence the bail decision. It would be beneficial to have them in court in case you need to be bailed out. If you are charged with a felony, your case may go before a grand jury.

You may plead guilty to a misdemeanor at arraignment and be sentenced right there or plead not guilty and return to court in the future. It's possible the judge may reduce or dismiss the charges at arraignment if you pay your bail, or releasing on your own recognizance, the judge assigns you a future date. It is now permissible to use a credit card to make bail. Then you are free, at least until you are arrested again or go to trial, whatever comes first.

Prisoner entering police wagon

Arrest Procedure

The felon will be transported in a prison van along with other prisoners to a penitentiary so designated by the state, such as Statesville. The prisoners will have a large leather belt on with a ring in the middle and he will be cuffed to it. The prisoner van will deliver the prisoners to the area used to accept new prisoners. This area is enclosed by a wall or a fence that can be raised and then closed after the van enters the prison area.

The prisoners are then escorted into the prison where they are turned over to the custody of prison guards. The guards will then strip-search the prisoners, checking once more for weapons and drugs. The prisoners will be taken to a main holding area with halls that are narrow and labyrinthine. There are locks everywhere, old ones opened by giant keys and new electronic ones opened by guards in booths. The floors are painted battleship gray, the bars and walls blue.

A stainless steel counter holds an older ledger and pen chained to it, used by a guard to log the prisoner in and assign him to a cell. A wrist or ankle tag with his identification will be attached to him, as well as a series of numbers issued for his prison garb. A medical technician screens the prisoner. This is fairly new, intended to weed out people with highly contagious diseases, such as TB.

After the medical screening, the prisoner is escorted to the shower room. There, he will be issued a cup of yellow liquid and told to rub it in wherever he has hair. The liquid is used for detoxification purposes.

A two-piece orange jumpsuit, orange socks, and orange sandals are then issued to the prisoner. After the shower, the prisoner is then taken to a twenty-by-thirty-foot room where the prison booking officer will then take his prints and photo. There is a chalkboard on the wall where the prisoner identification is listed along with what cell he is assigned to.

The prisoner will then be escorted to his assigned cell, which is probably occupied by another prisoner. At that point, the prisoner had better learn how to fight or dance.

Surviving Prison

John Dillinger was sentenced to ten to twenty years to a reformatory then a state prison for a robbery of a man going home from his grocery store. His accomplice was an ex-convict by the name of Singleton who received a sentence of two to fourteen years. Dillinger did not have an attorney when advised by court officials to plead guilty; he would have gotten a lesser sentence because it was his first offense. A judge gave Dillinger the maximum sentence. Singleton hired a slick lawyer from Indianapolis, pleaded not guilty, and had a jury trial before a different judge. As a consequence, even though he was an ex-convict, he received the lesser sentence.

The disparity between the severities meted out to the young Dillinger compared to the lenient sentence given to Singleton, the ex-convict, was total injustice. Singleton was released after two years; Dillinger served nine years. Judge Williams, who sentenced Dillinger to the maximum, defended himself by pointing out that the sentence he imposed was mandatory on a plea of guilty. However, Dillinger was not yet twenty-one years of age, was married, happened to be intoxicated when he and Singleton committed the crime, and had no previous criminal record. Judge Williams should have taken these facts into consideration, knowing that Dillinger had no legal counsel and was obviously unaware of what a guilty plea would entail. This injustice helped make a hardened criminal out of Dillinger. If Dillinger would have been given two years probation, based on the facts of his case, things may have turned out differently. His wife would probably not have divorced him, and he might have realized that committing crimes was not the best thing to do. Maybe he would have settled down and become a good citizen. This is highly unlikely, but possible.

The following information is based on informants of mine who did time in a correctional facility or had been thrown in solitary confinement at one time in their criminal career. Correctional officers currently working in jails or prisons in the Chicago area agreed to explain the operation of the prison system.

The first question usually asked by first-time convicts is, "Will I be assaulted or raped in the first twenty-four hours on the inside?" It's quite possible, so one must be ready to defend himself. In some joints, there may be an orientation program where you, one of the new fish, are issued an inmate rule book. These sessions are essentially dog and pony shows; most inmates learn the rules and procedures from other convicts. As a new prisoner, you are technically unclassified, have not received a work assignment, and are not allowed a phone call or commissary privileges. You are locked down twenty-four hours a day on the fish tier; this may take a few days until they decide which cellblock is available for your assignment. Where you end up depends upon your age, race, sentence, and crime. If you have been convicted of a violent crime or received a long sentence, you may go directly to the hole. On the other hand, if you are under eighteen, have declared yourself gay, or appear particularly vulnerable, you may be locked up in protective custody.

After you meet your new cellmates, they will probably begin sizing you up, trying to figure out if you are a friend or foe. Be careful about owing anybody because you never know when the bill may come due. Remember the rules discussed in orientation sessions, listed in the prisoner handbook and posted on the bulletin board. Keep to yourself as much as possible; project a cool, quiet aura of self-possessed confidence, and be prepared to back it up with action when needed. The other guy has got to know that if he messes with you, he's going to pay a price. Defend your rights early on, and it'll make the rest of your stay a lot easier. The beating you give to another con trying to make a move on you may very well earn you a few weeks or months of solitary in the hole. However, when you come out, it'll work to your advantage among the rest of the prison population.

If you are sent to the hole and raise hell while you are there, the guards may remove all of your clothes and throw you into a strip cell or they may let you cool your heels in a dark cell with no lights. If you continue to act up, they may strap you to a board or a chair with restraints. If they really get nasty, they can put you in a straitjacket and put a rag in your mouth. Under normal hole conditions, you will have one light bulb. In some prisons, it is common to be placed in the hole with no clothes, beds, or blankets. The worst is when the cell is cold or hot, you are naked, and the floor and walls are smeared with human waste.

It is imperative to try and stay focused; the lack of human interaction will eventually take its toll. Some inmates have passed the time by training cockroaches to race or to adopt mice or baby rats as pets. This may keep you busy for a few weeks. After a time, inmates will begin talking to themselves, assume different characters, and carry on terrific conversations. When the walls seem to be closing in on you, you've reached a low point. Inmates who have spent long periods in solitary confinement begin hallucinating, see ghosts, and even lose the ability to talk.

After Dillinger was sent to the Indiana State Prison at Michigan City, it became a learning experience for him. He joined up with Harry Pierpont and Homer Van Meter who were real bad guys. Dillinger learned how to lay out specific banks, learn who had control of the safes, and determine how many guards were present. must He was informed which banks were the best to rob, where to fence stolen goods, bonds, jewelry, and hot money. Dillinger was ready to get even with society; it had been a learning experience.

Surviving jail

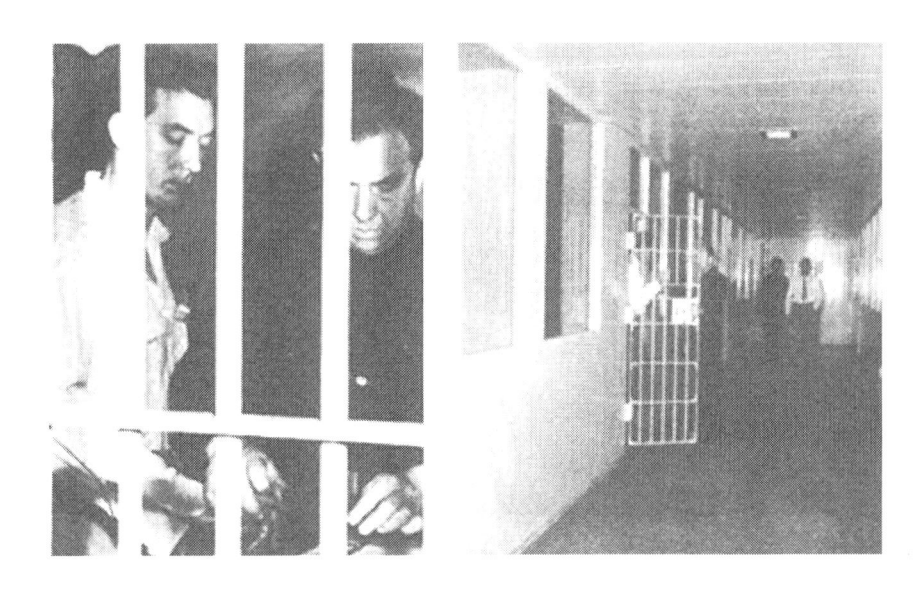

The Alcatraz Island prison facilities are shown in this aerial photo taken in the 1920s.

Prison Violations

- Using abusive language toward staff
- Failure to wear wristbands
- Failure to perform routine cleaning duties
- Failure to maintain personal hygiene
- Displaying of gang signs
- Not wearing of uniform at all times
- Failure to pick up and return food tray
- Trafficking of notes
- Displaying of obstructive materials in windows
- Not keeping hands outside of uniform
- Failure to comply with any order given by an officer
- Tampering with alarms and ventilation system
- Entering of any other inmate's cell
- Indecent exposure
- Possession of any medication not issued by jail

Three habitual minor violations will lead you to solitary confinement.

Disciplinary Rules of Indiana State Prison

1. Be quiet at all times.
2. The lights will be turned on at 6:00 AM. You must arise, make up your bed. see that the toilet and washbasin are clean, and make sure your cell is in neat and orderly condition.
3. If you are sick, notify the officer that unlocks the range or the shop officer as soon as you reach the shop. Do not remain in your cell without permission.
4. Be clean in your habits; keep your cell and clothing clean and in good order.
5. Do not mark, deface, or alter any of the state's property.
6. Do not slam your cell door when entering or leaving. Hold the door closed until the drawbar is thrown or until it is locked by the officer. Always stand at the cell door during count. You must sleep with your head toward the door. Do not go to bed during the daytime except by permission, and do not go to bed with your clothes on. Never put your shoes on the bed.
7. You must not enter any cell but your own. In passing along the range, do not stop, do not stop to look into a cell, and never pass any article into a cell.

8. You are not to talk or communicate in any manner with other men while marching or standing in line while at meals, except by such signs as to make your wants known to the waiter, while in the chapel; or at work in the shop, except when given permission by an officer. Do not talk or call to other men in other cells, whistle, sing, or make unnecessary noise.
9. You must not use vulgar or profane language.
10. You must not have a knife, tool, lead pencils, or any valuables whatever in your possession or cell except by permission of the deputy warden.
11. When you have a necessary communication or request to present to the board of trustees, board of state charters, warden, deputy warden, or chaplain, inform your officer who will make out your written request for an audience and forward it through the proper channel. In matters of minor importance, notify your officer of your desire to speak to the deputy warden when he next visits the shop. Do not step out of line to address the warden, deputy warden, or other persons.
12. You will not correspond or send money to relatives of other prisoners. Special letters will be granted by the deputy warden when urgent business requires it.
13. Obey the orders of your officer and directions of your shop foreman without reply or argument.
14. To attract the attention of your officer, raise your hand. Do not hiss, call to him, or make noise.
15. You must approach an officer in a respectful manner. Remove your hat and salute before speaking to him. In addressing an officer, if you do not know his surname, say "Mr. Officer" and proceed with your communication.
16. In speaking to an officer, stand at a distance of two paces and speak distinctly. Do not pass closely in front of an officer or between two officers who are conversing, and do not make an interruption unless sent by an officer with urgent and important business.
17. You are not to warn a prisoner of the approach or movements of an officer. Do not stare at officers or visitors. Imprudent staring will be considered and reported as insolent. Do not gaze around the shop, but attend to your work.

18. You are required to attend chapel service on Sunday and in no case to absent yourself without the written consent of the warden, deputy warden, or physician.
19. You must not leave the line or change places in line without permission of your officer. When marching, keep your place in line until the officer directs you. When you leave the cell, shop, or chapel, see that your clothing is in order and that your shirt is properly fastened at the neck. No ribbon, badge, or decoration will be allowed on your clothing. Place your cap on properly, and keep your hands out of your pockets. Avoid all insolence and dowdiness in your walk, manner, or gesture.

Louis Tragas—One of a Kind

Louis Tragas, forty-nine, of 3757 North Monticello Avenue, and a person identified by police as Hugh Ruttenberg, thirty to thirty-five, of 5308 West Eddy Street, Chicago, were found shot to death in an antique furniture shop loft at 2416 West Addison Street. The police theorized that the time of death was October 11, 1979.

When the police arrived at the scene on a Thursday afternoon, Tragas's estranged wife, Rita, ran screaming from the building to tell them where the bodies were. Both men were friends and were found fully clothed lying faceup on the bed.

Police described Tragas as "an old fence" who was well-known to the police. Three weapons were found: a double-barrel shotgun and two pistols, a .22 caliber and a 9 mm automatic. They were sent to the crime lab to determine if they had been fired. The men had been last seen alive near the Addison Street address on Wednesday night.

Police identified the establishment in which the victims were found as Sammy's, an antique furniture restoration business. The room was a large one, which, besides the bed where the bodies were found, contained junk furniture and stereo equipment. The police believed that Tragas had been fencing stereo equipment and might have interfered into someone else's territory.

When I found out about Louie getting whacked, I was really surprised. Louie always was one step ahead of everybody else and could talk his way out of any situation that he got into.

Louie and I grew up in the same neighborhood at North Avenue and Cicero in the '40s, '50s, and '60s. We used to hang out at a bar at Keating and North Avenue called Al-Tone's, which was owned by two guys named Al and Tony, naturally.

One of Louie's close friends was a guy named Frank Pecucci who was known to have a few beers from time to time at Al-Tone's as well. In fact when Louie joined the Marine Corps back in 1948, Frank enlisted two weeks later, but that's another story that will come later.

It so happened that Louie had another brother by the name of George who was a couple of years older than Louie. George was as wild as anybody in the neighborhood. He would take any dare you gave him, and do it without fear. I remember one day when a few of us were fooling around in an abandoned old building called the Malt House, which was about seven stories high in the area of Grand Avenue and Kilpatrick by some railroad tracks. I recall that the whole place was gutted, but there were some stairs you could climb to get to the top floor. When we got up there, George found a few steel cables that extended out past the building a few feet. Well, of course, one of the guys dared George to climb out and swing on one of the cables. "No problem," said George. Suddenly, we saw George swinging on this cable seven stories above the ground; he sure made a believer out of us.

Let me explain that George was not crazy; he just had more guts than anybody else, and he knew what he was doing every minute. He was a hardworking guy and was as smart as a whip.

In 1945, George, who was seventeen, and I, almost sixteen, decided to join the Marine Corps. I had changed my birth certificate so I could go. World War II was just about over when we went to a marine recruiting office at 321 South Plymouth Court in downtown Chicago. We signed up for four years. We both passed the physical, and my birth certificate passed as well. We were told to report back to the recruiting office on September 4, 1945, to be shipped out.

I met George on the corner of North Avenue and Cicero, and we were both excited about our future. We reported to the recruiting office with our overnight bags at 8:00 AM. There were about thirty-five other guys waiting with us to begin our new career as U.S. Marines. That is when I got a surprise. The recruiting sergeant who had sworn us in asked me to come with him into his office; he didn't look happy.

He asked me how old I was, and I said, "Seventeen, sir." At that point, he started yelling at me about being a damn liar and that he was going to have me arrested for falsifying my birth certificate. He told me that he had information that I was only sixteen and that I should get the hell out of his office and go back home. When I was leaving, he was smiling and said, "Hey, kid, nice try, see you next year." Before I left, I told George what happened, wished him luck, and went home a little depressed. George wound up in boot camp at Parris Island, South Carolina, and eventually went overseas to China, which was still friendly toward the United States.

The next time I saw George, he was getting discharged in 1949. He was a changed man and had really settled down compared to what he used to be. I guess the service will do that to you; in fact I know it will. In 1948, Louie followed George and joined the Marine Corps for three years; and when his good friend Frank Pecucci found out about it, he joined the marines two weeks later, also for three years. Both of them were shipped to Parris Island for boot camp, but they were in different outfits. Louie and Frank both attended mechanics school after boot camp and got separated. Louie wound up in Camp Lejeune at Jacksonville, North Carolina, and Frank went out to Camp Del Mar in California.

The Korean War started on June 25, 1950, when the North invaded the South. The next time that Louie and Frank got together was in Masan, Korea. Frank had participated in the invasion of Inchon with the First Marine Division and had gone up North to the Chosin Reservoir. Louie had also been up fighting the Chinese when they came across the Yalu River, which was the border between Communist China and North Korea. Both Louie and Frank, who were mechanics, were put into the infantry and had to fight their way out of the trap the Chinese had laid for the marines and the U.S. Army Seventh Division, which were part of the X Corps. They were both very lucky and came out of this battle in one piece. While Frank was waiting to ship out, one of his buddies came into his tent and told him that there was some gook in a truck outside that wanted to see him. Frank went outside. There was Louie with his fur hat on, driving a water truck. Frank said that he was the ugliest marine he ever saw, but the best-looking guy ever. Louie had a .45 strapped to his chest. He also had three gook broads sitting in the truck. He asked Frank to go to town with him and have a party with the gook broads, but Frank decided that that wouldn't be a good idea. Louie explained that his first Sergeant had sent him out yesterday to fill up the water truck, but he got sidetracked.

After a few days, Louie came back and met Frank; and this time, they went into town and had a few. Louie explained that he took care of the first sergeant when he got back to his outfit and there was no problem. One of the bars they went into was called the Black Cat. Louie told Frank that if and when he ever got out of the marines, he was going to open a bar in the neighborhood and call it the Black Cat. Louie and Frank both were honorably discharged from the marines in May 1952. Frank worked his trade as a mechanic, and Louie opened a body-and-fender shop across from Al-Tone's bar at Keating and North Avenue.

Louie and his brother George were excellent body-and-fender men and ran a successful business, for a while that is. George decided to get out of the business and went on to be an electrician. Our guy Louie stayed in the business and made enough money to buy a bar at 4735 West North Avenue. The bar belonged to a fella by the name of Harry Bloom. Harry knew everybody in the neighborhood, but he was getting too old to run the place, so he sold it to Louie. It was a small bar, and the people that frequented the place were mostly shot and beer drinkers and never caused any trouble in the neighborhood.

It was March of 1961 when the Black Cat was opened for business. Louie was in his glory and invited a lot of his friends to the opening. Some of his friends were shady-looking characters, and they looked like they had just got out of the joint. I had joined the Chicago Police Department on February 1, 1955, and was assigned to the old Twenty-eighth District, which is now the Fifteenth District at 5327 West Chicago Avenue. After walking a beat and putting my time in a patrol car for six years, which I really enjoyed, I was reassigned as a vice detective. One of the duties of a vice detective is to make premise checks on all liquor-licensed establishments in the district to make sure that they are being operated properly. Needless to say, this was going to be interesting.

At that time, I lived across the street from the Black Cat with my wife Gen and three children at 4752 West North Avenue in a second-floor apartment. Of course, I had a bird's-eye view of the Black Cat from my front-room window, which was something to see.

Before I get into further developments concerning the Black Cat, I would like to explain a few habits that Louie developed. First of all, Louie was a very good driver and, at the time, he owned a yellow convertible Cadillac. One of his favorite things to do was to drive in reverse on main streets and bet anybody that he could keep up with the normal flow of traffic. One night, while we were hanging around Al-Tone's bar and after a few cool ones, Louie came up with a wild idea. He said that he would bet anyone that he could drive his Cadillac in reverse all the way downtown to Union Station. Everybody called him goofy and told him that he didn't have the nerve to do that. Besides, he would probably get stopped by the police before he got a few blocks. Well, that was a big mistake on our part because Louie got in his canary yellow Caddy convertible and dared somebody to go with him to prove that he did it. Two of the guys that had a few too many beers got in the backseat, and away they went down North Avenue. We went back in the bar and waited for a phone call from some police station that was holding Louie for driving illegally and driving drunk. Much to our surprise, the call never came, but Louie did. He and the two guys that went with him, who were now sober and laughing like a couple of fools, parked the Cadillac in front of Al-Tone's. The whole trip only took forty-six minutes. The two guys, Roger and Bob, verified that Louie did in fact drive in reverse all the way down to Union Station and back and was never stopped by the police. Louie was laughing his ass off, and of course, we bought him drinks the rest of the night.

Louie's Black Cat bar was rated by some old-time police detectives I knew as one of the worst bars ever in the history of Chicago. I guess a few of the reasons for the Black Cat to get that reputation was the fact that it was a hangout for every thief and burglar on the north side of the city. Louie, being an accommodating bar owner, would let a few of his unsavory customers use his place for target practice. They would set up Chianti bottles on top of an amusement machine, and they would bet on who could shoot the corks off the tops of the bottles. They would use .45s, .38s, and .22s or whatever else they were packing that particular day. If that wasn't bad enough, when they started shooting some plastic violins that were hanging on the wall, the bullets began going through the wall. There was a machine shop called Panek's next door, and when the people that worked there arrived in the morning, they saw all these bullet holes in the wall so they called the police. That was the beginning of the end for the Black Cat.

Some of the burglars that hung around the bar made a serious mistake. It seems that they burglarized a stash house where some other mob burglars had hidden their stolen goods. I understand that these dopes liked to brag about the scores they had made. I remember that five of them were all found murdered in two weeks time. Some had been beaten and stabbed to death, and some were strangled as well as shot. I understand Louie also had a couple of dancing girls from Cicero strip joints dancing on the bar naked whenever one of his customers had a birthday. This, of course, would take place when the bar was supposed to be closed. Of course, the Black Cat met its demise before the year was out. Louie was depressed for about ten minutes, but then moved on to other things.

He decided to get back into the body-and-fender business. He needed a garage to get started, and he found one at 7254 North Harlem Avenue. This was a gas station that belonged to the Sinclair Oil Company and just so happened to have an attached garage, which Louie could use to start his body-and-fender business. Sinclair Oil, of course, expected him to pump gasoline from the four gas pumps that were on the premises. I don't think they had any idea that Louie's main interest was the body-and-fender work and had no concern about pumping gas.

Louie was doing fine for a while, repairing cars that had been banged up, and didn't give a damn about the gas customers that waited by the pumps. Before long, Sinclair Oil, of course, noticed that they were not selling too much gasoline at Louie's gas station and informed him of that fact.

Louie, being the diplomat that he was, bullshitted Sinclair Oil that things were going to turn around and his main goal in life was to sell their gasoline. It seems that Louie neglected another important fact: he hadn't paid the rent for a few months. This, of course, helped Sinclair Oil to make up their minds about Louie's future with them. The firm decided to evict him from the premises and informed him of this by written notice. In Louie's mind, this was a good example of big brother picking on the little guy. He decided to get even. Louie had to get even with Sinclair Oil, and a good way to do that was to hurt their business. Louie owned a tow truck, so he knocked down all four of the gasoline pumps that were on the property he was using. Of course, Sinclair Oil had a good idea who had performed such a dastardly deed and reported this to the police. The police arrested Louie and charged him with criminal damage to property. "OK," Louie said, "You want to keep fucking around with me. We will see who wins this battle."

Louie decided to torch the gas station and burn it to the ground. So a couple of nights later, he made his move and poured gasoline all over the station's office and set it on fire. Needless to say, the station was a total loss. Again, Sinclair Oil kind of had an idea as to who would want to cause harm to their property; Louie was first choice, of course, and the police picked Louie up again.

When they interrogated Louie about the arson, Louie readily admitted that he was the one that had set the fire in the gas station and burned it to the ground. He even agreed to sign a written confession that he did commit arson at 7254 North Harlem Avenue. Louie was indicted for arson and was given a court date to appear at the criminal court building at 2600 South California Avenue for trial. It seemed that Louie had finally screwed up and was going to jail for a few years.

Before the court date came around, Louie had another idea to get his revenge. He drove his tow truck downtown to the office of the Sinclair Oil building on Michigan Avenue and plowed through the front doors of the building. The doors were flattened, and all the windows were broken as well. This seemed to make Louie feel a little better when he saw a picture of the entrance of the Sinclair Oil Company in the newspaper.

A person who is charged with a crime has a right to ask for a jury trial or a bench trial. Louie decided that he would have a much-better chance with a jury than with some judge who would probably throw him in jail. Louie somehow attracted the attention of one of those scandal magazines, and the front page was all about Louis Tragas; they called him the Don Quixote of the Sinclair Oil Company. Louie was described as David and Sinclair Oil was Goliath. It was unbelievable how Louie became somewhat of a hero that represented all the little guys of the world that were fighting big business.

I was unable to attend Louie's trial, but I did run into him the next day at a sundry store at the corner of North Avenue and Cicero, which was owned by a fella called Shoes and a Chicago cop named Jimmy Norton. When Louie saw me, he started to laugh and said, "Don, you should have been there, I had the jury in tears when I was testifying." He went on to explain to them how he served in the Marine Corps, fighting the North Koreans and Communist China at the Chosin Reservoir at the Manchurian border. He said that he always believed in helping people that had been invaded by the Communists and was ready to give up his life to keep them free. He went on to tell the jury that all that he wanted when he got out of the service was to open up his own business and was thankful that he lived in a free country where he could do that.

Louie went on and on explaining that some of the women on the jury had handkerchiefs in their hands, wiping away tears as he told his tale of woe. Obviously, Louie beat the case even though he had signed a confession that he burned the gas station to the ground. I believe that Louie got the jury to believe that Sinclair Oil was like the North Koreans or Chinese Communists. He was just an ex-marine that fought for his country and had the right to operate his own business.

I recall a story Louie told me when he was with the First Marine Division, Seventh Regiment up near the Chosin Reservoir in North Korea. It was about thirty below zero with snow and the wind blowing, and some crazy Chinese Communist soldiers were trying to kill him and all the other marines they could find. He said that the bastards would blow bugles and make fanatic charges at them. The good news was that Louie and the rest of his outfit had the high ground and could fire down at the enemy; it was like shooting fish in a barrel. It seems that they fired their .30-caliber machine guns so much that they burned the barrels out and they had to replace them. When this battle was over, there were hundreds of dead Chinese soldiers stacked up below them, but that didn't seem to bother the Chinese because they had hundreds of thousands of other soldiers that were ready to start all over again. I knew Louie was lying because Frank Pecucci, who was also with the First Marine Division, Fifth Regiment, had also gone through this same type of combat, only it was on another hill near a place called Yudam-ni up at the frozen Chosin.

Louie was one of a kind, that's for sure. It seems that he just had a knack for getting involved in some form of illegal activity from time to time. As far as I know, he never hurt anyone.

(From left to right) Frank Pecucci, and Louis Tragas. U.S. Marine Corp – 1948

10-11-79

2 shot to death in loft of shop

By Andy Knott

LOUIS TRAGAS, 49, of 3757 N. Monticello Av., a one-time gas station operator who had frequent bouts with the law in the 1960s, was found shot to death along with another man Thursday in an antique-furniture shop loft at 2416 W. Addison St.

Police identified the other victim as Hugh Ruttenberg, 30 to 35, of 5503 W. Eddy St. Each man had been shot once in the head, and had been dead for about 12 hours, police said.

Investigators said they believe it was a murder-suicide but have not ruled out the possibility of a double homicide. They declined to discuss details.

The bodies were found lying on a bed. Police, who had been alerted by an anonymous phone call, said that when they arrived at the scene Thursday afternoon, Tragas' estranged wife, Rita, ran screaming from the building to tell them where the bodies were.

SGT. EDWARD Flynn, of Belmont Area police homicide unit, said a double-barrel shotgun and two pistols, a 22-caliber and a 9-millimeter automatic, were found near the bed. The weapons, Flynn said, were sent to the police crime laboratory to determine if they had been fired.

Lt. John Michaelson, Belmont District watch commander, described Tragas as "an old fence" who was well known to police. He said the victims were friends. Michaelson said the bodies were fully clothed and lying face-up when found.

THE MEN HAD LAST been seen alive near the Addison Street address Wednesday night, he said.

Police identified the establishment in which the victims were found as Sammy's, described as an antique furniture restoration business. Michaelson said the room was a large one which, besides the bed where the bodies were found, contained "junk" furniture and stereo equipment.

Michaelson said Tragas apparently had been fencing stereo equipment. Burglary investigators were at the scene inventorying the business' contents.

IN 1972, TRAGAS was indicted by a federal grand jury for committing perjury as a defense witness in the trial of Sam De Stefano, a reputed crime syndicate loan shark who later was convicted of threatening a government witness in a federal narcotics trial.

During the mid-1960s, Tragas battled the Sinclair Oil Co. after the firm evicted him from a service station he operated for nonpayment of rent. He was found guilty of criminal damage to property in December, 1964, after knocking down four gasoline pumps with a tow truck in his former Sinclair station at 7251 N. Harlem Av. He was acquitted of similar incidents la-

Newspaper article reference the execution of Louis Tragas in Chicago – 1979

Martin Luther King Jr. Assassinated— Chicago Burns

When Dr. King arrived in Memphis on a Wednesday afternoon, he was met by a Memphis police security detail of four men headed by chief of detectives Don Smith. Two other detectives joined the group later. Dr. King, accompanied by Ralph Abernathy, was taken to their usual lodging, the black-owned Lorraine Motel. Sources reported that Dr. King always stayed there because they treated him very well.

It seems that room 306 was the hotel's best, and Dr. King always stayed in that room, reported Ralph Abernathy. Originally, Dr. King and Abernathy were assigned to room 202 on the ground floor because someone else already occupied 306. Whoever occupied room 306 was moved out, and Dr. King and Abernathy were given their usual room. Walter Bailey, the hotel's owner, said that records showed that King had stayed at the hotel more than thirteen times and always occupied room 306.

Room 306 was located across the road from a rooming house, which would give an assassin a clear view of the occupants of 306 if he intended to shoot Dr. King. Half a block away, a law enforcement team was ensconced in a newly constructed fire station that had large glass windows, which gave the police a clear view of the hotel. FBI agents were also on the scene as well as several military intelligence officers. The two Memphis police officers most responsible for surveillance on April 4 were black, W. Richmond and E. Redditt. They recorded the names of people and times they visited King, as well as the license numbers of cars that came to the hotel. If King left the hotel, they were to follow him and report on his activities. Security seemed to be excellent and well planned out by law enforcement. Of course, the assassin still managed to shoot and kill Dr. King and make his getaway without getting caught.

King had been struck in the lower right jaw by a single .30-06 bullet. It was a fatal shot. Because of the angle at which King was standing, the bullet smashed his jawbone, pierced his neck, tearing major blood vessels and nerves including the jugular vein, and then severed the spinal cord before coming to rest in his shoulder blade.

It was instant pandemonium at the scene. Most of King's aides, guests, and reporters were scurrying about, trying desperately to find out what happened. Most thought the shot had come from across the street in the vicinity of a rooming house. The driver assigned to King told police it sounded like a firecracker, and he ran around the area to see if he could see anything unusual. He saw someone or something moving quickly through the bushes across the street, which raised the question for years that the assassin was hiding in the foliage.

A thorough investigation of the rooming house eventually revealed that the fatal shot was fired from room 5B; the tenant who had rented the room identified himself as John Willard. He appeared to be in his thirties, male, white, and had dark hair, blue eyes, and a thin nose. Willard drove a white Mustang. The Mustang was traced to Eric Galt, a.k.a. Harvey Lowmeyer. Hoover, FBI director, had assigned 3,500 FBI agents to the case. The clues they found from the Mustang and the rooming house finally identified an ex-con by the name of James Earl Ray as the assassin. Wanted posters were soon distributed around the country; some were printed in Spanish and distributed in Mexico.

Ray was now in possession of a passport under the name of Ramon George Sneyd. Ray had managed to get to Heathrow Airport in London and was trying to go to Brussels. An alert immigration officer checked a "Watch For and Detain" booklet that a Ramon George Sneyd was wanted by Scotland Yard for "serious offences." He was detained and searched. When they found a loaded .38 revolver in his right pants pocket, he was arrested, and the FBI was notified of his incarceration. After numerous hearings, Ray was extradited back to the United States to stand trial for the murder of Dr. King.

It was April 4, 1968, when Martin Luther King Jr. was assassinated on a balcony of the Lorraine Motel in Memphis; he was shot dead by a sniper. The country went into a state of shock, and the next day, riots broke out on Chicago's West and South sides and in 125 other cities. The blacks went nuts! They started burning buildings and looting stores, especially on the West Side. Everybody in the Organized Crime Division was detailed to the patrol division and sent to the West Side where it looked like everything was on fire. From our office on the thirteenth floor at 1121 South State Street, we had a view of the West Side, and it looked like every building was burning. The sky was almost black from the smoke.

Our unit was detailed to the area of Madison and Pulaski Road where a lot of looting was taking place. As soon as we got there, we began getting shot at by snipers; they seemed to be everywhere. A lot of the fire trucks in the area were catching hell also from the snipers, and some of the trucks got the hell out of there. It was an unbelievable sight to see scores of people of all ages taking television sets, radios, chairs, lamps, clothes, and even refrigerators. We grabbed some of the looters, and their excuse for taking whatever they had with them was the store was burning anyway so why let the stuff burn. Another story was that they were going to guard the stuff until the owner came back to claim it.

That first night was a little nerve-racking with all that damn sniping going on. The bad guys were using rifles, and all we had was our .38s and .45s. We certainly were not prepared for this kind of police work. We caught some teenagers with a couple of shopping bags full of clothes trying to run across Garfield Park. They intended to stash the stuff so they could come back for more. We looked at the evidence, and most of it was water-soaked and had soot on it. I decided to kick them in the ass and not arrest them. I let them keep what they had, on the condition that they stay home and not come back for more. They gave us their word that they would stay home and were grateful that they weren't arrested. We figured that they would be back within two hours.

After twelve hours of eating smoke and trying to prevent looters from getting into stores that had not been set on fire yet, we were relieved and told to report back in eight hours. Before we left, we heard that the mayor had requested assistance from the National Guard and that they would be on the scene the next day to help patrol the streets and try and stop any more arsonists from burning the rest of the city down. When we reported back to Madison and Pulaski Road the next day, there was a command post set up in a Goldblatts Department Store at the corner. This was a pretty sharp move on Goldblatts' part; they were getting more protection than anyone else in the area. We needed a command post in the worst way so it was a good deal for everybody. I told the guys in my crew to bring any kind of weapon they could get their hands on, such as shotguns, hunting rifles, or U.S. Army carbines or M1s. We were in a war out there, and it wasn't getting any better; we had to protect ourselves any way that we could.

There was a Robert Hall's clothing store just east of Pulaski Road on Washington Boulevard, which had not been touched yet by looters or arsonists, so we decided to get up on the roof of the store and wait for the bad guys to show up. We liked it better up there because at least we had the high ground and had a better firing angle to return fire in case somebody wanted to use us for target practice. I understood that a huge Sears warehouse at Homan and Arthington Avenue had their security force set up with rifles to keep any looters away from their building. They eventually had National Guard soldiers on the roof with a machine gun. I don't think they would have used it, but who the hell knows? The way things were going, the whole city could burn down around us.

While we were up on the roof of Robert Hall's, we spotted a couple of dudes walking down the alley in the back of the clothing store. They each had a two-gallon can with them, and it looked like they were about to torch the store as soon as they got around the back. I used to be a pretty good shot in the army with an M1, so I borrowed Frank's who just happened to have it with him. I was going to scare the dogshit out of these two guys by shooting one of the cans right out of the biggest guy's hand. When they got about fifty yards away, I let a round go and hit the can dead center. It flew out of the guy's hand, and he let out a yell that scared the hell out of us. His partner threw his can away, and they both were running, screaming obscenities about somebody's mother, and disappeared down the alley. That was one of the funniest sights I ever saw, and under the circumstances, we needed a laugh in the worst way. My guys even congratulated me on my marksmanship. After another twelve-hour tour, we got relieved and went home with orders to report back the next day.

The next day, we saw that the National Guard had arrived, and they even had Sherman tanks with them as well as machine-gun jeeps, radio jeeps, and half-tracks. That was one goofy sight seeing Sherman tanks driving down Madison Street. Before it was over, there would be a total of three thousand national guardsmen patrolling the streets of Chicago. The fire department was busy trying to put out the fires using over two thousand firemen. During our patrol duties, we saw the smoldering ruins of the Robert Hall clothing store that we kept out of harm's way for a day. I guess our two guys got some more cans and torched the place anyway. By the time the whole thing was over and peace was restored, nine blacks were killed and over 350 persons were arrested for looting. A lot of policemen were also hurt, as well as firemen. Of course, everybody's days off were canceled as well as leaves until the city got back to normal. A lot of policemen were detailed to Chicago's Loop area to protect the stores and businesses should the blacks go downtown for revenge.

Mayor Daley and Fire Chief Quinn flew over the Chicago area where the fires were raging and the looting was out of control. It was reported that Daley said, "I never believed that it would happen here." Fire Chief Quinn goaded him during the flight, pointing out looters, urging that they be shot on sight, that anybody starting a fire be shot. His firemen were in danger, he said, especially his white firemen. Allegedly, Daley called the superintendent of police, Conlisk, and demanded to know why police had not been ordered to shoot arsonists and looters. Conlisk said, "Because you issued no such orders, Mr. Mayor."

Daley called a press conference and told the press that an order had been issued by him to the superintendent of police that he emphatically ordered that police were instructed to shoot to kill any arsonist or anyone with a Molotov cocktail in their hand because they are potential murderers. Also, an order was given for the police to shoot to maim or cripple anyone looting any stores in our city. This turned out to be Mayor Daley's most famous statement. He was assailed by the liberals, blacks, churchmen, and moderates. How can a policeman be sure he will merely wound a looter? Are they such fine shots that they can avoid hitting an artery in the leg? Or maybe aiming higher and hitting somebody in the spine for running away with a radio or toaster?

After a few more days, the riots ended with the West Side ruined by fires and looting. It sure was a bad time for Chicago. We managed to survive the ordeal, and nobody got shot in our crew, but maybe some arsonists and looters got a lesson that they soon wouldn't forget. I hope we never have to go through something like that again. More than a hundred American cities were hit with riots in the aftermath of the King assassination. Some 50,000 army and guardsmen assisted local law enforcement during the seven to ten days of violence. Two of the cities struck worst were the nation's capital with 11 dead, 1,200 injured, 7,600 arrested, and 1,200 fires; and nearby Baltimore with 6 dead, 700 injured, 5,800 arrested, and 1,000 small businesses destroyed. Little did I know that the Democratic National Convention was fast approaching, and we would be in for another nightmare.

Mayor Richard J. Daley later told reporters that he had ordered police "to shoot to kill any arsonist or anyone with a Molotov cocktail in his hand . . . and . . . to shoot to maim or cripple anyone looting any stores in our city." In the first two days of rioting, police reported numerous civilian deaths but were unable to determine whether they were caused by the riots or other crimes. No official death toll was given for the tragedy, although published accounts say nine to eleven people died during the rioting. Three hundred fifty people were arrested for looting, and 162 buildings were destroyed by arson. Bulldozers moved in to clean up after the rioters, leaving behind vacant lots that remained empty three decades later.

▲ *On the first day of rioting, smoke from fires on Madison Street fills the sky above the West Side.*

▼ *Chicago police, rifles at the ready, crouch behind a patrol car to take cover from a sniper.*

The Bell Brand Ranch Scam—Chambers, Arizona

A Chicago disc jockey by the name of Howard Miller had one of the most popular radio shows in the '50s, '60s, and '70s on WIND, WGN, WCFL, and WMAQ. In the late 1950s, he commanded Chicago's largest audience and was the nation's biggest influence on record sales.

He always spoke well of the police and fire departments, which, of course, was an attraction to every cop I knew, as most of them all listened to his radio show. Some of us even carried transistor radios with us in our squad car when we were working so we could listen to his show, which was 90 percent music.

Of course, he had to play commercials during his show, one of which caught my attention. Wally and I were driving around Chicago in February. It so happened that it was colder than hell and we were sliding all over ice-covered streets. On the radio I heard Howard Miller raving about the weather in Arizona. He mentioned a wonderful location in Arizona located near the Painted Desert and the famous Route 66. It was called the Bell Brand Ranches and was being subdivided into one-acre lots. The price was $795 per acre and was a great deal, according to Miller. It was great for golfing, hunting, and fishing. The company that was selling the land was called Arizona

Properties Inc., and their main office was at 322 South Michigan Avenue in Chicago.

The next time I heard about the Bell Brand Ranches was on television; a movie star named Forrest Tucker was talking about the acre of land he bought on the Bell Brand Ranches and was in the process of building a ranch house on it. Tucker became famous by playing a cavalry sergeant in a TV series called *F Troop*. He also appeared with John Wayne in the *Sands of Iwo Jima* and many other films. He seemed like a very nice fella to me.

I remember the following week when Wally and I were cruising around downtown Chicago looking for a walking bookmaker in the area of Jackson Boulevard and Michigan Avenue. When we passed by 322 South Michigan Avenue, I remembered that the Arizona Properties office was located in the building. I told Wally that as long as we were in the neighborhood, we ought to drop in their office and take a look at some of the photos they had of the Bell Brand Ranches. They kept saying everyone was welcome. Wally agreed and we checked the directory; they were on the fifth floor. We found their office, which was really a combination of three offices. It was covered with large photos of Arizona at sunset and sunrise, cactus plants, and many other beautiful scenes. Two well-dressed gentlemen were busy showing some models to four elderly couples. The tables were set up with cactus, homes, small lakes, and streets. The two salesmen were both in their middle forties. One had a beard, was five feet eight inches tall, and weighed 190; his partner was six feet, thin, and had a thick mustache and glasses. I noticed they both wore cowboy boots, giving the impression they were Western dudes.

The taller cowboy introduced himself to us. He said his name was Sid and would be happy to show us around the office. We explained to Sid that we had heard about the Bell Brand Ranches on the Howard Miller radio show and saw Forrest Tucker on television talking about the lot he had bought and how happy he was. Sid then invited us into an inner office where he had other land plots and catalogs. All the time, he kept talking about what a great deal the Bell Brand Ranches was.

On his desk, I happened to see a sports schedule; it was called Doc's. This sports book contains the names of both college and pro basketball teams. It gives the times of scheduled games and the home team and even lists telephone numbers of the college teams. It is used by both bookmakers and sports bettors who record point spreads of coming games. We found a lot of these sports schedules on numerous gambling raids we made on wire rooms throughout Chicago and suburbs.

While Sid gave us his best sales pitch, I caught Wally's eye and motioned with my eyes at Sid's desk. Wally spotted the schedule and kind of half smiled at me and walked Sid over to a table where there were more catalogs of the Bell Brand Ranches. Taking advantage of Wally's diversion, I got a closer look at the schedule that had a code number 55 and a telephone number underneath it with the hours of the day, ten thirty to one and five to six thirty. The hours specified when the wire room was in business.

I memorized the phone number and gave Wally a thumbs-up and motioned that we had to leave. We told Sid that the ranch really looked good and that we would be back to see him after we talked to our wives. We headed back to our office at police headquarters at 1121 South State Street called the Illinois Bell security office and requested the name and address of the phone number we got from the sports schedule. In 1968, subscriber information could be obtained from the security section of the phone company without too much trouble. After we got the listing, which was an alleged real estate office in the 5200 block of West Madison Street, we typed up a search warrant with the necessary information to have a state attorney and a judge sign it.

We informed our lieutenant that we had a search warrant to serve and left the office. We requested another crew to meet us in the area of the search warrant. The address appeared to be a vacant real estate office with shades pulled down on the windows and front door. A mail slot was at the bottom of the door. I opened the cover and could see a guy seated at a desk at the back of the office with a telephone in his hand and a coffee percolator on the desk. We informed our partners to cover the back of the building for us and proceeded to break down the front door with a sledgehammer. Of course we knocked on the door and announced that we were the police armed with a search warrant and to open the door. To be honest, the only knocking we did was with the sledgehammer.

It took three whacks with the hammer to bust the door down. We were on the bad guy in seconds, but he had enough time to pick up his bets and drop them into the boiling hot coffee percolator. We did recover a Doc's sports schedule with point spreads and a piece of water-soluble paper that must have fallen on the floor during all the excitement. The paper contained bettor's code numbers with plus and minus figures designating who was winning or losing. I noticed number 55 was plus $1,500; our guy Sid was doing okay. The bookmaker identified himself as Carmen Antonelli; he was about forty-five, five feet six inches, 145 pounds, and claimed he had just walked in the place to visit his cousin Vince. He said Vince asked him to watch the office while he got some cigarettes and then we busted in. The two telephones he had on the desk were ringing constantly. We answered the phones, and some of these dopes gave us their code numbers and bets on horse races and basketball games to be played that night. I informed Carmen that for some reason I didn't believe his story and that he was under arrest for boiling water in a percolator without a license on a Monday. He was transported downtown and sent to the lockup.

Wally and I felt pretty good about busting up Carmen's bookmaking operation. While we were talking about it, our transistor radio was on, and Howard Miller was talking about the Bell Brand Ranches again. We had a good laugh about that. That night, I talked to my wife about Howard Miller and the Bell Brand Ranches and that maybe it would be a good investment for the future. She just stared at me and said nothing.

A couple of days later, Wally and I happened to be back on Michigan Avenue, looking for that walking bookmaker. As we passed by 322 South Michigan Avenue, Wally mentioned that he heard Miller bragging about Arizona again and what a great place it would be to live in. I told Wally that I would like to go back to the Arizona Properties office again and look at their brochures of the ranch and ask them how many acres have been sold and how many were left. Wally agreed with me and admitted that Miller was getting to him about the ranch as well.

When we entered the showroom, there were seven other people looking at the tables with the miniature cactus plants and streets with names like Wells Fargo Trail, Howard Miller Boulevard, and Pinto Trail. Sid and his partner Myron were still wearing Western-style clothes along with their cowboy boots. They both waved at us and smiled. I mentioned that we just needed some brochures and they should take their time with their customers while we looked at some other photographs. Sid said that he just received some new photographs and they were on his desk and that we take a look at them.

Not wanting to offend Sid, we walked in his office and found some beautiful photos of the Painted Desert and more sunset views. I couldn't help but notice the same Doc's sports schedule on the desk as well. A closer look at the schedule revealed that the old telephone number that we had found had a line through it and a new number was written underneath it. I nudged Wally, and he saw the number as well. We both memorized the number, trying to be very nonchalant about it. Sid and Myron were still pitching their sales talk to the other customers. With brochures in our hands, we smiled at Sid and Myron and told them we would be back. We returned to the gambling unit office and contacted Illinois Bell security for a listing, name, and address of the telephone number we just got. This number was listed to Helen Circello, of Apartment 2, 4800 block of West End Avenue, Chicago. We typed up the necessary probable cause to get a search warrant for that location, had it approved by a state attorney, and signed by a friendly judge.

We knew we needed some backup when we hit the apartment, so we got two guys from another crew to assist us, John Spellman and Frank Kelly. We informed them where we were going and asked them to cover the rear of the building when Wally and I hit the front door. When we got up to the second floor, we could hear a radio playing a Frank Sinatra song. Wally was ready to hit the door when I stopped him and pointed to the lock on the door. Whoever was in the apartment had left the key in the door when they shut it. I tried the door, but it was locked, so I tried the key. I'd be damned if it didn't open. We entered the apartment and found ourselves in the front room – which had a chair, a couch, a couple of lamps on end tables, pictures on the walls, and a television set in the corner of the room – but nobody was in the room. There was a closed door next to a bathroom. We tried the door, but it was locked. Listening at the door, we were able to hear telephones ringing and a male voice talking very low. It was my turn to hit the door. When I did, the sledgehammer bounced off the door. Obviously, the door had been barricaded from inside. After about ten more whacks on the door, the door began to splinter. A voice inside said, "OK, OK, just a second, I'll open it for you." By this time, Wally and I were calling this guy every obscene name we could think of. When he opened what was left of the door, we were face-to-face with our newfound friend Carmen Antonelli. He was as upset as we were. We found that he had a three-quarter-inch sheet of plywood covering the door, with two-by-fours across the door for braces.

He had a card table with two telephones on it; each phone had a towel underneath it to keep the rings at a minimum. This time, he cut the phone lines. Of course, the percolator was boiling away as usual; he destroyed all the bets he had taken. Antonelli kept asking why we were after him and why we weren't out chasing Communists or rapists. At that point, I dumped the water from the percolator on his shoes and smashed the percolator with the sledgehammer. This time, we called for a wagon to transport Carmen downtown to be processed. The last thing he said to us was that he was quitting the business and we would never see him again.

Of course, the weather in Chicago was getting very nasty, which made me think about the weather in Arizona and the Bell Brand Ranches. Of course, Sidney's sales pitch was getting to me as well. I told Wally that I needed another look at Arizona Properties, and being a Friday, we'd visit Sidney again and find out about property taxes and when the streets were going in. Wally agreed, and back we went to Michigan Avenue. When we walked in the office, Sidney was busy marking Sold on some lots on a large map of the Bell Brand Ranches on the wall.

He gave us his undivided attention and answered my questions about taxes, streets, schools, and when things would start to begin to develop. He even told us about Forrest Tucker buying four lots on the ranch. Sidney then invited us to his office and showed us a contract. He said that if we bought an acre from him if and we weren't satisfied, he would return our money, which was no problem.

At that point, two elderly couples walked into the outer office. Sidney told us to think about it and excused himself as he had to greet the customers that came in. Wouldn't you know that his sports schedule was sticking out from underneath his telephone? I couldn't help myself but pick it up, and sure as hell, the last phone number was crossed out and a new number was written under it. I jotted the number down and replaced the schedule under the phone. Sidney was deep in conversation with the elderly customers as we waved good-bye. I told him that I was going to buy an acre and would see him on Monday.

Wally and I wondered who we would find using the phone number now that Antonelli had quit the business. We got a listing from telephone security, and the subscriber was J. Quigley located at a third-floor apartment at 300 block of North Laramie Avenue, Chicago. We had the warrant signed and requested the assistance of Spellman and Kelly once again. The building was a multi-unit apartment building.

For some reason, I decided to check the phone lines going into the third-floor apartment. We located two phone lines coming out of the apartment that were hidden under a rug in the hallway. Luckily, we were able to trace the lines to a basement apartment that faced the alley. The odds were that no one was in the third-floor apartment. They were in the basement apartment, but the problem was that we didn't have a warrant for the basement apartment. I thought, "Oh well, shit happens sometimes, we'll just have to improvise." I decided that if they wanted to play games, we would just have to break down both apartment doors simultaneously.

I had Spellman and Kelly hit the third-floor apartment while Wally and I kicked in the basement door. I couldn't believe my eyes; Carmen Antonelli was sitting on a couch with two phones on a coffee table in front of him. No percolator was in sight, but he didn't need one because all I saw was a flash of fire go up in front of him. The little bastard was using flash paper. The bets burned away in a second.

Spellman and Kelly reported that the third-floor apartment was empty except for two phone jacks in the wall. When we entered the basement apartment, we noticed a flashing light above the door that started flashing. When Spellman and Kelly hit the third-floor apartment, Carmen would get the hell out of the basement apartment. It was a good thing that we found those phone lines.

I told Antonelli that we were going to charge him with lying to the police about quitting the business, and we were also going to charge him with arson by creating a fire hazard with his flash paper. It was the third time that we busted Mr. Antonelli in five days. He kept asking me who the stool pigeon was that was turning him in. He said he would give us anything we wanted if we told him. I told him he had a deal. "Just give me who you're working for and who you lay off too." His eyes opened very wide and said, "Are you nuts? Why do you want me to wind up in a trunk.? Forget about it, I'm really gonna quit this time." We sent him to the lockup in a wagon and told him we would see him next week.

The bad news was that I had been in the Arizona Properties office too many times, and their sales pitch had gotten to me. I convinced my wife that this would be a great investment for $995 for an acre of land on the Bell Brand Ranches in the Valley of the Sun. The taxes were under $4 a year as well. Our acre was located on Maverick Drive just north of Howard Miller Drive. I should mention that this real estate bonanza was in 1968. When I mentioned the Bell Brand Ranches deal to one of my partners at the time, Frank Kelly, he bought an acre of land as well.

It is now 2009, and we still own this desirable acre of land on the Bell Brand Ranches. The taxes have gone up though; now they are $16.48. About ten years ago, we had an opportunity to pass by the old Bell Brand Ranches, which of course was nothing but desert and weeds about eight feet high. An elephant could hide in there and never be seen. I don't think Forrest Tucker built a ranch house on his acre like he said he did back in 1968. We do get a response from some realtors from time to time who claim they have interested buyers from Korea and would get us $500 for our acre. Having spoken to Kelly recently, he still owns his acre in the Land of the Sun as well. Of course, he also asked me if I had any more good real estate deals for him.

Oh well, at least Carmen Antonelli went to jail three times in five days. I suspect that Carmen was working for the Chinatown crew run by Angelo LaPietra who was a South Side mob boss at the time. I never saw or heard of Antonelli again, but I never went back to that damn real estate office either. The bad news is that I recently got on e-Bay and saw an acre of land for sale on a place called the Bell Brand Ranches in Chambers, Arizona. The owner opened the bidding at $25. I almost made a bid for $26 just for the hell of it, but I didn't. Maybe I'm getting smarter? Naw.

PLAY ONCE...STAY FOR A LIFETIME

Horse Race Wire Service

A newspaper called the *Daily Racing Form* was started in Chicago in 1894. It was dedicated to horse racing. The small publication listed the names of horses that were racing that day along with information about their previous performances. ML "Moe" Annenberg bought the business from a former sports editor of the *Chicago Tribune* for $400,000.

In 1927, Annenberg made a business decision that would turn out to be the most lucrative he would ever be involved in. Annenberg purchased 48 percent of the shares in Mont Tennes's General News Bureau, known as the race wire service. Tennes was being squeezed by the Capone mob in Chicago to relinquish control. Annenberg envisioned great potential in this operation. Jack Lynch, a tough Chicago gambler, purchased 40 percent. Tennes's nephew bought the remaining shares.

Annenberg then hired his old neighborhood pal James Ragen to run the operation. Ragen soon mapped out plans to make the General News Bureau the only race wire service in the country. Annenberg contributed heavily to the Democratic machine that ran Chicago, just like Capone did. He bribed the politicians as well as the police with a fund called "widows and orphans" which came to $150,000 a year.

The General News Service controlled by Annenberg and Ragen had hired goons to force other smaller wire services out of business. In 1929, organized crime figures decided to operate a national wire service. It was reported that Capone offered Annenberg a proposition that Annenberg flatly rejected.

In a short time, Annenberg's wire service went national, stretching across the United States into Canada, Cuba, and Mexico. A crime reporter for the *Chicago Tribune*, Alfred "Jake" Lingle, reportedly helped Annenberg with politicians, police, gamblers, and bootleggers. Lingle was a master fixer until he was murdered in an underpass on his way to the Washington Park Race Track on June 30, 1930.

In 1932, Annenberg began to squeeze out his partners. He created Universal Publishing Company, which printed "wall sheets" and "hard cards." The wall sheets listed races, horses, jockeys, and the morning odds that bettors used in deciding which horses to bet on. The wall sheets were posted on the walls in book joints for customers as well as clerks taking the bets. The hard cards were a smaller version of the wall sheets, which could be carried in a bettor's pocket.

Annenberg then attempted to force his partners out of the General News Bureau completely. It is amazing why Annenberg wasn't whacked by the mob or any of his partners at this point. He did hire bodyguards to protect him around the clock. Later he decided it would be to his advantage to get out of Chicago and head for Miami to be with his old friend Meyer Lansky.

Jack Lynch, Annenberg's old partner, joined forces with the Capone organization against Annenberg. Frank Nitti approached James Ragen in an attempt to get him to change sides. It was reported that Nitti told Ragen that if he went along with them, they would kill Annenberg in twenty-four hours.

While in Miami, Annenberg bought the *Miami Tribune* and soon battled the *Miami News* and the *Miami Herald* for circulation supremacy. Lansky, who helped Annenberg bring his wire service to Florida, was getting a piece of the action by keeping Annenberg from getting shot. In 1936, Annenberg reached an agreement with his old partner Jack Lynch and the Capone syndicate. He paid $1 million for protection to stay alive.

Annenberg then bought a newspaper, the *Philadelphia Inquirer*, that had prestige and class which his other ventures lacked. Under his leadership, the paper became a successful tool for the Republican Party. His son Walter made the right contacts with the Republicans, which would lead him to be appointed ambassador to Great Britain by President Nixon.

Annenberg was indicted for income tax evasion in 1939. At this point, he ended his association with Nationwide News Service to improve his image in court. In June 1940, he agreed to pay $9.5 million in taxes, penalties, and interest. He was sentenced to three years in the Lewisburg Federal Prison. After being released in July 1942, he died soon after of a brain tumor.

After Annenberg walked away from the Nationwide News Service, it went out of business. Five days later, the Continental Press came into being under new leadership.

James Ragen was the new owner of Continental Wire Service, an essential element of any bookmaking operation that provided immediate horse racing results. In 1946, the mob wanted to take over the business. When Ragen resisted, Lenny Patrick, Davey Yaras, and Willie Block shot him on the street. But there was a problem: he didn't die and could identify his attackers. Patrick, Yaras, and Block were arrested for the attempted murder of Ragen who was recuperating in the hospital from gunshot wounds. It was reported that there were three other witnesses to the shooting who could also identify them.

Believe it or not, but somehow the mob was able to poison James Ragen while he was recuperating in the hospital and he died. The other three witnesses of the shooting had other strange things happen to them. Number 1 was found shot to death, number 2 just disappeared, and number 3 had a lapse of memory. All charges were dropped against Patrick, Yaras, and Block.

[TRIBUNE Photo.]

Sergt. James McInerney (left) and Prosecutor Alexander Napoli with telephones found in race joint at 2503 East 79th street. *(Story on page 1.)*

Modern Wireroom - Suitcase phones
Bookmaker: Ray Tominello
Sgt Don Herion VCD Gambling

Jiggers, the Cops!

 A dope dealer and his brother, who happened to be a bookmaker, set up their respective operations in a thirty-flat apartment building in Cicero, Illinois. Being frugal, they wanted to cut expenses, so they rented a two-room apartment, which they could both use. This way, they only paid one rent instead of two. The dope dealer, Frank, picked out this apartment because it had a front door and a back door. Frank would use the back door to greet his coke addict customers, and his brother Tony would use the other room to set up his telephones to take laid-off sports bets from other wire rooms in other parts of the city and suburbs. He also had to stay in contact with Las Vegas oddsmakers to get the latest sports lines, which he would disseminate to the other wire rooms.

 Tony has been working for the Chicago Outfit for many years and has learned many tricks throughout the years to fool the police. They both have been busted a few times in their criminal careers and have spent some time in the slammer, but they blame bad luck on getting caught and not because they were stupid or careless. Tony was doing Frank a favor by letting him operate his business in the same apartment where he was operating his wire room layoff office. If Tony's boss, Joey Aiuppa found out about the setup, he would probably break Tony's legs because he was putting his gambling business in jeopardy by letting Frank deal dope in the same apartment. They also decided that it would be better to set up their operation in the suburb instead of Chicago because they were told by Aiuppa that the Chicago police were not allowed to make any more raids in the suburbs.

Tony, the bookmaker, made arrangements with the telephone company to have three telephones installed in his room in the apartment. The installer would meet him at apartment 21 the next day at 9:00 AM. Actually, the apartment was 12. Tony changed the numbers on the apartment just before the installer arrived so when the installer made out his work sheet, he recorded the three phone numbers to apartment 21. Anyone that checked the phone numbers for subscriber information would be informed that the three phone numbers were installed in apartment 21, not in apartment 12. In the event the police obtained a search warrant for apartment 21, the warrant would be invalid because they would have the wrong apartment. Beside that, they probably would get in a jam for busting down the wrong door.

Frank conducted his business in the other room in the apartment. He also took precautions to protect his operation. He installed scissor gates on the rear door and set up a security camera so he would be able to observe anyone lurking in the area. He also installed a three-fourth-inch sheet of plywood that he would slide behind the door leading to Tony's room and his room in case of a raid by the police. His narcotic stash was in a bag hanging outside a bathroom window so that when the window was opened the wrong way, the bag would fall to the ground and he couldn't be charged with possession of narcotics.

I got lucky one day when I was watching a cigar store where gamblers frequented on occasion to meet and settle up their accounts for the week. I spotted Tony coming out with some other mutt and watched as they gave each other a hug when they split up. I observed Tony get in his town car at Austin Boulevard and Roosevelt Road. He headed south toward Cermak Road then east near Cicero Avenue where he parked in a lot and walked through an alley into a large apartment building with about thirty apartments. I couldn't get near enough to see what apartment he entered, but the way the building was set up, I knew there would be a problem finding where he was operating. I decided to hang around and see what time he came back to his car. Sure as hell, he came waltzing back to his car after bookmaking hours. Now all I had to do was to find out where he was in the building.

The last time I had busted Tony, which was about a year ago, he had phones installed in the third floor and had run the phone lines down into a basement apartment. Luckily, we had checked the phone lines before we broke down the door in the third-floor apartment and traced them to the basement where he had set up his wire room. Of course, the basement door was barricaded, so before we knocked it down, Tony had destroyed all the wagers that were on soluble paper. He even broke the three telephones so that we couldn't take any bets from his customers.

That night, my partner Bill Mundee and I got in the building to check it out. We had exterminator jackets on, which I borrowed from a pal of mine, and carried a couple of empty canisters so if anyone in the building became suspicious of us, we just told them we were exterminating some vermin that had infested the building. Actually, the building was full of roaches and mice and really needed an exterminator. We checked for anything suspicious, like new locks on a door or phone lines coming out of an apartment. We couldn't find anything unusual on any of the apartment doors, so I decided to check the basement where the telephone box for the building was located. Just by chance, maybe Tony had new phones installed in an apartment in the building. The Illinois Bell telephone installer would have to activate the phone lines in the box. The box was so screwed up from lines being taken out and installed we couldn't figure out anything that would make sense. I began to think this was going to be a headache trying to find this mope. Besides, we were out of our jurisdiction. It wouldn't be a good thing if we got caught and our bosses found out about our little escapade.

Then I remembered a saloon on Taylor Street that was calling Tony's number in the past. We caught the bartender pushing parlay cards and were going to bust him for it until he begged us to charge him with a misdemeanor instead of a felony. In return, he would give us a wire room number he had been calling. So we played let's make a deal. The number he gave us turned out to be Tony's operation. We paid the bartender another visit, and sure as hell, we caught him with some sports bets. I made another deal with the bartender, and in return, he gave me Tony's new phone number. But knowing Tony, it wouldn't be much help because we were never going to find him in that building even if we got a listing from Illinois Bell. The bastard would be somewhere else. And for sure, he was still using soluble paper, so we probably wouldn't catch him dirty again.

We were screwed anyway because we were not allowed to make any raids outside the city limits. I often wondered about that. Something smelled a little fishy to me. We had been making a lot of raids in the suburbs with no problem in the past. I did hear rumors that we were embarrassing the Cook County Sheriff's Office. Apparently, they didn't make too many raids because they were tied up working on other crimes. I decided, the hell with it; I thought of an old trick I used in the past that worked and we got our bad guy. All we needed was a little luck. There wasn't any use notifying the local police of Tony's whereabouts because they were also busy fighting crime in the streets of Cicero.

I decided to contact the Illinois Bureau of Investigation (IBI). I had worked with them before on a few gambling raids in the suburbs. They were reliable guys, and I was sure they would like to bust some outfit bookmaking operation, especially in Cicero. The only problem I had was that we were to remain anonymous. Because there were only two ways out of the building, I decided to give Tony an anonymous call and told him I was calling for a friend of his who told me to call him and tell him that he had observed the police getting a search warrant signed and that his name was on the warrant. Obviously, they knew where he was operating and that he had about ten minutes before they got there. He should get his stuff and get out of wherever he was. I also told him that his friend wanted $200 for the tip. Then I heard him call out to Frank and tell him that they had to clear out as there was heat coming. Tony wanted to know my name; I told him his friend would meet him later and explain everything.

When I informed the IBI agents about the plan, they looked at me like I was a little goofy. They probably thought that they were going on a raid, breaking some doors down and then going to have a few beers. I explained that all they had to do was stay undercover and watch the front and rear doors, which were the only way out of the building. I told them to be aware of anybody leaving the building in a hurry and to grab them.

Sure as hell, Tony and his brother came racing down the stairs into the arms of the surprised IBI agents. Tony, of course, had warned his brother Frank to clean up and grab his stash as there was heat. Frank came running out with his bag of dope in a gym bag. Tony got caught with all his bets written on soluble paper hidden in his shorts. Only he was not near any water this time, unless he pissed in his pants. As things turned out, Tony got charged with felony gambling, and his brother was charged with possession of narcotics. I told the IBI to ask the brothers where they were going in such a hurry, was the building on fire or what? Then ask them if they had been warned that the cops were coming and to give IBI the name of the informer who told them. They both denied knowing anything about anything!

The IBI was happy even though the case would probably be tossed out of court because they didn't have a search warrant. They did however aggravate some mob people who were going to be curious about narcotics being found on Frank and question what the hell Frank was doing with Tony anyway. Somebody was going to catch a beating!

Bill Mundee and I made sure our names were not on any reports involving the raid, or we would have some explaining to do ourselves. I was glad that Tony didn't get scared enough to piss in his pants, or the bastard would have beaten us again.

Bookmaker fleeing wire-room before raid by police.

Angel-Kaplan Sports News Inc.

The original owner and creator of Angel-Kaplan Sports News was William Kaplan, a handicapper. The business was located at 236 North Clark Street in downtown Chicago. He started the Kaplan Sports Service in the 1930's. It provided football line information to his subscribers. Kaplan started his business in the Croydon Hotel. Surprisingly, he listed his business in the yellow pages under "Football Service." Pierce was a South Side mobster in Chicago's Fifth Ward. It was represented by Sidney Korshak's brother, Marshall, who answered to the current mob boss Sam "Momo" Giancana. Allegedly, Pierce was believed to be a top suspect in several gangland murders and other extortion plots.

In 1957, Pierce and two other mobsters, Al Frabotta and Gus Alex, allegedly suggested to Kaplan that he take on a partner by the name of Donald Angelini, better known as Don "Wizard of Odds" Angelini, another handicapper. When Angelini joined Kaplan, their handicapping service became Angel-Kaplan Sports News Inc. At sixty years old, Kaplan was starting to get weary from all the pressure and agreed to hire Angelini, a Chicago mobster. Kaplan told people that the new partnership was voluntary and that he would now be in a position to spend time in Miami during the winter months.

They became associated with Sam Minkus, sixty-nine years, who owned the National Publications in Miami a sports line service and the largest producer of football parlay cards in the country at the time. Sam Minkus had a residence at 1127 West Albion Avenue, Chicago. In 1967, I had been investigating the Angel-Kaplan Sports News Inc., because it had come up on some gambling raids we had made on sports wire rooms around Chicago. Our investigation revealed known gamblers and bookmakers visiting Angel-Kaplan frequently. Sam Minkus was kept under surveillance and was observed leaving his residence every Monday. He'd drive downtown and meet with Anthony Verlick, male, white, fifty-five, residing at 6051 North Maplewood Avenue, Chicago, Illinois, at the Conrad Hilton Hotel on Michigan Avenue. We had arrested Verlick in the past for conducting a large-scale parlay-card gambling operation when we caught him with twenty-five thousand football parlay cards. There, he would give Verlick the sports line information that would be used by Verlick to print football parlay cards.

The Angel-Kaplan Sports News Service Inc. was going full blast. Another handicapper was hired by Angelini. He was Frank "Lefty" Rosenthal, male, white and thirty-nine. Rosenthal had appeared in front of Senator John McClellan. His Permanent Subcommittee on Investigations conducted hearings into gambling and organized crime. Rosenthal was accused of fixing both basketball and football games. Rosenthal took the Fifth.

Angelini was considered the best sports handicapper in the business and had the best record for setting the line. Kaplan told another sports handicapper, Bob Martin, that the Angel-Kaplan line was going great and it was the best move he had ever made. Kaplan was making more money now than he ever did, but there were some drawbacks. His new exposure got him subpoenaed before a federal grand jury in Indianapolis, Indiana, that was investigating a Terre Haute gambling syndicate. Kaplan admitted that he had traded information, such as handicapping, with some Terre Haute people and they paid him during the football season. Angelini became Rosenthal's mentor and became a great sports handicapper. He left on his own accord after two years. Rosenthal was getting a reputation of betting as much as $100,000 on a game. It was the opinion of many that anyone that would wager that much on one game had to have inside information.

In September 1960, Rosenthal was indicted for attempting to bribe a halfback at the University of Oregon prior to a 1960 football game against the University of Michigan. Rosenthal and a friend offered Michael Bruce $5,000 for his help in throwing the game, which was to be played the following day. If Bruce could solicit the help of the quarterback, he would get an additional $5,000. Bruce told his coach about the offer, and the coach called the police. Rosenthal was arrested. When the case was to begin, Bruce refused to testify in court against Rosenthal, so the case was dropped. However, Bruce testified before the U.S. Senate Subcommittee on investigations in 1961 and told about the offer Rosenthal made.

When Rosenthal was confronted with Bruce's charges, Rosenthal took the Fifth, and he was never indicted. Our surveillance of Angel-Kaplan Sports News continued revealing known bookmakers and gamblers frequenting their office regularly. Information from reliable informants told us that a large bookmaking operation was being operated out of Angel-Kaplan. Subscribers to their sports schedules were paying $50 weekly to get the sports line and the changes in the line during the week.

I presented our probable cause of illegal gambling at Angel-Kaplan to the state attorney's office and obtained a search warrant for Angel-Kaplan for illegal gambling. We executed the warrant in November 1967. Two employees were on the premises when we served the warrant. Kaplan and Angelini were not present. That wasn't a problem because our main purpose in making this raid was to gather as much intelligence as possible from the addressograph press. It revealed plates that contained the names and addresses and the number of A-K sports schedules that each subscriber received every week.

Of course, the subscribers were gamblers; many of them were bookmakers not only in Chicago but also throughout the country, including Canada. This turned out to be a great source of intelligence involving the outfit's operation in Chicago as well as Las Vegas and Minnesota. We confiscated the plates and returned to our office at police headquarters at 1121 South State Street. At that point, I was told by my lieutenant that a couple of attorneys had called him, requesting the return of the plates we had confiscated. They were not considered gambling contraband.

At that point, I thought it would be a good time to make copies of the plates we had before some attorney served us with a subpoena to return the plates. The police department had a unit that printed various police orders and notices in the building, so I took the plates to them and was able to convince the officer in charge that he would be doing mankind a great favor if he would make copies from the plates. I didn't tell him where they were from, and he would be better off not knowing.

When we got back to the office, there was a well-dressed guy in the lieutenant's office with a briefcase, waving his arms around and appearing to be upset. We put the copies we just made from the plates in my locker. We sat down at our desks with the plates, an inventory book and the box that we had the plates in. I went into another room and called the lieutenant on his phone and told him that we had accomplished our mission and we would be in the process of doing an inventory of all the plates. All he said was 10-4 and hung up the phone. I then knocked on his door and told him in front of the well-dressed guy "who was an attorney" that we were going to start inventorying the plates we confiscated from the raid at Angel-Kaplan. Of course, the attorney who heard what I just said objected to the lieutenant and demanded that the plates be returned to him as he represented Angel-Kaplan.

The lieutenant went along with our charade and informed the attorney that if the plates were not gambling paraphernalia, he would release the plates to him after he informed the state attorney's office of the plates and what they contained. He then made a phone call to the state attorney's office and spoke to an assistant state attorney and explained the situation to him. After a few minutes, he hung up the phone and told us to release the plates to the attorney as they were not considered to be gambling paraphernalia. The attorney had a big grin on his face when we gave him the box with the plates, and he scurried out the door. The lieutenant then gave us a weather report he just got from the call he just made. I told him that he was a pretty good actor. He said, "Yeah sure, I missed my calling. OK, boys, get busy with those names and addresses. I expect big things from you guys."

When we checked the names, we found that some of these subscribers were known to us as bookmakers we had busted in the past; others were names who had forty or fifty sports schedules mailed to them. Subscribers were dealing with Angel-Kaplan from all over the country as well as Montreal, Toronto and other cities in Canada.

When we were through investigating all the leads we had from the plates, we made numerous raids all over Chicago. I found one interesting location at 18 East Elm Street, which was an apartment hotel in the Rush Street area of Chicago. Angel-Kaplan sent twenty sports schedules to this location with the recipient's name and apartment number. When I checked out the building, I found that there was a clerk sitting at a telephone switchboard in the foyer of the building. The clerk was busy answering switchboard calls that were being made from the different apartments. When the clerk asked if she could help me, I told her that I was waiting for a friend of mine to come home from work. She accepted that answer and smiled and continued answering the switchboard.

I casually asked her if the switchboard was always that busy. She then explained that the building was quite old and all the telephones in the building were connected to the switchboard and anyone that wanted to make a call out from their apartment had to ring her and give her the number they wanted and she would then dial the number for them. She would then write down the phone number in a daily logbook with the date and time and the apartment number that made the call. The occupant would be billed at the end of the month. The apartment I was interested in was 711; the occupant's name was Ben Oshansky whom I recall was involved in a gambling raid we made two years ago.

I had to figure out a way to get that logbook from the clerk for a few minutes without telling her the number of the apartment I was interested in. I decided to leave and come back when another clerk was on the switchboard at night. I waited until the next week to make my move, whatever that was going to be. I decided that everybody hates obscene phone calls, so when I went back to 18 East Elm Street on a Sunday night, another woman clerk was sitting at the switchboard, so far so good. I identified myself as a police officer and told her that I was working out of the Prostitution and Obscenity Unit investigating sexual deviates and pedophiles. I explained to her that someone in the building was making obscene phone calls to elderly ladies and we traced the number to this building. I explained that we knew the number of the victim but that was confidential and we couldn't release that information to her. I asked if she would let me look at the telephone log sheet to see if I could recognize the number if it was there.

At this point, she started telling me that she really hated these sex fiends that call people and they should all be locked up. That's when she told me that she couldn't let me look at the log sheet. I started to tell her a few horror stories about some sexual predators we arrested and that

that did the trick. She made me swear that I would never tell anyone that she let me look at her logbook. I raised my right hand and swore to go blind if I ever gave her up. She gave me the log, and I checked 711. Well, 711 only made calls during bookmaking hours and called the same numbers repeatedly. I wrote the numbers down without the clerk seeing me and gave her back her precious logbook. I just told her that I didn't recognize any of our victim's numbers, but I would probably be back in a week or so. I thanked her and left a happy man.

When I checked the four telephone numbers through Illinois Bell, I found that two numbers were listed to a basement apartment on Taylor Street and the other two numbers were listed to a vacant store on Twenty-sixth Street in Chinatown; both locations were in Chicago and not the suburbs. Our surveillance of these locations revealed that they were being used for wire rooms, as two men were observed entering both places during bookmaking hours. At closer observation, we could hear telephones ringing and being answered by men talking about the sports line and accepting wagers on a Monday-night football game. After obtaining search warrants for both locations, we executed the warrants on Monday night. We had to use necessary force to gain entrance to the vacant store, which had been barricaded with plywood and two-by-fours. The two mutts that were inside destroyed all the evidence in a bucket of water. We busted them anyway, threw them in a wagon, and went to the other location on Taylor Street.

The two guys on Taylor Street were not as prepared as the other mutts were. We busted the front and the rear door of the basement apartment at the same time because they weren't barricaded like the vacant store was. When the doors came flying in, they froze. Even though they had a bucket of water and the bets were written on water-soluble paper, they didn't have a chance to destroy them. We caught them with the whole week's action, over $900,000. It's the old story; the harder you work, the luckier you get. Needless to say, I did return to 18 East Elm Street many more times.

A lot of schedules were mailed to suburbs surrounding Chicago. We made a few investigations at these locations and observed known bookmakers entering these buildings. At the time, we were not allowed to make any raids outside Chicago, so we gave this information to the FBI for further investigation. If they ever investigated any of the locations we gave them or made any raids, they never reported back to us about anything.

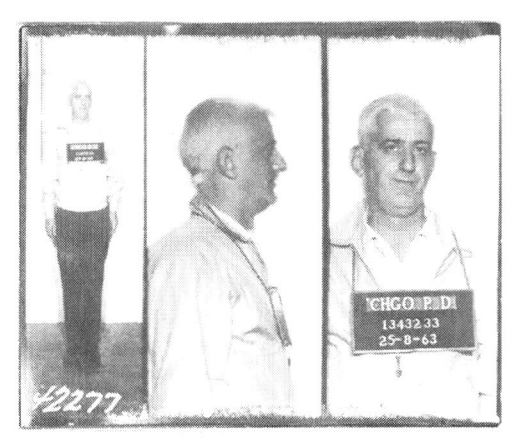

#42277-8/25/63

Donald Angelini

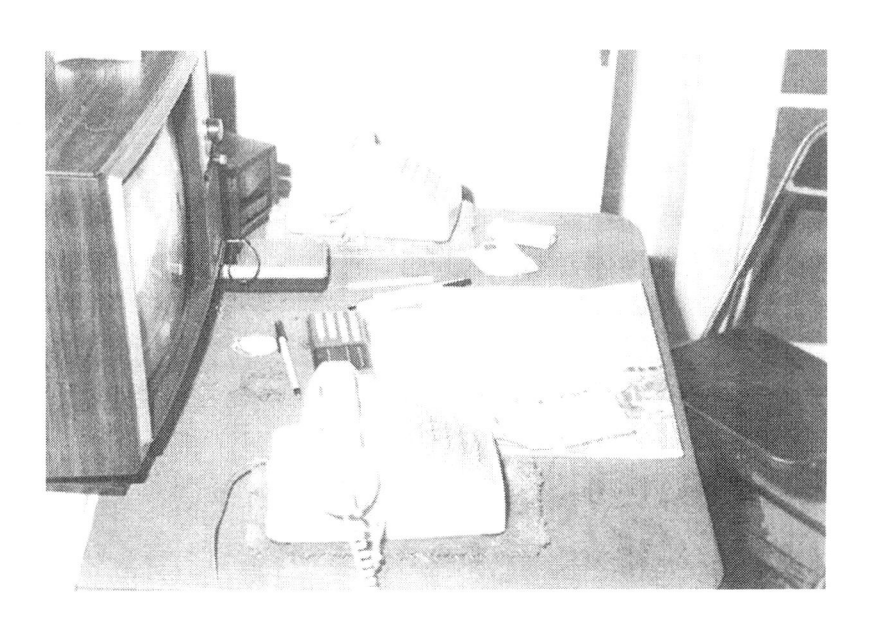

The Friendly Card Game

Often, the general public may display a certain amount of apathy toward the "friendly" card game, regardless of the fact that some money may exchange hands. However, this apathy will quickly disappear if it is learned the friendly game involves marked cards.

The Chicago Outfit had a good operation going with card games like poker and blackjack. All of their games were fixed, of course. Chicago mob boss Rocky Infelise was in charge of the games and used two of his best underlings to set up and control the games. Jimmy Nicholas and William Jahoda took care of the locations where the games would take place and even provided a limousine service for the unsuspecting suckers who played in the games.

The outfit had "two mechanics," gambling cheaters who resort to sleight of hand to accomplish their crooked work. They also had a "shill," which is a player who bets house money to stimulate the action. A reliable informant told me that Nicholas and Jahoda were deciding how much money would be given to the person that brought in a certain number of players to the game. Jahoda was telling Nicholas about the "shill" he had been using for the past few years and that he gets excellent business for the game. He mentioned a man who owned a thriving business in a suburb and was one of his clients. Another guy that owned a motel was a good customer and loved to play blackjack and poker. He's always good to blow from twenty to forty thousand. Plus, he's Greek, and he always brought a couple of players with him.

And all these guys thought it's on the square; nobody had any idea what's going on. I mean nobody.

"Who are the two guys?" Nicholas asked. Jahoda replied that they're all right and he would vouch for them. "One guy is good to blow $20, $25,000." "OK," Nicholas said, "You get half of whatever they blow. Fair enough?"

Nicholas was responsible for setting up the game in a local hotel room or suite and provided food and drinks for the players. He also made arrangements with a local madam by the name of Rose Laws who would provide hookers for any of the participants in the game. On occasion, the game could last two to three days at a time and would involve twenty or more players. Most of the players were restaurant owners of Greek descent.

The mechanics that worked for Nicholas were real professional card cheats. It should be noted that, as compared to the use of crooked dice, cheating at cards often requires considerable sleight of hand. Simply knowing certain cards are marked is valuable, but it is much more advantageous to also be able to deal certain cards to certain players. Furthermore, cheating may be effectively accomplished without marked cards; but with palming cards, second or bottom dealing, or use of signals to a confederate. The detection of such techniques by skilled card mechanics is next to impossible. Thus the game may be crooked although the cards are straight.

Players should not be fooled when an apparently new deck is opened and dealt. It's common practice for crooked gamblers to unseal the cellophane wrapper carefully at the seam, to slit open the box usually at the seam on the box, and to mark the cards. Then the deck may be resealed using colorless glue so that the deception is hardly detectable with the naked eye. New decks should be thoroughly shuffled prior to dealing as all new decks are packaged in the same value-suit order. If they are not shuffled completely, the player can tell what many of the other players may be dealt simply by the cards he possesses.

Nicholas said that he wanted to knock the fucking Greeks off first. He had seventeen or eighteen players for sure. This was going to be too many, so he wanted to start the game at two or three in the afternoon. Some guys would take a couple of hours break and leave their business. Jahoda guaranteed Nicholas that he could get his guys to come in the afternoon. These guys were degenerates; all they wanted was the action.

The most popular games they played were seven-card stud and Texas Hold'em. The betting structure was from $10 to $20 on the turn of a card. Some of the players would remain at the table for as many as twenty-four hours without a break, pausing only to attend to such necessities as going to the bathroom. Others would sit in for only six to eight hours and leave when their luck went bad. The smart players got in and got out. The game didn't sound like much, just six to eight players seated around a table. However, the game represented thousands of dollars for the keepers of the game and their mob bosses at a minimal investment. Jimmy Nicholas and Jahoda cut each pot for 5 percent for services. Each pot in the game averaged $800, so the house got $40. It was estimated that there were, on the average, twenty hands that played an hour, generating twenty pots.

That much action yielded the house about $19,000 a day. If the game lasted three days, the house grossed about $56,000. With card mechanics in the game, the house was guaranteed a very profitable day. On occasion, a player that got caught cheating in the game was treated with respect in front of the other players in the game. He was informed that the house didn't approve of his card playing, and he was asked to leave the game. The crooked player left the room and thought that he had gotten away with something. As soon as he walked out of the building, he was followed. At the first opportunity two men with masks on would take him to the nearest alley and give him a beating with blackjacks. He would then be relieved of his valuables and given a warning to never show his face in the area again or he would be killed.

In February 1988, Jahoda had been arrested for operating an illegal blackjack game at the Arlington Hilton Hotel in Arlington Heights, Illinois. Infelise told Jahoda that something could be done on the case. Jahoda had a series of conversations with Infelise, DeLaurentis, and Maltese regarding payoffs they were offering the three judges to fix Jahoda's case. Judge Thomas Hett's name had been mentioned along with two other Cook County judges. Judge Hett recused himself because he knew one of Jahoda's family members. After Hett recused, Infelise told Jahoda that Maltese had met with Hett and that Hett would have been given $7,500 to take care of the case. Maltese was one of twenty mobsters indicted in February 1990. The state eventually dismissed the case on its own motion.

James Nicholas was also indicted in February 1990. He was released on his own recognizance from the charges placed against him. Of course, he got back in business right away and ran an illegal crooked card game at the Hellas coffee shop at 334 South Halsted Street in Greek town. We had an undercover officer inside the coffee shop, and he observed Nicholas collecting a cut of the card games. We raided the coffee shop and arrested Nicholas for gambling as well as being a keeper of a gambling house.

Shortly thereafter, Nicholas was incarcerated again for violation of his personal recognizance bond. A jury found James Nicholas guilty in the criminal court at 2600 South California. Nicholas was sentenced to serve another six months in jail; that, along with his federal charges, came to a total of almost four years. Nicholas is out of jail now but still hangs around Greektown even though the Greeks know that he had cheated them all these years with fixed card games.

Richard "Dick" Cain

Richard "Dick" Cain joined the Chicago Police Department in 1956. After getting out of police academy, he was assigned to the Thirty-fifth District, now the Eighteenth District. This is the Rush Street area of the city with numerous nightclubs, the magnificent mile on Michigan Avenue, as well as the Gold Coast. This was considered to be a good assignment for a rookie just out of the police academy. It should also be noted that in 1956 Cain was assigned to the vice squad in the district. Obviously, Cain was well connected.

Reliable sources reported that Cain was connected to the First Ward alderman John D'Arco who was suspected of being associated with the Chicago Outfit. A reliable informant stated that Cain had been instructed to join the Chicago Police Department so he could be a valuable asset to the Chicago mob. While assigned to the vice squad in the Eighteenth District, he soon became the mob's bagman in the police department. He became partners with Gerald Shallow and a spy for the mob. Then he began to get involved with a jackroller that was shaking down homosexuals who frequented the Rush Street area. Cain and Shallow apprehended a jackroller and reportedly beat the man to death.

Another incident involved a raid on a whorehouse where the madam reported that the police "Cain and Shallow" had confiscated her money stash. Whatever money confiscated was never inventoried by the police.

In 1960, Cain took a furlough from the police department, which was dominated from top to bottom by Mayor Richard J. Daley, a Democrat. He was finally compelled to quit the force in 1960, when he and Gerald Shallow were discovered wiretapping the offices of Mayor Richard Daley's commissioner of investigations to secure possibly damaging information that could be used against the mayor in a political campaign. For two years afterward, Cain was a private detective, and he developed his skills in electronic eavesdropping. Cain claimed that he was hired by a private detective agency in Miami, Florida, who were training former military officers and law enforcement people for the invasion of Cuba, known as the Bay of Pigs fiasco. In 1962, he returned to Chicago where he worked for the election of Richard Ogilvie as Cook County sheriff. Cain said that he told Ogilvie, "I know the hoods, I'm not afraid of the hoods, and I hate the hoods." Despite warnings about Cain's mob connections, Ogilvie hired him and later made him chief of investigators. While holding this position in the sheriff's office, Cain was reportedly receiving $1,000 a month from mob boss Sam Giancana to divert Ogilvie's attention from mob activities and to feed inside police information to the outfit. But he also told the police about out-of-favor mob figures whom he wanted to have arrested in order to solidify his position within the Chicago Syndicate.

At first, things were going quite well for the double-dealing Cain. He made gambling raids all over unincorporated Cook County, knocking down doors while the press was a witness to this type of action. Most of the raids were set up by the mob. He soon was being called Super Sleuth of Cook County. Cain could do no wrong.

I do recall the splash Cain was making in the newspapers back in 1962. I was working as a vice detective in the old Twenty-eighth District, Austin, at the time and recall seeing a photo in a local newspaper showing Cain coming out a door, carrying an alleged policy wheel from a gambling raid the sheriff's police had just made. Actually, it wasn't a policy wheel at all; the wheel he was carrying was used to pick numbers for bingo games.

In the fall of 1963, the Zahn Drug Company in Melrose Park was burglarized of $250,000 worth of drugs. This theft was headline news for a few days and then faded away. It seemed the police had no clues. Then one day out of the blue, four newspapers were called as well as local TV stations to meet Dick Cain at the Caravelle Motel in

Rosemont, Illinois. The previous owner of the motel was Sam Giancana who used it many a night with his current girlfriends.

When the press arrived, they met Cain who warned them to stay behind his raiding party because there could be some gunplay. "But don't worry, we will protect you." At that point, Cain approached a particular door and proceeded to break it down with an ax as his men stood by, armed with machine guns at the ready. The door came down; Cain rushed in with his men. That's when they found $43,000 worth of the stolen drugs. There was no one in the room and no arrests, of course, but at least someone had finally done something about the major theft.

The favorable press of the raid was amazing. Cain was on the front pages of all the papers; he was requested to do interviews on TV. He was the man of the hour, but not for long. It seems that someone had thought to check the registration card to the room where the drugs were found. What a brilliant move. It was discovered that the room had been rented by one of Cain's own deputies!

Soon Cain and two of his deputies were indicted for perjury, conspiracy, and obstruction of justice. They were all convicted in 1964. Of course, Ogilvie admitted his error in making Cain his chief investigator and fired him.

During the investigation brought on by Cain's dismissal, it was discovered that while on the sheriff's staff, he had helped the mob smoke out a suspected stool pigeon in its midst by having a lie detector test administered to five bank robbers – for the benefit of the mob. While Cain was still with the sheriff, there had been a bank robbery at the Franklin Park Savings and Loan. The six robbers got away with $43,000. Due to the fact that the offenders were apprehended soon after the robbery, a mob boss, Willie "Potatoes" Daddano, suspected that someone had been an informant in their crew. Daddano contacted Cain, who was out of town at the time, and told him that he wanted to give lie detector tests to the robbery crew. Cain contacted Bill Witsman, one of his subordinates in the sheriff's office, and told him to meet with Daddano and administer the polygraph tests. Witsman was a qualified operator. The tests were administered in a suburban motel to all the robbers. Witsman determined that the informant who flunked the test was Guy Mendola. He informed Daddano of this, and Mendola was immediately shot to death outside his home in August 1964.

The FBI agents working on the case, of course, found out about Witsman's participation in the lie tests and interrogated him. Witsman, of course, confessed, and a charge of conspiracy in the robbery of the Franklin Park Bank was filed against Cain and Daddano. They were charged for ordering the lie detector examination of the robbers, and Witsman was to be the key witness against them.

Cain was jailed in 1969 on charges of conspiracy, concealment of evidence, and acting as an accessory to a robbery. Paroled in 1971, he resumed his role as Giancana's right-hand man, serving both as international courier and scout for gambling operations and investments in corporations in Europe and elsewhere. For reasons not clear, Cain's influence in the outfit had diminished by early 1973. It was the opinion of some longtime Mafia observers that Giancana and Cain had a serious dispute. Another reliable source reported that mob boss Marshall Caifano found out about Cain's informant status and received permission from Tony Accardo to murder Cain. Some say one of the masked killers was hit man Harry Aleman. The real reason will probably never be known; but Richard "Dick" Cain was shotgunned to death on December 20, 1973, in Rose's Sandwich Shop at 1117 West Grand Avenue, Chicago, Illinois.

Dick renewing a policy wheel during one of many gambling raids
Big Six wheel
Not a policy wheel

Dec 20, 1973
RichaRD Dick`Cain
Shot gunned to death
1117 W. Grand Ave.

Sam Giancana and the Rosemont Hotel

Mob boss Willie "Potatoes" Daddano was running the River Road Motel in Rosemont, Illinois, in 1953. This was before Donald Stephens became the village president of Rosemont. Daddano had numerous prostitutes working out of the motel. Giancana bought the motel, remodeled it, and named it the Caravelle and then the Thunderbolt. He wanted it operated on the square. He bought it through a crooked banker at the Southmoor Bank. The banker was Leon Marcus. He had been indicted earlier that year for misappropriation of bank funds.

Marcus got some wild idea that he could blackmail Giancana, which would put some heat on the outfit and they would come to his aid and get him acquitted. Marcus even boasted to other mobsters that he had enough information about Giancana that would put him in jail for life. Of course, Giancana heard about this threat and contacted Daddano with orders to get rid of Marcus.

Daddano picked one of his own men to do the job, a former Chicago Park District cop who was now a hit man for the outfit; his name was Sal Moretti. Moretti had a brother by the name of Vince Moretti who was also a former Chicago Park District cop and now a mob member as well. Sal Moretti was told to kill Marcus and retrieve a document receipt indicating $150,000 cash payment for the motel. If the document was found by law enforcement, it would be embarrassing for Giancana.

Moretti decided to take along three understudies of his so they could watch him in action. All they had to do was sit in the car and watch the show. On March 31, 1957, Moretti grabbed Marcus on the street, shot him dead and then drove away with his flunkies. However, he forgot to search Marcus and retrieve the receipt. This was a fatal mistake. The gangland murder hit all the newspapers as well as television. The incriminating receipt caused a major headache for Giancana, and the story remained in the newspapers for another week. He was brought in for questioning about the receipt and many other murders in Chicago. This notoriety infuriated Giancana.

The indictment of Giancana for conspiracy to commit gambling in a place called the Wagon Wheel in the suburb of Chicago in 1951 was set to be heard. The indictment was quashed by Judge Wilbert F. Crowley on the grounds that the federal laws relied upon for the conspiracy count was obsolete. Everything looked like the headlines were finally over for Giancana, but they weren't.

On April 17, 1957, Sal Moretti's tortured and bloated body was found stuffed in the trunk of a Chevrolet on Caton Farm Road, southwest of Chicago. Moretti's pockets had been emptied and turned inside out and his labels had been torn from his clothes. His knees had been tied, he had been beaten with a hammer or pistol and strangled with a rope. Moretti was shot four times in his battered head to make sure he was dead. The only thing that was left was a comb. This might have been a warning for other mob guys or wannabes that you better do the job right and go over everything with a fine-tooth comb. If not, you might wind up like Moretti.

Everybody knew that Willie Potatoes had taken care of Moretti for screwing up the hit on Marcus, but nobody wanted to talk about it. Even mob guys were nervous about Daddano and the way he liked to torture people. Reliable mob guys told me that Daddano was a real sadist and got his kicks by torturing guys like Sal Moretti.; as did Sam DeStefano, Fiore "Fifi" Buccieri, and Teets Battaglia. It has also been reported that Daddano liked to give lie detector tests if he didn't trust somebody. God help the guy that failed the test; they were history.

Mob boss Tony Accardo's house in River Forest was burglarized in January 1978 while he and his wife were vacationing in Palm Springs. Needless to say, he was very upset. Accardo had a sophiscated alarm system installed in his home and thought it was burglarproof. Accardo contacted Jackie Cerone, his protégé, who was running the outfit in Accardo's absence. Cerone ordered Tony Spilotro back from Las Vegas to take care of things. Spilotro learned that there was only one person good enough to circumvent the alarm on Accardo's house, and that was a burglar by the name of John Mendell. Mendell's associates were Vince Moretti; Donald Swanson, a.k.a. Donald Renno; Bernie Ryan; Steve Garcia; John McDonald; and Bobby Hertogs. It appeared that Vince Moretti was running into some bad luck.

I had had trouble with Vince in the past. I thought he would have gotten a little sharper, but obviously he didn't. Vince and another dope by the name of Donald Swanson (a.k.a. Donald Renno) were found in the backseat of Swanson's Cadillac in a parking lot of a restaurant called Esther's Place at 5009 South Central Avenue in Stickney, a suburb of Chicago. Moretti's face was burned off with acetylene torch; he was also disemboweled and castrated. Swanson was found with his throat cut from ear to ear.

On January 20, 1978, a man by the name of Bernie Ryan was found in his 1976 Lincoln parked on a side street in Stone Park; he had been shot four times, and his throat was cut from ear to ear. A known burglar and a pal of Ryan's, Steve Garcia, was found on February 2, stuffed in the trunk of a rental car in the parking lot of the Sheraton O'Hare Hotel on Manheim Road. His throat had been cut numerous times. John Mendell's body was found February 20, 1978, in the trunk of his 1971 Oldsmobile parked at 6304 South Campbell. He had been tortured, and his throat was also cut from ear to ear.

Then we have two more dopes that should have enlisted in the French Foreign Legion after they had heard about the other burglars getting whacked, but they didn't. John McDonald's body was found on April 14, 1978, in an alley behind 442 North Racine Avenue. He was shot in the head, and of course, his throat was cut from ear to ear. Now we have the last dope. I had busted this guy when he was eighteen years old; I thought he too would have gone straight. Forget about it. Bobby Hertogs was his name. He had been shot numerous times, and of course, his throat had been cut as well.

I guess the only people happy during this murder spree were the undertakers of Chicago; they were having a field day. I don't imagine there were too many people attending the wakes for fear that someone might think they were close friends of the deceased. I'm sure a lot of wise guys learned the lesson from Professor Accardo that Crime Doesn't Pay. We have been trying to teach that for years but haven't had a lot of success. Maybe we should look at this happening as sort of a crime-preventive measure and thank Big Tuna. Look at all the crimes these seven burglars would have committed in their careers if they were still on the loose. Even if we captured a few of them, we would have to have long trials that would tie up our court system with paperwork, etc. If we sentenced them to prison for any length of time, that would cost thousands to keep them locked up. I think Accardo might have the right system after all.

THE CHICAGO WAY

Sam (Momo) Giancana

During the mid-1960s, Sam Giancana frequented the Cal-Neva Lodge in Lake Tahoe, Nevada, which was partly owned by his pal Frank Sinatra. One of several Chicago hoods whose name was in the Nevada Gaming Control Board's so-called "black book," Giancana's presence at Cal-Neva got Sinatra in considerable hot water, forcing him to sell his various Nevada gambling interests.

The Rat Pack pose in Las Vegas, in the same order as the names on the sign. The Giancana led Outfit shared girls and good times with Sinatra and his pals. While the others may have used mob connections to advance their careers, Sinatra appears to have been a gangster "wannabe." Among other things, he intimated to Chicago that he could get the Kennedy family to help them out, but did not deliver on that promise.

STUDY MARCUS 'MOB' LOAN

Marcus' Pockets Bulged with Cash at Slaying

Leon Marcus, the ex-banker, was almost a traveling bank when he was slain.

His pockets yielded enough cash, travelers' checks, cashier's checks and other documents to fill a large size manila envelope and make it bulge. Police expressed amazement that he found room for it all in his pockets.

The inventory included $1,650 in cash, $3,600 in traveler's checks and four cashier's checks for $200 each, drawn on the Southmoor Bank and Trust company, of which Marcus once was board chairman.

Carries Nine $100 Bills

The cash included nine $100 bills, 70 $10 bills, one $20 bill and three $5 bills. The remainder was in loose change.

The travelers' checks included 25 of $100 denomination and 22 $50 checks.

The other documents included two checks for $2,800 each drawn on the Southmoor bank and made payable to W. L. Randall, but not signed; a $40 check drawn on the First National bank of Phoenix, Ariz., and a $100 check drawn on the First National bank of Lake Geneva, Wis., on a blank check of the Luzern hotel, also unsigned.

The unsigned $100 check on a check form of the Luzern hotel was explained last night when it was disclosed that Marcus owned the hotel at the time of his death.

A hotel spokesman said the check was on an account which the hotel maintains in the First National bank of Lake Geneva, and would have been good if Marcus had signed it. A hotel spokesman said that all reports of the hotel's business are made directly to the Southmoor Securities company, which Marcus headed, and that Marcus seldom visited the hotel, a modernized resort on the shore of Lake Geneva.

Killed in Accident

Then there was a $300,000 check, dated last June, drawn on the Society National bank of Cleveland, payable to Marcus, and signed by J. O. Harmon, a former oil land promoter.

Harmon was killed in an auto accident last September, and his death made the check worthless. Had it been for a legitimate debt, Marcus might have presented his claim to Harmon's executor, but there is no evidence that he did so. Nor was there any explanation of why he never attempted to cash the check, while it was good.

An even greater mystery to police was why he carried it. If he kept the check as evidence of a claim against Harmon's estate, it would have been more logical for him to keep it in his safe deposit box in the Southmoor bank.

Has Copy of Receipt

Also in his pockets was a carbon copy of a receipt apparently given to Sam [Mooney] Giancana, a syndicate hoodlum, acknowledging a payment of $100,000 on a $150,000 mortgage Marcus appears to have carried on a west suburban motel.

Several other documents found on Marcus' person were not disclosed by police because they are still the subject of investigation.

Marcus' possession of a total of $6,049 in cash or readily negotiable checks gave rise to speculation that he might have been planning to leave the country in view of his forthcoming trial in federal District court on charges of misapplication of bank funds, and making false entries in bank records.

Police discounted this theory, however, on the ground that Marcus had extensive business interests here which he could ill afford to abandon, and that there is no evidence of his having transferred assets out of the country, altho police conceded this would be difficult to check.

Found in Slain Man's Wallet

Check for $300,000 signed by John Harmon, an oil promoter now dead, which was found in wallet of Marcus.

BANKER'S LIFE: TANGLED TALE OF SCHEMING

BY FRANK HUGHES

Leon Marcus, murdered banker and figure in the Orville E. Hodge scandal of last summer, was in the center of a tangled web which led to syndicate hoodlums, politicians big and little, and "manipulations" for contractors, as well as the multi-million dollar construction business.

Marcus was a Latvian immigrant who came here with his parents at the age of 12. He had little formal schooling, but a depression era real estate venture eventually won him ownership of the Southmoor Bank and Trust company. Marcus' connections and friendships were amazing.

Knew Many Persons

His gangland connections, some think, may have been in some way responsible for his slaying, altho others point to the fact he was facing federal trial on the same misapplication charges which sent Hodge and two others to prison. He may have been shot to death to insure silence.

"Marcus knew a lot of people, but he never introduced them to me," Edward A. Hintz, ex-president of the Southmoor bank, now serving a three year federal sentence in Joliet prison, said in an interview yesterday.

Hintz confirmed that Lionel Isaacs, alias Ives, who has a Chicago police gambling record, was one of those who played a part in organizing the bank with Marcus in 1948. He was a depositor also, Hintz said.

Retirement Forced

Ives, a native of Alaska, came to Chicago in 1931 from Los Angeles and became an automobile salesman. Later he became an extensive handbook operator in the Hyde Park and Woodlawn districts. He became so successful in this enterprise that he attracted the attention of syndicate gamblers, who forced his retirement to Florida in 1952. Since that time, as far as police can learn, he has been living in Surfside, Fla.

Early in his career here, Ives became a friend of Marcus. Early in 1948, Marcus had told acquaintances, Ives and two other men came to him with a plan to organize a bank to be operated in the old Stony Island bank building, which Marcus had acquired during the depression. However, their financing plans fell thru, and Marcus took over the organization of the bank himself, with Ives as a stockholder.

Police said they would like to question Ives, altho so far as they can learn, he has not been in Chicago since 1952.

Finances Brothel

But this was only one of the minor gambling connections in the career of Marcus.

A $100,000 receipt made out to "Mr. Sam Giancana," for partial payment of a mortgage on the River Road motel, 5400 N. River rd., Schiller Park, shows that he was financing what was formerly the syndicate's biggest house of prostitution.

Giancana is Sam [Mooney] Giancana, also known as "Mr. Mooney." He is the leader of the younger faction of syndicate hoodlums, known as "the young bloods," a group of killers. Giancana lives in Oak Park.

Giancana holds the syndicate gambling rights in the northern section of Cook county and has influence in Cicero. He is said to be the No. 3 man in the syndicate to those who rate Paul [the Waiter] Ricca as No. 1, and Tony Accardo No. 2.

Made Into Motel

Giancana's River Road motel is the old Sunrise club, a syndicate house of prostitution flattened three years ago after a Tribune investigation. The same building was converted into the motel, and Rocco Potenza, who manages Giancana's gambling houses, is the reputed operator.

Another Marcus link to the syndicate lies in the old Fort, near Glenview, and Ralph's Place, on Waukegan rd. north of Glenview, the sites of the syndicate's biggest gambling operations.

Received from Mr. Sam Giancana, $100,000.00 to apply on mortgage in the amount of $150,000.00 on the property located at 5400 North River Road, Shiller Park Post Office.

Utitals and Kowa on River Road Motel.

SOUTHMOOR SECURITIES COMPANY

Copy of receipt from Sam Giancana for $100,000 found on the body of slain Leon Marcus, former board chairman of Southmoor Bank and Trust company.

The River Road motel, on which Marcus reportedly had made a $150,000 loan to Giancana.

Alfred Rado, with whom Marcus had dined Sunday evening, testifies at inquest of seeing Marcus seized by two men a few moments before he was shot to death.

Giancana was meant to appear before a Senate committee investigating CIA and Mafia links to kill Castro. Whoever decided to carry out an assassination plot on the former Mob King did so to perhaps insure that Sam didn't reveal anything too incriminating on his return to Chicago.

On 19th June, 1975, in the basement of his home in Oak Park, Illinois, an unknown assassin shot Giancana in the head seven times with a silenced .22 caliber handgun. He was found with a wound to the back of his head and six bullet holes in a circle around his mouth. Some suspect the CIA was responsible, others the mob carried out the act with its tradition of Omerta – the vow of silence adhered to by all mob members. CIA Director William Colby was quoted as saying, "We had nothing to do with it."

In fact many researchers believe that Giancana's onetime friend and Chicago Mafia boss Joseph "Joey Doves" Aiuppa ordered the hit on the disgraced "Momo" because he had become too talkative. Aiuppa may have feared Giancana would reveal everything he knew about Chicago mob operations. Giancana has been the subject of many biographies. One of them 'Mafia Princess', was written by his daughter Antoinette and filmed as a TV movie.

The body of Mooney Giancana, where it was found in his basement on June 18, 1975.

1147 S. Wenonah
Oak Park, Il.

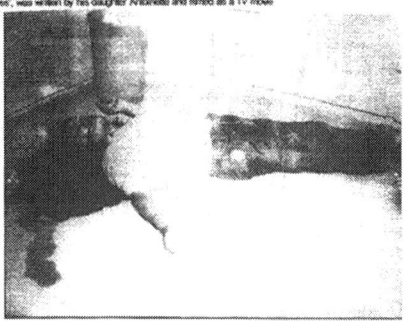

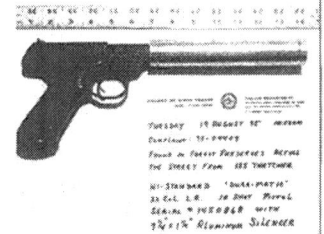

The weapon used to kill Giancana, a .22 automatic with homemade silencer, found alongside the road on the way to aide Butch Blasi's home.

Home of Sam Giancana
Chicago Mob Boss
Murdered in basement
Oak Park, Il. June 1975

Mafia Initiation Rites

Some of the names characters, places, and incidents in the following have been changed to protect reliable sources of mine.

Chicago, Illinois

"Paulie," the nasal, raspy voice of mob consigliere Salvatore Rovelli asked. "Do you got any brothers?"
"Yes," Paulie Saracco answered.
"Do you have sons?"
"Yes."
"If I were to tell you that one of them was an informer," Rovelli, a police informer, continued, "gonna put somebody in jail, and I told you, you must kill him, would you do that for me without hesitation?"
"He has gotta go," Saracco replied.
Rovelli's cocksure voice and Saracco's, at times nervous and hesitating, boomed over a loudspeaker in a U.S. district court here Tuesday. It was the first time that a tape recording of the Mafia's centuries-old quasi-religious initiation rite had been played in public.
The courtroom was silent except for the recorded voices. Jurors listened over headphones and followed the conversations intently from a typed transcript. The eight reputed Rocky Infelise – crime family members and associates being tried on racketeering charges

did the same. About two dozen reporters and the packed gallery also strained to hear.

Propped against the evidence table was a chart with fifteen color photographs that were taken on a quiet Sunday morning in the Chicago suburbs. They depicted a tidy home at 1705 Guild Boulevard in the suburb of Elmwood Park. The trees in the yard carried the last bits of autumn's color.

The FBI agents and Organized Crime Division detectives that were scattered around the neighborhood hid nervously. Down the street, in a hastily assembled command post, another agent worried over a tape recorder, listening to the goings-on within 1705 Guild Boulevard being provided by at least one secretly installed transmitter.

As noon approached, a big Lincoln stopped repeatedly in front of the home. It deposited groups of mostly middle-aged men. All but one were wearing business suits or sports jackets and ties.

The eavesdropping agent heard the coughing and small talk of seventeen sworn DiVarco family members and the scraping sound of furniture being moved before Rovelli took the floor. He initiated four new members into Chicago's dominant criminal organization. Paulie Saracco was the fourth.

"We have to ask, say once more," Rovelli continued, questioning Saracc., "This thing you're in, it's gonna be the life of heaven. It's a wonderful thing, the greatest thing in the world. If you feel that way, want to be part of it, as long as you live?"

"Yes," Saracco said, "I do."

There was one difficulty Saracco was compelled to mention. He had an uncle on the Chicago Police Department.

"But I don't think he ever made a pinch in his life," he said.

"That's all right," Rovelli said.

Then the voice of Biagio DiGiacomo, with a thick Italian accent, filled the courtroom.

"Good luck, Paulie," DiGiacomo said.

Then as he had for those inducted before Saracco – Carmen Federico, Vinnie Tortora, and Robert DeLuca – he administered the Mafia's blood oath in Italian.

"Lo, Paulie, voglio entrare inquesta organizzazione per proteggere la mia famiglia per proteggere e per proteggere I miei amici." I, Paulie, want to enter into this organization to protect my family and to protect all my friends.

Saracco repeated the oath as it was administered by DiGiacomo. He swore never to betray the Mafia's secrets and to obey with love and omertà, the Sicilian code of silence.

"Which finger do you use to pull the trigger?" DiGiacomo then asked.

Saracco showed him, and the FBI said the finger was cut to draw blood. Then in an elaborate numerical ritual similar to a game children play when choosing sides for ball games, the mob selected a *compare* or buddy for Saracco, someone to stand beside him during the next phase of the ritual.

As a paper card bearing the image of the DiVarco family's patron saint was burned in Saracco's cupped hands, he swore in Italian, "As burns this saint, so will burn my soul. I enter alive, and I will have to get out dead."

"Come in alive, and go out dead," one of the mobsters assembled around Saracco interjected.

The FBI considers the recording one of the most important pieces of evidence ever collected in its decadelong fight against the nation's organized crime families. For years, reputed mafiosi have said the Mafia exists only in the fevered imaginations of government agents.

Agents and government prosecutors say that the recording is the best possible proof that the Mafia is a continuing enterprise designed to further its interests by breaking the law. The government's principal weapon against organized crime, federal antiracketeering laws, requires that the existence of a criminal enterprise be proven.

Prosecutors hope jurors hearing the case in Chicago, as well as those who will hear testimony in a related trial in Boston later this year and others elsewhere in the United States, will consider the recording just that – proof.

Begin Optional Trim

The recording did not end with the conclusion of the fourth initiation on October 29, 1989. DiVarco, DiGiacomo, one of five mob capos at the ceremony, and other high-ranking gangsters instructed the freshly initiated Mafia soldiers in the rules of La Cosa Nostra.

"All the friends of ours, this family, we help each other because you people became outlaws, you know," the initiates were told.

The phrase *friend of ours, amico nostra* in Italian, is an important aspect of communication in the Mafia, the four new soldiers were told.

They were ordered never to introduce themselves as Mafia soldiers except to another soldier and then only when the introduction was arranged by a third mafioso friend with both parties.

Non-Mafia members should be introduced as "a friend of mine," DiGiacomo said. Then DiGiacomo, in a kind of charade, mimicked how the introduction of a mob capo, or captain, should go.

"Then he's a captain, and I say, 'Vinnie, he's a friend of ours and a captain,'" DiGiacomo said. "Then you shake hands. You don't kiss him. Years ago, we used to kiss each other."

The practice of men kissing one another attracts too much attention, particularly from FBI agents, he explained.

"Right away, they're going to make it," DiGiacomo said. "They say it's a wop, they do something with this guy."

Each new inductee was also introduced to the men at the ceremony identified as the five DiGiacomo family capos. They were Bobby Carrozza, Charlie Ferrera, Vince Quintana and DiGiacomo of the Chicago area, and Mathew Gugieletti of the Detroit area. Gugieletti has been identified by the FBI as the leader of the family's Midwest crew.

He was originally among those on trial for racketeering in Detroit but pleaded guilty. He is scheduled to be sentenced in the near future.

The four new members were instructed in other rules.

"Another thing," Russo told them. "We're very protective of our women. You have a sister? Unless our intentions are superhonorable, marriage, of course, that's all.

The same applies to wives and girlfriends," he said.

"A woman is sacred," Russo said, adding, "the only way to get out of that, you die. You die."

Joe "Nagall" Ferriola, who was then the mob's boss, warned the new members not to get carried away with their newfound prestige.

"Stay the way youse are," he warned. "Don't let it go to your head."

The Mafia is an international organization, the new members were told. Members can obtain assistance anywhere or any time. There are families in cities all over the country.

"All families are related, all over America," Russo said.

"Throughout the world," DiGiacomo said.

But once a member joins, there is no way out, DiGiacomo said. Particularly if he betrays the secret.

"It's no hope, no Jesus, or Madonna," he said. "Nobody can help us if we ever give up this secret to anybody, any kinds of friends of mine, let's say."

[Begin optional trim]

"This goes back about three hundred years," an unidentified speaker said. "Right, Biagio?"

"More," he answered.

"Around the twelfth century, wasn't it?" Quintana said. "Ah, the Sicilian vespers."

Explaining the background of the Mafia, DiGiacomo said that it started in Sicily "because there was a lot of abuse to the family, to the wife, to the children."

"Until some people, nice people, they got together, and they said, 'Let's make an organization over here, but let's start to do the right thing. Who makes a mistake, he's gotta pay.'"

The induction ceremony ended a little after noon.

[End optional trim]

"Only the [expletive] ghost knows what really took place over here today, by God," Quintana told his pal as they left.

Ken "Tokyo Joe" Eto

February 10, 1983, was Eto's lucky day. He had been set up by mob bosses Joe Arnold and Joey DiVarco who told him to meet two friends of his, Jasper Campise and John Gattuso, at an American Legion Hall at Narragansett and Addison avenues. Then they would meet Solano for dinner around Grand and Harlem avenues. Eto told investigators that he smelled a rat, but there was nothing he could do about it.

He met the two mob guys in the parking lot, and they suggested that they use Eto's car. Gattuso sat in the back, and Campise sat next to Eto in the front. The conversation revolved around a great Italian restaurant they were going to. The only problem was there probably wouldn't be any parking in front because the place was that busy. Gattuso suggested Eto park in the back lot behind the restaurant, which he did. After Eto parked, Gattuso shot him three times in the back of his head, Eto stated that. He heard all three shots and pretended to be dead by lying on the seat. After he heard the car doors open and close, he waited a few minutes before he got out of the car. Eto realized that he was bleeding profusely and wasn't sure how bad he had been injured.

He staggered to a drugstore and asked the manager to call the police and an ambulance as he had been shot in the head. When the ambulance arrived, they looked at Eto and couldn't believe he was still alive. Investigators believed that the killers had used faulty ammunition or the silencer on their gun was faulty; in any case, Eto was very much alive and ready to get even with his assailants and mob bosses.

Eto, sixty-three, told investigators how Jasper Campise and John Gattuso tried to kill him under orders from his mob boss Vince Solano. He also gave detailed information how he split gambling proceeds with Solano, Joseph "Joe Nagall" Ferriola, Joseph "Joey the Clown" Lombardo, and others. Eto, his head ringed in bandages applied to three bullet wounds, gave the FBI a firsthand look at how he ran the bolita gambling operations for the mob. Two former pals of Eto's were arrested and charged with attempted murder after Eto identified them as the pair that tried to kill him.

Gattuso was identified as a Cook County deputy sheriff assigned to the civil section as a process server. He and Campise appeared in court where their bail was set at $500,000 each. They both were released later in the day after posting 10 percent of their bonds in cash. The two men were offered protective custody, but they turned it down. They apparently thought that they were in good shape with their mob bosses and they wouldn't get whacked for their fouled-up hit. They were wrong; five months later in July 1983, the bodies of Gattuso and Campise were found in the trunk of Campise's car in a parking lot in Naperville, Illinois. Both had been stabbed numerous times. I remember locking up Campise in his store at 4820 West North Avenue where he was running an offtrack betting parlor. He was a smart-ass then and called us a few nasty names. Bye-bye, Jasper. In 1982, gambling boss Ken Eto and his top lieutenant, Ray Tom, forty-five, were served with a Cook County grand jury subpoena concerning a high-stakes game called Monte. It is a game similar to blackjack in which players try to beat the house, in this case Eto and the mob. Sgt. Ray DelPilar and his squad made the raid in a house at 4868 West Concord Place. "At the time, I lived in a house at 4907 West Concord Place, which was across the street about seven houses west of the game." DelPilar said that the game would have netted the mob at least $1 million a year and was organized by Eto.

The raiders had a search warrant signed by the state attorney's office Richard M. Daley Special Prosecutions Unit. The raiders, in a tactical move, elected not to make arrests and instead served Eto, sixty-two, and his top lieutenant, Ray Tom, forty-five, with subpoenas, directing them to appear before a county grand jury. Police also obtained the names of fifty players, of which some would also appear before the grand jury as it investigated Eto's latest gambling operation.

Police said that bets on a single card ranged from $50-$5,000 during the game. The players ranged from young people with incomes in the $30,000 a year range to those with incomes of more than $125,000 a year. The game, which changed locations, was so professional it was played with chips that can't be counterfeited. An undercover detective reported that on one occasion, a player hit a hot streak and won more than $30,000. When the player balked at playing further until he could be assured that any further winnings could be covered by the operators, Eto was called. He arrived shortly with a suitcase containing $100,000 in cash to prove to the player that his winnings could be covered. The player resumed playing and ended up losing the $30,000 he won.

Due to the fact that Eto had been recently convicted of operating a lucrative bolita ring, the mob might have felt that Eto could have thoughts of informing on other mob members in return for a lighter sentence. On January 18, 1983, Eto – of 116 Rockhurst, Bolingbrook – and another man were found guilty of operating a $70,000 a day bolita ring. Evidence showed that Eto and Walter Micus of Hillside operated the illegal numbers betting ring and collected bet in Illinois and Indiana. The gambling operation employed more than one hundred people and grossed $3 million a year. Eto's sentencing was set for February 25; he faced a maximum penalty of ten years in prison and a $30,000 fine.

Eto is the highest-ranking Oriental in the Chicago mob. He began his rise in the syndicate during the '40s as a Rush Street gambling lieutenant for the late North Side gambling boss William Goldstein, better known as "Bill Gold." Eto's shooting followed by only three weeks the January 20 gangland-style execution of insurance millionaire Allen Dorfman whose insurance companies handled the scandal-tainted Teamster Central States Pension Fund.

Bolita is a gambling game in which a bettor wagers that a number chosen by him will be the winning number. A form of lottery similar to Chicago's policy racket, bolita was considered at first to be a relatively harmless amateur sport to raise money for clubs and fraternal groups. During the late 1950s and the early 1960s, however, Eto and others drew bolita under the syndicate's umbrella of activities and raised the financial stakes.

Ken "Tokyo Joe" Eto, who was now a government informer, testified for the first time against some of his former crime syndicate pals. Eto was surrounded by U.S. marshals and FBI agents that guarded the courtroom on the twenty-first floor when he took the stand. Eto's testimony drew attention from the Department of Justice officials and mob defense attorneys. They made their own judgments as to whether Eto was a good courtroom witness whose testimony would be valuable in other cases.

Eto was the government's star witness at a sentencing hearing for Joseph "Big Joe" Arnold, seventy-two, of 2724 West Winnemac Avenue, and Joseph Grieco – fifty-four, of 4600 North Overhill, Norridge, Illinois – before U.S. District Court Judge John Nordberg. The two were convicted of buying the silence of a grand jury witness called to testify on the mob's loan shark racket. Grieco was a reputed mob juice loan terrorist. Eto, who was in charge of the mob's bolita racket in Chicago and three states, was expected to detail mob activities of Arnold and Grieco while the government presented testimony aimed at winning lengthy sentences for the two mobsters.

Eto, who was in the federal witness protection program, would probably enjoy testifying against Arnold, one of the mob chieftains who allegedly ordered his assassination, investigators said. Arnold and Grieco were found guilty of obstruction of justice and conspiracy for manipulating the grand jury witness, Ralph Carazzo, not to testify before the grand jury. Arnold and Grieco faced up to ten years in prison and $10,000 in fines. In January 1980, Carazzo was sentenced to eighteen months in jail for refusing to testify before a federal grand jury despite a promise of immunity. Carazzo, a former Rush Street parking lot attendant who worked for Arnold, was not called as a witness at the trial.

Electronic eavesdropping equipment was placed in Arnold's store, Odds and Ends, at 913 North Rush Street to show that Arnold and Grieco conspired with Carazzo to thwart the grand jury. Prosecutors reported that after the two defendants became aware of the grand jury investigation, they won Carazzo's cooperation by promising to wipe out a $15,000 loan he owed Grieco.

I testified at the President's Commission on Organized Crime in New York, New York, on June 24-26, 1985, as an expert witness on the Chicago Outfit. After I testified about the outfit, Ken Eto testified; he was dressed in a hooded black cloak to keep his identity a secret. He explained how he had been the victim of an assassination attempt on his life when he was shot three times in the back of his head by John Gattuso and Jasper Campise. Through a miracle, the bullets were faulty or the silencer was faulty and Eto survived. He told the commission that the two assassins were under orders of mob boss Vince Solano.

In February 1986, Eto testified in Milwaukee, Wisconsin, U.S. Eastern District Federal Court as a government witness describing four gangland murders he had been associated with. The testimony revealed how the crime syndicate dealt with unwanted gambling competitors in the 1950s and 1960s. Among the four was Eugenio Lopez who was strangled under orders of Ross Prio, North Side mob boss. Eto testified that he fingered Lopez (a.k.a. James Crizell) because Lopez was opposing North Side syndicate bolita operations. Eto said that he lured Lopez to a building at 642 North Clark Street where Anthony DelMonte, a man named Frank Orlando, and Vincent "Saint" Inserro strangled Lopez with a wire.

Gonzalez was resisting syndicate efforts to take over bolita in his Puerto Rican community. Eto testified that he and mob associates attempted to drive to Gonzalez's headquarters, but due to street-gang members in the area, they cancelled the plan. Eto said that he contacted Gonzalez, met him and drove to an alleged meeting at 1813 North Washburn Avenue. It wasan industrial area where mob hit men Angelo "the Hook" LaPietra and his brother James knifed him.

Investigators in the case said that the LaPietras were suspects in the case, which could be reopened if witnesses could be found. Eddie Robinson, a black man, was shot to death on August 7, 1962, by the syndicate because he was running bolita on the West Side and wouldn't yield that turf to the mob's bolita game, Eto said. Robinson was killed right after leaving his car at the Eisenhower Expressway and Independence Boulevard. The hit men included Joseph "Joe Shine" Amabile and Vincent Inserro. Robinson's body was never found, but Robinson's family reported him missing on the date of the slaying provided by Eto.

The fourth slaying was indirectly related to bolita. The victim Padone was forcing romantic attention on the wife of a mobster important in syndicate bolita operations. He was, in effect, interfering with the mobster's concentration on his work. The victim, known only as Padone, was shot to death on North LaSalle Street. Eto stated that he reported to mob boss Ross Prio about Padone causing problems with their bolita operation, upsetting bolita operator Cruz Pinzon. Eto said that Prio ordered him to provide Padone's description, address, and phone number. Mob hit men did the rest.

Ken "Tokyo Joe" Eto reportedly passed away January 23, 2004 in Atlanta, Georgia, at 84 of natural causes.

Ken "Tokyo Joe" Eto died in January 23, 2004 of natural causes at 84 in Atlanta Georgia.

Crime lab investigators look for clues near the car in which reputed mobster Ken "Tokyo Joe" Eto was shot three times Thursday night. The attack took place in a parking lot at 7129 W. Grand Ave.

Casinos

Gamblers and their money are the main attraction drawing organized crime to casinos. In those instances where the mob exerts a direct influence over casino operations, the casinos generate cash for redistribution to organized crime. But skimming is only one of the reasons that casinos continue to be a prime target for organized crime.

Casinos can also serve another purpose for organized crime, perhaps just as important. Increasingly organized crime has used casinos like private banks to launder the proceeds on narcotics trafficking. The potential for this kind of abuse is staggering. The estimated gross revenue for gambling casinos in Clark County, Nevada, for 1983 was approximately $1.85 billion. Atlantic City's nine casinos grossed $1.77 billion in 1983, and in 1984, ten casinos grossed $1.95 billion. The estimated gross for eleven casinos in 1985 was $2.1 billion.

The vast majority of casino patrons are law-abiding citizens. Some are not. Investigation conducted by authorities revealed that $28.2 million was deposited directly by patrons with the casino cages in Atlantic City in June 1983. During that month, 356 individuals made cash deposits in excess of $10,000. Of the 356 individuals, 55 had serious criminal records for drugs, extortion, bookmaking, etc. In September 1983, over $43 million (an increase of 52 percent over June figures) was deposited with the casino cages in Atlantic City, with 460 individuals making deposits in excess of $10,000.

This cash flow and some patrons of questionable backgrounds were among the reasons that casinos in Las Vegas and Atlantic City are required to report currency transactions in excess of $10,000 as of May 7, 1985. Casinos in Atlantic City file currency transaction reports (CTRs) directly with the Department of the Treasury, while casinos in Las Vegas first file with the state of Nevada. They (CTRs) are then forwarded to Treasury.

As in the case of other financial institutions, casino owners should take measures to discourage money laundering and should notify law enforcement of suspect transactions. Otherwise, casinos will continue to be used as conduits for drug money, especially those in Atlantic City that are close to the large heroin and cocaine markets in the Northeast. According to the Department of Justice, in 1984, 37 percent of all heroin investigations nationwide by the Organized Crime Drug Enforcement Task Forces were initiated in the two regions contiguous to Atlantic City.

A review of over a dozen investigations by the Drug Enforcement Administration reveals similar methods that have been or are being used to launder illicit drug money through casinos. One method simply involves the exchange of small-denomination bills commonly obtained through drug transactions and other illegal activities for larger denominations. In this way, cash proceeds can be converted into a less conspicuous and more easily transportable form. A second method, somewhat more intricate, involves using the casinos as a banking operation. The client gives money to a casino official who in turn invests the money, retains the money for safekeeping, wires the money to offshore accounts, or provides loans back to the client. A third method involves the use of two or more casinos to transfer funds between clients. For example, the recipient of a drug shipment in the United States can give money to a casino in Las Vegas or Atlantic City for transfer to a designated account in an affiliated casino outside of the United States. Once transferred, the receiving casino can issue credit to the appropriate amount to whoever controls the account, in this case the source of the drug shipment. In many instances, money that has been passed through a casino can later be declared as gambling winnings for tax purposes, thus legitimizing the narcotics money. Peanut King provides a case study of these techniques.

Maurice "Peanut" King, a Baltimore heroin trafficker, used the Resorts International Casino in Atlantic City, in effect, as a bank. He invested over $400,000 in heroin street money in businesses and real estate, also exchanging small bills from street sales for one hundred dollar bills. This is often the first step in the laundering process.

Peanut King, then Baltimore's major heroin trafficker, and two accomplices frequently visited the Resorts International Casino in Atlantic City during 1980 and 1981. At first, Resorts International classified King as a class 5 gambler, an off-the-street gambler. Later, as his heroin business grew and more money flowed to the casino, his status changed to that of a class 1 gambler or high roller. This entitled King to as many as twelve rooms at Resorts International with complementary food and drink.

The King group originally cashed chips and checks but then asked for cash, specifying one-hundred-dollar bills. In practice, King and his cohorts went to gambling tables, exchanged cash for one-hundred-dollar chips, and then gambled. At the end of their stay, each turned in his chips and requested that three checks totaling $118,000 be sent to individual accounts at Legg Mason, an investment firm near Baltimore, Maryland. King and his accomplices then formed a corporation and purchased two grocery stores through the Legg Mason account for $124,500. Later, the grocery stores were renovated at a total cost of $443,600, paid primarily in cash.

Searches of properties owned by one of King's accomplices resulted in the seizure of over $300,000 cash from a safe in his home and from a safe-deposit box. The cash was in five-thousand-dollar stacks of one-hundred-dollar bills with Resorts International wrappers. All told from the period of August 1980 through May 1982, the Drug Enforcement Administration seized or verified the expenditure of over $870,000 of which $418,000 in cash was laundered through Resorts International.

The Golden Nugget

A recent investigation by the Drug Enforcement Administration and the Internal Revenue Service resulting in indictments of Anthony Castelbuono, Gaetano Giuffrida, and others in the Eastern District of New York involved over $3 million in cash from heroin and cocaine sales being deposited at cashier's cages at four Atlantic City casinos – the Tropicana, Caesar's World, Bally's Park Place, and the Golden Nugget. According to the indictment, which was pending in the

Eastern District of New York, Giuffrida and his accomplices conspired to support a heroin-importation network by utilizing an international system of money laundering. The system worked this way: Small denominations were obtained at various Atlantic City casinos. In turn, the heroin cash, its bulk in weight considerably reduced, was transported to places outside the United States, including Bermuda, Canada, and Switzerland.

The conspiracy was initiated in the spring of 1982 when Antonio Turano and several other accomplices counted a large quantity of money. The first apparent movement of heroin cash took place on May 28, 1982, when Anthony Castelbuono, a Harvard-trained lawyer who used the alias of Anthony Cake and Tony Cake, transported approximately $1 million to Atlantic City, New Jersey. The deposits of the majority of the money, over $2.5 million, began on May 28, 1982. There were three transactions on three separate days at the Golden Nugget beginning on November 26, 1982, the day after Thanksgiving.

Five days after the last transaction at the Golden Nugget, on December 16, 1982, one of Castelbuono's accomplices deposited approximately $1 million into an account at the Credit Suisse bank in Switzerland, a bank which was also used by the Pizza Connection heroin traffickers to launder money in 1982.

On February 7, 1985, the Bank of Boston pleaded guilty to currency-reporting violations for failing to report currency received from Switzerland. In 1982, Credit Suisse shipped more unreported cash to the Bank of Boston than any other Swiss bank. In 1984, at a commission hearing on money laundering, Giuffrida and his Sicilian Mafia accomplice, Antonio Turano, were identified as customers of Eduardo Orozco, now convicted of laundering $97 million in drug money through the Deak-Perera foreign exchange firm in New York City.

In October 1984, when the subject was Asian organized crime, the commission heard how Giuffrida and Turano used banks to move money from New York and Milan, Italy through Zurich, Switzerland. Their contact in Hong Kong, headquarters of the criminal Chinese triad societies and a major laundering point, were likewise identified.

Turano was found murdered on March 3, 1983, in Queens, New York. Giuffrida was prosecuted and found guilty in Italy for trafficking in eighty kilos of heroin destined for the United States. It was seized in Florence, Italy, on January 21, 1983, less than five weeks after the last Golden Nugget transaction.

The experience with the Giuffrida network demonstrates several points: First, the versatility and sophistication of one heroin money laundering operation, which used a foreign exchange firm, banks, and casinos in New York, Hong Kong, Atlantic City, and Switzerland. Second, the absolute need for organized crime to have access to financial institutions of all kinds. Last, financial institutions must play a crucial role in closing their doors to the money launderer if there is to be a successful interdiction of the flow of cash into the coffers of organized crime.

The staff of the commission continues to believe that the impetus for effective internal antilaundering measures must come from the top in the form of clear, articulated management policy. We should be reminded of the prior testimony of Eduardo Orozco whose institution was used as a launderer for the Giuffrida organization. During the commission hearings on cocaine trafficking in November 1984, Nicholas Deak, chairman of Deak-Perera, gave these responses to questions about a laundered deposit made at Deak-Perera in New York on October 5, 1981.

He was asked, "Would you consider it suspicious, in your many years of experience, for somebody to bring into your company a deposit of $3,405,000, weighing 230 pounds, consisting of 13,300 one-dollar bills, 6,200 fifty-dollar bills, 79,900 twenty-dollar bills, and 17,100 ten-dollar bills?" Mr. Deak's answer was "Yes, I would consider that suspicious, of course."

Mr. Deak was then asked if a money launderer came to one of his companies, that he could expect to be turned away if he presented the kind of deposit that was described. Mr. Deak said, "I don't think that they will be turned away. I think that they should be reported."

Las Vegas Casino

ETTE TABLES
ILTON CASINO

The Japanese Mafia—Yakuza

I had always heard that the Japanese had a criminal organization that operated like our Italian Mafia, but I never realized how many members belonged to their organization, better known as the yakuza. I've already told you about a gambling boss in Chicago by the name of Ken Eto, a.k.a. Tokyo Joe, Joe Montana, or the Pizza Man. At one time, Eto was called the legendary "Chinese" mystery man of Chicago's policy racket. In the early '60s, the Chicago police and federal agents smashed the outfit's numbers racket, arresting more than forty men. The raids revealed one of the best-kept secrets of this organization. The outfit was now using Orientals as gunmen. Six Orientals – five Japanese and one Chinese. The outfit used them to carry money and gambling receipts because they were clean, had guts, and kept their mouths shut.

The basic charges against the racketeers were conspiracy to break federal gambling laws. Major income tax evasion cases were also involved. Two printing firms, several currency exchanges, and a large bank were involved in the investigation, which was then known as Cadillac numbers.

Syndicate hood Joseph "Cappy" Capizzi was alleged to be the manager of the game. He had a record of narcotic violations as well as policy. Capizzi had been seen in the company of syndicate hoodlums Ross Prio, Dominick Brancato, Jimmy Allegretti, Dominick Di Bello, Joey "Caesar" DiVarco, and Tony De Monte. In addition to Eto being arrested, other Orientals brought in were Raymond Choy, Chinese, Oda Tsutomu, Kazutoka Moto, Stanley Imoaka, and Cecil Shiki, all Japanese. It was not known if they were members of the yakuza.

When I appeared at the President's Commission on Organized Crime in New York City in June 1985, I met other people in law enforcement that had been involved with the yakuza and had firsthand knowledge of their illegal operations.

Like the Mafia in the United States, the yakuza is a source of popular lore for many Japanese. It enjoys a cachet abroad as well as at home, enhanced by images of barrel-shaped men whose razor-sharp suits cover bodies plastered with tattoos. Some gang members are missing parts of fingers, the result of self-mutilation designed to show their allegiance to their leader if they fouled up an assignment.

Theirs is said to be a multi-billion-dollar empire based largely on gambling, prostitution, drug dealing, gun smuggling, and loan-sharking. The more adventurous have expanded operations into seemingly legitimate consumer-finance companies that are often the last resort for credit-starved Japanese.

It has been reported that American authorities have expressed concern that yakuza groups, as well as other Asian criminal societies, have begun to make inroads in the United States. The name *yakuza* is derived from an old card game, similar to blackjack, whose object was to draw three cards adding up as close to nineteen as possible without exceeding it. *Ya-ku-za* represents the Japanese words for 8, 9, 3, which total 20, a useless number. Basically, *yakuza* now means "good for nothing."

In January 1985, a funeral was held for a man known as Japan's godfather, who had been gunned down in the street in Osaka. Two of his lieutenants were also killed. Masahisa Takenaka, fifty-one years old, led the Yamaguchi-gumi, by far Japan's largest underworld clan with a membership estimated by police at 10,400. He was slain by men who fired from a black car as he left the apartment house of an Osaka woman said to be his mistress. With more than one thousand black-suited gangsters as mourners, a Buddhist funeral service was held, which was also televised. The Japanese police also turned out in force, carrying riot shields, bracing themselves for a long siege of revenge and violence within the country's underworld. The Yamaguchi-gumi had been racked by blood feuds for four years after Mr. Takenaka assumed control of this faction of the yakuza. A dissident faction broke away and formed a group called Ichiwa-kai. A member of the Ichiwa-kai group had been arrested for the killing, and three others were being hunted. The yakuza have set themselves apart as guardians of chivalry and honor. Actually, the police say that they are nothing more than social dropouts.

A National Police survey in Japan estimated that in the middle eighties, there were 98,000 yakuza belonging to 2,330 distinct groups. In Chicago, we would call them street crews. The yakuza's tribal features are compelling, like those of an alien life-form: the full-body tattoos, missing digits, and pseudofamily appearance.

The Japanese National Police estimates that the yakuza currently have eighty thousand members. The most powerful faction is still the Yamaguchi-gumi group; they reportedly have close to forty thousand members. In Tokyo alone, the police have identified more than eight hundred yakuza front companies: investment and auditing firms, construction companies, and pastry shops. The mobsters even set up their own bank in California, according to reliable underworld sources.

The yakuza have also moved into finance. Japan's Securities and Exchange Surveillance Commission has an index of more than fifty listed companies with ties to organized crime. The commission is currently reviewing all listed companies and will expel those that have ties to the yakuza. The fact of the matter is that Americans have billions of dollars in the Japanese stock market. So it's possible that U.S. investors could be funding the Japanese mob.

Japanese law enforcement explains that they are aware of the yakuza and what they are involved in but their hands are tied as far as making arrests because "they don't have a RICO Act." They don't have plea bargaining or a witness protective program either. If the government gave law enforcement the tools they needed, they would be able to shut their operations down.

Unlike their Japanese counterparts, U.S. law enforcement officers are sharing tips with Japan. In 2003, the Tokyo police used information from U.S. law enforcement and the Nevada Gaming Control Board to seize $2 million in cash from a safe-deposit box in Japan, which was leased to Susumu Kajiyama, a boss known as "the Emperor of Loan Sharks."

The yakuza made most of their money in recent times from prostitution, drugs, street taxes, and child pornography. Tokyo's red-light district, known as Kabukicho, is swamped with child pornography. Due to international pressure, Japan's officials outlawed child pornography reluctantly. But there was a flaw in the law: it criminalized producing and selling child pornography, not owning it.

The United States has referred hundreds of cases to Japanese law enforcement authorities, but the Japanese authorities report that they cannot open an investigation because possession is legal. In 2007, the Internet hotline center in Japan had more than five hundred local sites displaying child pornography. There was talk in Japan of criminalizing simple possession, but some political parties (and publishers who are raking in millions) opposed the idea.

U.S. law enforcement wants to stop the flow of yakuza-produced child porn into the United States and would support such a law. But they can't even keep the yakuza themselves out of the country. The reason being that the Japanese National Police refuses to share intelligence. In recent years, the National Police had turned over the names and birthdates of about fifty yakuza members – "fifty out of eighty thousand."

The lack of cooperation was partly responsible for a deal made with the yakuza and U.S. law enforcement in 2001. A notorious Japanese gang boss, Tadamasa Goto, who some federal agents called the John Gotti of Japan, needed a liver transplant in the worse way. Goto offered to inform the U.S. government about Yamaguchi-gumi front companies and mobsters in exchange for the transplant. An FBI representative in Tokyo brokered the deal; he neglected to tell Japanese law enforcement, which they resented. You can't monitor the activities of the yakuza in the United States if you don't know who they are.

The operation was a success, but Goto only gave a fraction of what he had promised, but it was better than nothing. When the $2,000,000 was confiscated in the safety-deposit box, the lead did not come from the Tokyo police; they got some of the information from Goto. According to U.S. law enforcement, the Kajiyama case was probably not an isolated incident; if we had some more information from Japanese authorities, we would probably find other cases like it.

U.S. law enforcement has requested the Japanese National Police Agency to provide a list of all the members of Goto's organization so that we could stop them from entering our country. The Tokyo police file lists more than nine hundred members, so then why is it that the Japanese don't share intelligence on the yakuza with the United States?

Could it be because the Japanese government is ashamed of the fact that they let the yakuza become so powerful in Japan they have lost control of Japanese organized crime?

Reliable sources reported that a journalist in Japan was going to write an article about Goto concerning his need for a liver transplant, which he got in the United States. Sources reported that the journalist was threatened by some of Goto's henchmen. He was told to cancel the article or he would be canceled and so would his family. The journalist took some advice from the Japanese police who told him to forget about the story, which he did.

Yakuza activity in the United States is mostly in Hawaii. They use Hawaii as a way station between Japan and mainland America, smuggling crystal methamphetamine into the United States and smuggling firearms back to Japan. They fit easily into the local population. The yakuza were estimated to control around 99.9 percent of the methamphetamine trade in Hawaii as of 1988. They also work with local mobsters, funneling Japanese tourists to gambling establishments both legal and illegal. The yakuza are also suspected of using various operations to launder money in the United States.

It has been reported that the Bank of America is owned jointly by the Vatican, the Jesuits, and the Rothschilds. The parent holding company of Bank of America has been reportedly largely bought out by the Japanese Mafia, the yakuza. Most every bank in California is reportedly owned by the yakuza. Seldom mentioned by the news makers: the yakuza is the main force in West Coast dope trafficking.

'ORK TIMES, FRIDAY, FEBRUARY 1, 1985

Members of Japan's largest gangster organization surrounding coffin of their slain leader, Masahisa Takenaka.

TV Funeral for Japan's Slain Godfather

By CLYDE HABERMAN
Special to The New York Times

TOKYO, Jan. 31 — With more than 1,000 black-suited gangsters as mourners, a Buddhist funeral service was held today for a man known as Japan's Godfather, who was gunned down last weekend by rival gang members.

The Japanese police, who also turned out in force carrying riot shields, braced themselves for a long siege of revenge and violence within the country's underworld, known as the yakuza. Several minor skirmishes, including one involving a man who wielded a sword, already have occurred at several gang headquarters in central Japan.

"We must kill," one mourner said today after leaving the services held in Kobe for his fallen leader, Masahisa Takenaka.

"Total slaughter," said another gangster, his voice a rumble.

Led Largest Crime Clan

Mr. Takenaka, 51 years old, led the Yamaguchi-gumi, by far Japan's largest underworld clan, with a membership estimated by the police at 10,400. He was slain Saturday night by men who fired from a black car as he left the apartment house of an Osaka woman said to be his mistress. Two of his lieutenants were also killed.

The Yamaguchi-gumi has been racked by blood feuds for the last four years. When Mr. Takenaka assumed control last August, a dissident faction broke away and formed a group called Ichiwakai.

An Ichiwakai member was arrested in the Takenaka killing, and three others are being hunted.

Officials of the National Police Agency said they hope that they find their men before the Yamaguchi-gumi does. Many of Mr. Takenaka's followers, the police said, ascribe to a philosophy that he once summarized as "guns instead of butter."

Many Covered With Tattoos

Like the Mafia in the United States, the yakuza is a source of popular lore for many Japanese. It enjoys a cachet abroad as well as at home, enhanced by images of barrel-shaped men whose razor-sharp suits cover bodies plastered with tattoos. Some gang members, a declining number, are missing parts of fingers, the result of self-mutilation designed to show their fealty to the leader.

In their own eyes, according to people who study them, yakuza like to think of themselves as latter-day "ronin," the masterless samurai of Japan's feudal days who supposedly came to the rescue of the defenseless. They have set themselves apart as guardians of chivalry and honor. Actually, the police say, they are nothing more than social dropouts in a country that puts a premium on conformity.

A national police survey in 1983 concluded, with customary statistical precision, that there were 98,771 yakuza, belonging to 2,330 distinct groups.

Theirs is said to be a multibillion-dollar empire based largely on gambling, prostitution, drug-dealing, gun-smuggling and loan-sharking. The more adventurous have expanded operations into seemingly legitimate consumer-finance companies that are often the last resort for credit-starved Japanese.

In 1983, the police said, 19 people were killed and 77 wounded in gang-related shootings. Recently the American authorities have expressed concern that yakuza groups, as well as other Asian criminal societies, have begun to make inroads in the United States.

Means 'Good for Nothing'

The name "yakuza" is derived from an old card game, similar to blackjack, whose object was to draw three cards adding up as close to 19 as possible without exceeding it. Ya-ku-za represents the Japanese words for 8, 9, 3, which total 20, a useless number. Basically, yakuza now means "good for nothing."

Despite worries about imminent warfare, the authorities believe they have begun to bring the gangs under some control. The number of members is said to be about half what it was 20 years ago.

Moreover, the Yamaguchi-gumi has been in disarray since the death of a towering leader, Kazuo Taoka, in 1981.

The clan had hoped to restore order in August when Mr. Taoka's wife, Fumiko, conferred leadership on Mr. Takenaka by handing him a dagger as symbol of his authority. But an archrival, Hiroshi Yamamoto, seceded from the clan, taking thousands of allies with him and forming Ichiwakai, the group blamed for the Takenaka killing.

The underworld behaves somewhat differently here than in the United States. Mr. Takenaka's investiture was seen on national television, as was his funeral today. When Mr. Yamamoto seceded, he announced it at a brief news conference.

Roger "The Dodger" Riccio

The first time I met Roger was when we busted him for operating a sports wire room at 1616 West North Shore Avenue in a second-floor apartment. It was the first time I found a door barricaded with three-fourth-inch plywood. The front door was like any other front door. It looked like we could give it a couple of whacks with our sledgehammer and it would fall apart; no such luck. Roger had a frame on top of the door where he slid a piece of plywood behind the door. When we hit the door, the hammer went through the front door then bounced off the plywood and almost hit me in the head. Meanwhile, Roger was busy inside, gathering up all his bets and sports schedules, which he put in a bag and threw it out the side window. The only problem was, one of my crew, Frank, who was covering the back of the building heard a window opening. He saw the bag come out the window and retrieved it. Of course, Roger figured that he was clean, removed the plywood from the front door and let us in. All he said was "I thought burglars were breaking in. I didn't know you guys were the police, or I would have opened the door for you." I asked him what the plywood was for. He said that he was going to build a workbench for his crippled uncle who he was visiting in the apartment.

When we showed him the bag with over $50,000 in wagers in it, he got a little pale and said that he never saw the bag before and we were framing him. Of course, we arrested him for syndicated gambling and for building a bench without a license – only kidding about the license. The wheels of justice move very slowly at times, and Roger's case had been continued seven times before I had to appear in court to testify about the case. The judge decided that the case should be heard in front of the grand jury for possible indictment.

I met with an assistant state attorney, Tom Regan. He was going to handle the case, which was now over a year old. He asked me questions about the arrest and if there was another apartment on the second floor of the building. My search warrant specified the second floor of the building where we found Roger in. If there was another apartment on the second floor, the warrant would be faulty and the case thrown out of court. To my recollection, there was only one apartment on the second floor, but after a year I wasn't positive. Mr. Regan informed me that if in fact there was another apartment on the second floor, he would have to throw the case out and probably charge me with perjury. I told him again that there was only one apartment on the second floor.

Mr. Regan told me that he was going to send an investigator to the building on North Shore to see if there was only one apartment. This, of course, made me a little nervous, so I decided to recheck the building myself to make sure my memory was still working. Thank goodness I was right. After that, I began drawing a diagram of every raid I made. I began to wonder who the hell was the bad guy – Riccio or me.

The grand jury indicted Roger. When the case was heard in court, they threw it out because we didn't actually see who threw the bag of bets out of the window even though Riccio was the only occupant in the apartment at the time of the raid. Riccio smiled at me after the case was tossed out of court. I smiled back and wished him good luck. I reminded him to keep looking over his shoulder as he might see someone he knows.

Roger was getting a reputation as a big money mover for the outfit; he had been seen in the company of Joseph "Joe Spa" Spadavecchio, a big-time sports bookmaker, and Dominic "Large" Cortina who was considered along with Donald Angelini to control sports bookmaking in the Chicago area. I guess Roger didn't quit his day job after we busted him.

Of course, Roger couldn't get a regular job, and he continued his bookmaking operation with the outfit. Only this time, the FBI was involved and had wiretaps up on his bookmaking business. In 1974, Riccio was indicted along with his companions Anthony Turzitti, Augie

Lazzerini, Charles Naponelli, Vincent Palucci, and Hal Smith. The government proved that these offenders were fused together through layoff bets and betting lines. The business was in operation for more than thirty days and accepted $2,000 or more daily.

Hal Smith gave betting lines to Turzitti who then relayed the information to his associates (Riotto, Naponelli, Palucci, and Riccio). Turzitti acted as a beard for Riccio. On one occasion, Riccio past posted Augie Lazzerini on a daily double. The first horse won and paid $45, and Riccio had it connected to five horses in the second race, which one of them won. The payout was about $20,000. Riccio made the bet fifteen minutes after the race started. Lazzerini screwed up and accepted the bet. When he realized the trick, Riccio pulled on him. He refused to pay, but of course, Riccio convinced Lazzerini it would be better if he paid up.

When the case was resolved in court, two offenders were sent to prison. Riccio was acquitted because the government couldn't prove that he was anything more than a bettor. This guy had a horseshoe up his rear end. I decided to keep an eye on Roger just for fun. He lived in the 1300 block of Lee Street in Melrose Park, which is not a good place to set up surveillance without creating heat on yourself. I managed to track him when he left his house on a Saturday morning. He drove to the Town & Country Bowling Alley at 141 East North Avenue in Northlake, Illinois. I couldn't go in the place because I had no idea where the hell he was inside, and I didn't want him to know that I was on his trail. I hung around until about 1:00 PM when he came out and drove back home. Sure as hell, he was booking in the bowling alley, the little scumbag.

A new system was set up by the intelligence unit and the gambling unit to work together on mob-controlled gambling operations. The gambling unit would give a target that we were working on to the intelligence unit. Then they'd assign one of their surveillance teams to keep the target like Roger Riccio under observation. I, of course, gave the intelligence team Roger Riccio as a target.

I gave them any information I had on Roger, like his address, vehicle, photograph, and possible locations he frequented. I was informed that Roger was followed to a popular restaurant called the Rosebud at 1500 West Taylor Street. This restaurant is well-known, and celebrities have been known to eat there when they are in town. Local outfit guys have been seen frequenting the Rosebud as well.

But Taylor Street has had a reputation of being a mob neighborhood since the '20s.

An undercover intelligence unit detective reported that when he was in the front part of the restaurant near the bar, he observed Riccio talking to a couple of wise guys. At one point, Riccio handed one of them a paper bag. The guy dropped the bag, and when the bag hit the floor, a large amount of U.S. currency fell out. It was quickly retrieved by the unknown bad guy who was about half-drunk. At this time, all concerned left the restaurant. Riccio was kept under surveillance and followed to the Town & Country Bowling Alley at 141 East North Avenue in Northlake. Roger was up to his old tricks again.

I decided to give Roger a visit at the bowling alley, which he had been using to conduct his business. Wayne "Rico" Lloyd, a former robbery/homicide detective who was on my crew, was unknown to Riccio and was able to check out the bowling alley without being detected. Riccio's car was parked in front so we knew he was in the bowling alley, but Rico was unable to find him. We decided to wait until he returned to his car before we grabbed him.

When he came out and saw us approaching him, he dropped the valise he was carrying and was heard to say, "Oh shit." Of course, the valise was loaded with thousands of dollars in sports wagers, sports schedules, and slough sheets, which contained code names of customers and figures of who won and lost for the week. He had nerve enough to ask me if we had a search warrant. I just answered him by saying, "Are you goofy? Do you think that we would violate your God-given rights as a good citizen? Forget about it." The valise also contained a quantity of Cuban cigars. Roger claimed he had no idea where they came from and offered them to Rico who mentioned that he did smoke cigars on occasion.

Roger was arrested and processed once again. When the case was heard in court, it was of course discharged. We seemed to have violated Roger's rights because we didn't have a warrant. Roger seemed to have finally learned his lesson and was keeping a low profile. Maybe he saw the light, went straight and got a job. Forget about it.

I checked with a few informants of mine about Roger's behavior and was informed that he was back in action and was seen at the Rosebud Restaurant on Taylor Street. I decided to keep the restaurant under surveillance from time to time to see if Roger showed up.

After a couple of days of surveillance, we spotted Roger sneaking up the back stairs of the Rosebud Restaurant just before bookmaking hours. After the basketball games started, Roger would slither back down the stairs, with his head acting like it was on a swivel to see if any heat was in the area. We got in touch with our most reliable informant who disliked Roger, and he said that he had a source who could get the telephones Roger was currently using to conduct his business. This time, we obtained a search warrant for Roger at the rear office of the Rosebud Restaurant on the second floor. We kept the restaurant under observation, and sure as hell, here comes our guy Roger "the Dodger" walking down Taylor Street. His head was bobbing around, checking for a tail. He probably parked his car a mile away from the Rosebud to be on the safe side.

We saw him go up the back stairs and into the rear door. After two minutes, he came out and looked around to see if anyone was on his tail. Apparently satisfied, he went back in and shut the door. I waited until I was sure he was in business and climbed the rear stairs. The door, of course, was locked. I gave the sledgehammer to Rico Lloyd, and he battered the door a few times before it gave in. We found another door that was also locked and beat that one in, all the time we were yelling, "Police, we have a search warrant." After that door gave in, we were met by another door, also locked. Finally, the third door gave way, and we found ourselves in a rear office of the Rosebud Restaurant. Roger was seated in a chair with his hands in the air. That's when we heard someone running down some stairs in an adjacent building. I called on my radio to Bill, who was watching the front of the Rosebud to make sure Roger didn't get out the front. He said that some guy left the adjacent building in a hurry and headed west on Taylor Street.

Roger told us that he was in the office applying for a job and didn't know anything about the sports schedules or bets we found under the desk. While searching the desk, I found a couple of photographs of the alleged owner of the Rosebud Restaurant Alex Dana shaking hands with Chicago mob boss John "No Nose" DiFronzo. They were accompanied by Marco D'Amico, Elmwood Park gambling boss, Mike Caracci, and another mobster. Another photo was of Frank Sinatra surrounded by a waiter and four waitresses at the Rosebud. When I showed Bill the photo of Alex Dana, he said that was the guy who left the building next door in a hell of a hurry. Very interesting situation, it's too bad we couldn't get in the office fast enough. It would have been nice to meet Mr. Dana in his office. Maybe he could explain his alleged interview with Roger "the Dodger" Riccio.

I retired from the Chicago Police Department in 1992 after thirty-eight years. Thirty-two of them were busting up mob-controlled gambling operations. I was told by a few informants of mine that some guys were quite happy about that. But as things turned out, I was back in the hunt, working for the sheriff of Cook County Mike Sheahan who was having a problem with mob gambling operations throughout Cook County. I was given the title of director and was allowed to form my own vice unit to combat the outfit. We were able to make hundreds of raids in the county as well as in the city of Chicago.

I had almost forgotten about Roger "the Dodger" Riccio and wondered how he was doing. I hadn't heard his name from some guys I still had that hung around Rush Street bars; maybe he gave up and was driving a cab or something. Naw, no way.

I got a tip that he was hanging around a health club on the North Side on Lehmann Court near Diversey Avenue. I had a new face on my crew, a sharp detective, Jim Kondilis, who had been with the Cook County Sheriff's Office as a corrections officer. Riccio wouldn't know him so Jim came in handy on close surveillances on Roger. I gave Jim a photo of Riccio and the car he was driving and we split up, checking out some of Roger's old haunts on Rush Street, like Gibson's and a few other watering holes some of the wise guys liked to hang out in. As luck would have it, Jim spotted Roger getting in his car with another guy. Jim contacted me on my cell phone and informed me that he was tailing Roger who had parked by the Swissotel at 323 East Wacker. They entered the hotel where they probably had a room to start booking. I told Jim to try and at least find out what floor they got off on but to not heat them up.

Jim called me again and said not to worry about what floor they got off on. They're in the lobby of the hotel, sitting at a table near a bar, smoking Cuban cigars and working their cell phones. The pair had sports schedules and basketball bets on the table; their phones were ringing, and they looked like a couple of out-of-town business guys doing business. I couldn't get near the table where they were sitting, so after about a half hour, I told Jim to sit at a table next to them and open up a newspaper he had but to not look at them. I told him it would be a good experience for him to actually witness big-time bookmakers in action. I gave him a few minutes and then started to walk over to their table. Jim got up and said, "Good evening. Police. You're under arrest." When Roger saw me, he just shook his head and said, "That's it for me, Herion. I'm going to New Orleans." We recovered $50,000 in wagers and $29,000 in cash, two cell phones, and sports schedules.

Roger Riccio, fifty-nine, of 1300 block of Lee Street in Melrose Park, and his associate Robert Najman, fifty-five, of 1200 block of Lake Shore Drive, were charged with syndicated gambling. It seems Najman operated the health club on Lehmann Court near Diversey Avenue. Reliable sources said that Najman sold the club for $5 million, but he owed $3 million. He walked away with $2 million then got divorced. His wife got half of that, and bookmakers got the rest. Then he got rid of his residence on Lake Shore Drive and the bookmakers got that as well.

Riccio joined forces with a small-time bookmaker by the name of Demitri "Jimmy" Stavropoulos and taught him how to move sports lines, lay off bets, and a lot of other tricks, like using water-soluble paper in case of a raid. I had the pleasure of busting Demitri "Jimmy" a few times. The first time was in a second-floor attic apartment at 2105 South Lombard Avenue, Berwyn, Illinois. Demitri, Tony Orlando, and Albert Galluppi were running a large-scale sports bookmaking operation.

They had two barrels of water where they locked their cell phones, cut the wires with wire cutters, and threw them in the water with sports wagers and five calculators. Riccio and Demitri became very close friends and were seen at the racetracks together, and Demitri eventually had a big home built in Oak Brook, Illinois, reportedly at a cost of $1.2 million. Things were good. Until one day, he got a call that Roger "the Dodger" Riccio was found dead in a hotel room in New Orleans, Louisiana. Allegedly Roger was in New Orleans to pick up some money from his gambling ventures. The New Orleans Police reported that it appeared that Roger died of natural causes.

A reliable source reported that Riccio was not alone when he died; he was allegedly with a receptionist from the Lehman Courts Health Club. There was also a question of $50,000 that was missing from the room. The source also reported that when Riccio's wife was notified of her husband's death, a sympathetic mob associate accompanied her to pick out a casket and make funeral arrangements. This sympathetic gesture was really to get her out of the house so that other mobsters could search the house for a large sum of money that Riccio had hidden in the house that belonged to the outfit. If the money was found, no one knows, but reportedly one of the searchers was found murdered gangland-style three months later.

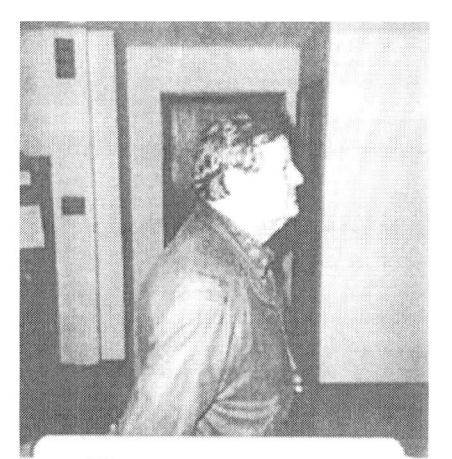

Wireroom operator
Robert Najman
Swiss Hotel
323 E. Wacker Dr.

Roger "Dodger" Riccio
Rosebud Restaurant
1500 W. Taylor St.

Dimitri Stavropoulos
12-2-98
Riccio's understudy

John DiFronzo 1
Alleged Mob Boss

Alex Dana

Marco D'Amico 2
Elmwood Pk mob boss

Alleged owner

Frank Sinatra ^employee's
Rosebud Restaurant

Rosebud Restaurant
1500 W. Taylor St.
2nd Fl rear office
Sports wireroom

Roger Riccio Bookmaker

Rosebud Restaurant
1500 W. Taylor St.
Front view
Roger Riccio

Sgt. Don Herion

Rosebud Restaurant

Gregory "Emmett" Paloian—The Paper Eater

I remember the first time we busted Emmett. His real name is Gregory, but he liked to be called Emmett for some reason. Anyway, Emmett had a bullshit job at Riis Park on Chicago's northwest side and had plenty of time to run his bookmaking operation from the field house. Of course, this was before cell phones became so popular. Emmett had to use the landline phones in the field house, which made him easy prey for the good guys.

The next time we ran into Emmett was in his house in River Forest, Illinois, and here I thought he would have seen the light and gave up bookmaking after we arrested him at Riis Park. Forget about it. Emmett was now equipped with cell phones and water-soluble paper. He proved to me that you can't die from eating bets written on soluble paper; he was getting good at it.

Emmett was involved in a Super Bowl party at the Carlisle Banquet Facilityin Lombard, Illinois. Bookies like to invite high-rolling customers to big onetime events. The cost of getting into the party was $1,000. Bettors and their guests enjoyed good food and a chance to bet on the game for a big payout. When the police raided the place, Emmett was found shoving more soluble paper in his mouth. He was successful once again in destroying the evidence. The next time

Emmett had to swallow his bets was when the Chicago Police were tailing him and he became aware of their presence. When they tried to stop him on the street, he ignored them and kept driving until he had eaten all the incriminating evidence that was in his possession. The police confiscated sports schedules, point spreads, and other gambling paraphernalia but were unable to find any bets. Emmett appeared on television that night as a mobster involved in a large-scale gambling operation in the Chicago area. The arresting officers asked me to look at the gambling evidence they confiscated to find anything illegal. I was sorry to report that Emmett did not possess anything illegal; apparently he ate the bets before they could stop him.

The next time I had the pleasure of busting Emmett was at the Elmwood Park Civic Center where one of his kids was involved in an athletic event. We kept him under surveillance, and we could observe him answering a cell phone and writing down sports wagers while he was watching the game in progress. At one point, I had one of my men, Phil DiPasquale, stand near Emmett while he was writing down the bets and overheard him repeating the bets back to his customer.

I decided to wait until the game was over before we would arrest Emmett for bookmaking. The game ended, and Emmett and his family left the gym area and walked toward the parking lot. At this time, we were no more than a few feet from him when we made our move. I had assumed that Emmett would more than likely put the bets he wrote down in his pocket. Forget about it. The bastard had the bets in his hand all folded up. He kept looking around but didn't see us because of the crowd of people walking toward the parking lot. When I put my hand on his shoulder and called him by name, his right hand shoved the bets into his mouth. At this point, we tackled him and fell into a pile of snow. I had my hand on his mouth, but he would not open it; he just kept chewing away and finally swallowed the bets. While this was going on, his cell phone kept ringing. I think I might have broken the phone by accident.

Emmett swallowed the bets, but we had a witness that overheard Emmett taking the bets when he wrote them down when the game was going on, so we locked him up anyway. Cell phones and water-soluble paper are the bookmaker's savior. I hated both of them. We had another occasion to bust Emmett when he was booking while sitting on a lawn chair watching one of his kids playing soccer in Westchester, Illinois. He had two cell phones going while he was watching the game. I had one of my partners (unknown to Emmett) get close to Emmett while he was taking bets, and this time, we caught him dirty. He was very surprised and screwed up by sitting in a place where someone could get close to him. What the hell, he can't win them all. This time, we were the winners.

Bookmakers like Emmett began using voice mail to set the betting line on a game and take bets the same way. Every call made to a bookie's voice mail gave the time of the bet so that the bookmaker couldn't get past posted. Emmett had cell phones listed to a store at 7100 West North Avenue in Oak Park, Illinois. Of course, they were under phony names as well. With voice mail, Paloian rarely had to talk directly to his betting customers.

Emmett also came up with a gimmick to hide the source of his income. He set up a phony corporation called U PICK 'EM SPORTS Inc. The company's stated legal purpose was to provide the betting line on games to callers.

Emmett teamed up with some other bookmakers who had their own customers. This way, the agents, as they were called, handled their own bettors and split the take evenly with the boss. Emmett earned more operating this way than he would by working alone; besides that, he was insulated from the new bettors. A bookmaker such as Emmett can earn $500,000 or more in a year. His agents can make $1,000 a week; for successful bookmakers like Emmett, their payoff to the outfit could run about $10,000 a month.

When Emmett first started booking in the late 1970s, it was a little rougher line of work then. If a bettor couldn't pay his debts, Emmett might refer him to an associate of his, James "Jimmy I" Inendino, for a juice loan, which called for an exorbitantly high rate of interest. Inendino was a close associate of mob hit men Harry Aleman and William "Butch" Petrocelli. As a matter of fact, Jimmy I was a scary guy himself. In a phone conversation that was secretly recorded, Inendino once threatened to break every bone in a man's body if the guy didn't pay up. But bookmakers today have finally realized that that type of violence only creates a lot of heat and is bad for business. Now they just cut off the deadbeats.

I had the pleasure of busting every one of Paloian's wire rooms. Ralph Strocchia (a.k.a. Dave), fifty-one, of 507 West Twenty-seventh Street, Chicago, who ran "an office," meaning a location set up to operate an illegal gambling business – accepted and recorded wagers from customers and at times collected money from bettors in payment of debts. Edward Gorniak (a.k.a. Felix), forty-nine, of 2708 South Wallace Avenue, Chicago – not only accepted bets on cell phones but he tallied, charted, or recapped the results of the crew's betting operation. Then a wiseass punk by the name of Steven Jasinski – twenty-seven, of 1604 North Twenty-fourth, Avenue Melrose Park, Illinois – worked as an agent for the crew and collected money from various bettors in payments of debts. Another member of the crew was Fred DelGiorno (a.k.a. Roger), who was an agent but passed away before the outcome of the indictment.

Gregory Emmett Paloian (a.k.a. Pete), forty-six, of 1825 North Seventy-second, Elmwood Park, Illinois, organized and led the Paloian bookmaking crew and directed its affairs. I had the pleasure of being part of the raiding team along with the IRS and FBI agents when we arrested Gregory Emmett Paloian in his house on July 2, 2001. Paloian was arrested along with his crew on racketeering and gambling charges for allegedly operating a sports-bookmaking business between 1985 and 1998.

When Emmett appeared in federal court, he swore that his involvement in bookmaking was over. Then he pleaded with the U.S. district judge Charles Kocoras to throw the book at him if only somehow he could be allowed out of prison for a few hours each day to look after his two teenage children. In the end, Emmett's attorneys and letters people wrote to the judge about what a good citizen Emmett had been didn't help. The judge told Paloian that he knew that bookmaking was illegal and knew that it could hurt his children. "You ran the risk," Kocoras said, sentencing Gregory Emmett Paloian to forty-one months in prison.

Paloian had another gimmick going on the side in the Hired Truck Program with his firm called Ruff Edge Inc. Like Jimmy Inendino, Paloian ran a small trucking company out of his house in Elmwood Park. The money came at a good time; the city had hired five trucks from him. That year, the city paid Gregory Emmett Paloian about $182,800. Only when Paloian pleaded guilty in federal court and was sent to prison for forty-one months, did the city stop using Paloian's trucks.

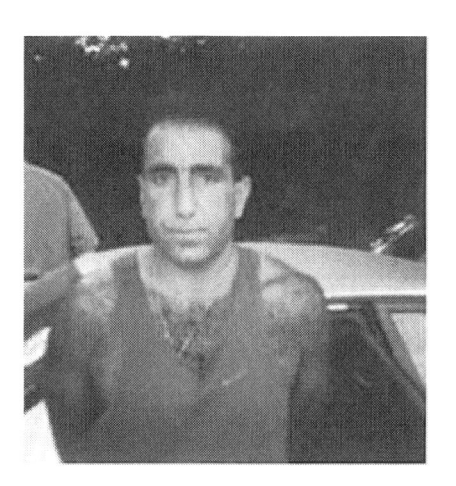

Gregory Emmett 'Paloian
Gambling - Overseer

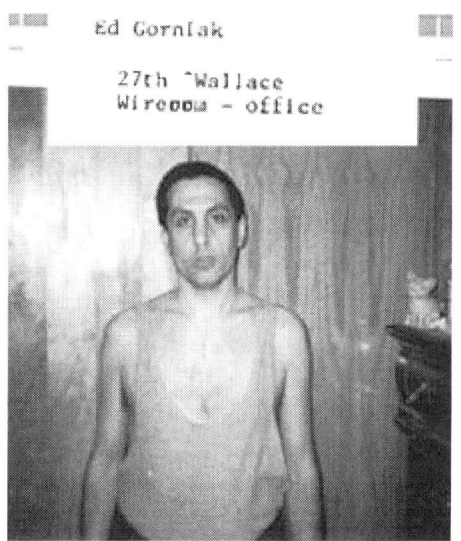

Ed Gorniak
27th ~Wallace
Wireroom - office

Gabriel Caliendo
Emmetts collector

Steve Jasinski
Wireroom

Mobile sports wireroom
3 arrets
Det Rico Lloyd Sgt Herion

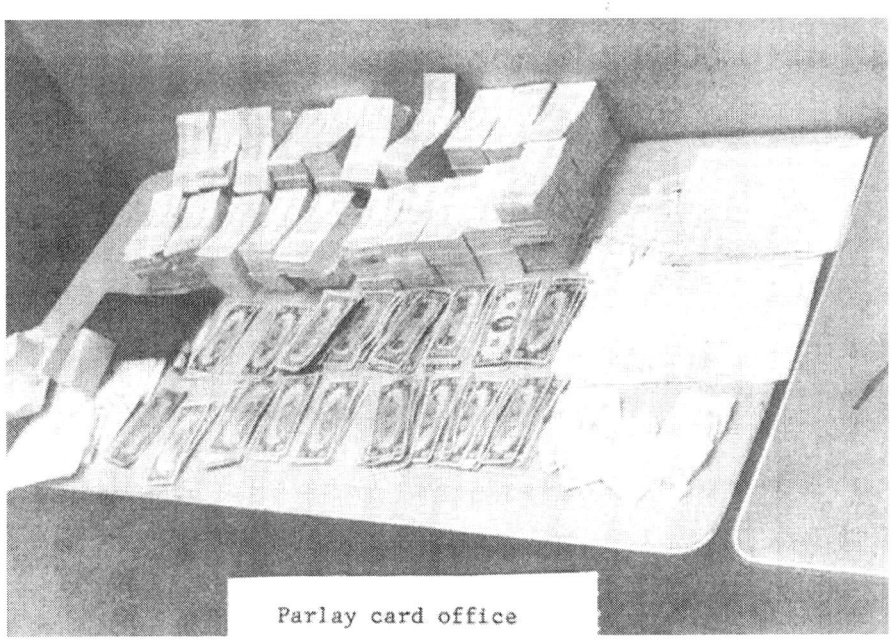

Horse/sports wireroom

Parlay card office

Sports wire-room of known Organized Crime Bookmaker Emmet Paloian

Undercover Methods

Wire Rooms

When my district commander, Mike Foley, appointed me as vice detective in 1961, I didn't have a clue of what I was getting into. The police department was changing their methods of operations since we had a new superintendent of police, O. W. Wilson. Some changes were that district detectives were now assigned to an area headquarters and not in each district station. Vice detectives were now the detectives in the district; they were responsible for any and all vice operations in the district, such as gambling, prostitution, narcotics, and liquor law violations.

Commander Foley told me the top priority was gambling, organized crime-controlled gambling. He wanted bookmakers and wire rooms raided. The one thing he didn't tell us was how to find these operations. At that time, gamblers bet on horses more than anything else. There were some bookmakers that took bets on sports like football, basketball, and baseball games. Of course, football parlay cards were popular at that time as well. They were the blue-collar bettor's way to bet sporting events.

The majority of horseplayers bought a scratch sheet or racing form from a local newsstand so that they could handicap the races that were being run that day. In Chicago, the newsstands sold a scratch sheet that listed out-of-town races, tracks, and what horses were running that day. I figured I would go to the source of the scratch sheets and see who would buy one. Obviously, they were interested in playing the horses, so I would pick out a guy and keep him under surveillance. Some customers drove up to the stand in a car, got a sheet and drove to a nearby location where he could study the sheet and figure out what horse he was going to bet that day. Sometimes he would write down some horse bets on a piece of paper with an amount of money he was going to wager on a horse or horses.

The suspect would then usually go to a tavern, barbershop, cigar store or return to the newsstand and give the bets to the news guy. This type of operation was called a handbook. Or maybe he would find a public telephone where he would call a wire room and make his bets. Cell phones were not around at this time, of course.

After the gambler was through making his bets, we would approach him, identify ourselves as police officers, and tell him that he was under arrest for bookmaking. Of course, he would deny it and tell us that he was only a bettor and was making mind bets.

After intense interrogation giving him our good cop/bad cop routine, we would tell him that if he were only a bettor, we weren't interested in him. We wanted the guy that he called on the phone. Whatever he would tell us would remain between him and us, and we would guarantee him that no one would ever find out that he gave up the wire room number to us.

It was amazing to me how many of these bettors would refuse to give us the wire room number he called. I guess it was for fear he would wind up in a trunk or the river. If the gambler did cooperate with us, I would request him to make another bet on a race in our presence after I dialed the phone number he gave us. It was necessary to do that because if you just accepted any number the subject gave you, he could lie about it. I instructed the subject to hold the phone in such a way that I could overhear both sides of the conversation. If that worked out, we would release the bettor with a warning. If he warned the bad guy that his number was in police hands, or if the bad guy had his phone disconnected or suddenly went out of business, we would visit him at his home or place of employment with an arrest warrant

Next, we would get a listing of the phone number, get a search warrant for that location, and probably kick in a couple of doors. If things went according to plan, we would have a good raid and everybody was happy, except the mob, of course.

Like I said, there were occasions when the bettor would rather fight you or tell you to go to bed with his wife, before he would come up with the wire room number. Then the bettor would swear on his dead mother that if we let him go, he wouldn't call the wire room and warn them that the police were on the way.

When working the day watch, it is the universal practice of police officers to go to breakfast right after roll call. That presented a problem for me with some of my crew. On occasion I insisted that we set up on a location like a newsstand or wherever scratch sheets or racing forms were sold. It was also necessary to be prepared to follow a car that would get a scratch sheet or racing form, especially in the winter months when the local racetracks were closed. The only place he could make a bet would be with a bookmaker. Because the form and scratch sheets were delivered around 9:00 A.M., that conflicted with the breakfast time. I just told them that maybe they better eat at home.

In the winter months, I found through trial and error that the best place to get wire room numbers were places that had a large number of public telephones inside large buildings. The LaSalle Street railroad station on Van Buren Street in Chicago's Loop was such a location. I found a bank of phone booths located in the lobby of the station that contained numerous offices on the upper floors. They were set up like a U, six on one side facing six on the other side with four others on one side.

The phones were accessible to people that came in from the street as well as people that worked in this multifloor building. I would sit in a booth on one side, which gave me a clear view of the six phones facing me. The best time to watch the phones was from 11:30 AM to 1:00 PM. Wire rooms usually were open from 10:30 AM to 1:00 PM, and workers in the building would use the phones on their lunch hour. I would have one of my partners sit across from me so that he could see who was using the phones on my side. That way, we could see anyone that had a scratch sheet, racing form, or a suspicious-looking piece of paper in their hand. We could signal each other as to where a suspect was and even sit in a booth next to him where it was possible to overhear his conversation.

There were days when I would sit in a booth for two or three hours. Sometimes, I was able to watch the gambler dial the number he was calling. If the line was busy, he just kept dialing it so he could get his bets in on time. The more times he dialed, the better chance

I had to cop the number. After the suspect made his bets, we would wait until he, or sometimes she, would walk away from the area of the phone booths. We didn't want to cause any suspicion around our method of operation. After a safe distance, we would stop the person and go through the routine I described before.

The greatest location that I found for gamblers was Soldier Field during the Bears home games. Soldier Field had public telephones all over the stadium. Some were in a cluster of six in a row or three and four in a row. It was like hunting fish in a barrel. Sports wire rooms usually operated from 10:30 AM to 12:00 PM. Then there was a break for two hours before they opened again at 2:00 PM to 3:00 PM for the afternoon games. Bear fans would have to leave their homes to get to the Bear game before the bookmakers opened for business, so by the time they got to the game, if they were going to bet on football, they would immediately go to the pay phones and call their bookmakers. There would be long lines at the pay phones waiting to get their bets in. Some of them had football schedules in their hands or some other type of sports lines so they would be ready to make their bets when they got to the telephone. Of course, my crew and I would mingle in with the bettors. We were equipped with football schedules and the latest point spreads for that day's games. Of course, no one suspected that we were the police.

While in the line, we would be attempting to copy what phone numbers the bettors were dialing. Usually when they got through to the bookmaker, they would identify themselves by a code number (e.g., R22) then proceed to make their plays. I've heard some guys made bets for up to ten dimes on a game. A dime is $1,000. Some bettors spoke very low and stood as close to the phone as possible, acting like they were Communist spies or something. Some even tried blocking the view of the number they were calling in case anyone would see or hear what they were doing. After we were sure we copied the right number, I would call my wife Gen or my three daughters, Nancy, Jayne, or Mary Ann at home and have them call the suspect wire room numbers to see how they answered the phone. They would then write down the following information: the number of times they had to call each number, how the person answered the phone, male or female, if the phone was constantly busy, or when it was answered, and if they could hear any other voices in the background talking about football teams, etc. They were instructed to ask for a girlfriend of theirs and then just say sorry wrong number. Having girls call a suspect number creates less suspicion with the bad guys than when a man calls the number; it makes them very nervous, and they have been known to run.

Other indications concerning wire rooms are when a guy answers the phone and he just says, "Hang on." Meanwhile, he's talking on another phone and can be overheard taking bets. The above kinds of investigations kind of went by the wayside when the cell phones were perfected. Wouldn't you know that when the first cell phones came out, that the outfit began using them? There were some bag phones, suitcase phones, and car phones. They were a real pain in the ass because they really couldn't be tracked down. They were still costing about $2,500 per phone. We thought we had trouble with pagers and call forwarding when they would have their calls sent to another location. With the pager, the bookmaker would give the bettor his pager number, which was listed to a vacant lot somewhere. So if a bettor got grabbed, all he could give the cops was the pager number. When the bookmaker would call the bettor back and we answered the phone, he would probably call us some nasty names and talk about our mothers. The bad guys then began giving eight hundred phone numbers to places like Aruba, Costa Rica, and the Dominican Republic where they had set up their operations.

Parlay Cards

Making an investigation on a parlay-card operation is a tedious, boring, aggravating experience. Whoever is doing it had better have a lot of patience because you could be sitting on a suspect for a long time until he gives you a lead.

The main objective of this type of investigation is to find out who is running this operation and take down everybody involved: the runners, distributors, and the office where the stubs are turned in with the money. If done right, the printing press can be found with a little hard work. The cards are usually printed late Sunday night after all the games have ended and the point spreads are determined. They can also be printed on Monday night, delivered on Tuesday to the distributors, who then give them to the runners who work in factories and office buildings. There are two types of football cards that are printed, one is for college football games to be played on Saturday and the other cards may contain both college and pro games on it.

Either way, the stubs have to be turned in with the money collected by noon Saturday.

I have had the good fortune to bust twenty-two presses throughout my career working on parlay presses. Some of the presses would print fifty thousand cards a week while other operations would print up to five hundred thousand. Many of them were controlled by organized crime, and some others were operated by independents. They, of course, had to pay the mob street taxes for the privilege of operating.

The card is usually three or four inches wide by eight or nine inches in length and printed on heavy paper. The back of the card lists the odds for betting on three teams' odds, paying 6 for 1. It doesn't say 6 to 1. There's a difference. The bets usually run from $1 up to $20. If you bet four teams, the payout is 11 for 1. The more teams you bet, the bigger the payout. By the way, all the teams you bet must win, ties lose.

The names of the football teams are printed on the front, such as Wisconsin – 3 and Ohio State. The other college games are listed with different point spreads. Pro football teams are listed below the college games. Usually they play on Sunday, with one game on Monday night.

Each team listed has a number in front of their name. Depending on what team you think will win, with the point spread, you would circle the number in front of the team that you pick will win the game. The minimum number of teams you can bet is three. The handicappers that make the point spread for each game try and make every game as even as possible with the point spread.

At the bottom of the card, there are numbers listed exactly as they are on the top portion of the card. That is, if you pick three teams at the top, such as 4, 22, and 30, you have to circle the same numbers on the bottom portion of the card. The card is usually perforated about two inches from the bottom of the card, which contains numbers 1 through 60 on the back.

The front bottom portion of the card has a place for your name, number of teams that you bet, and the amount of money you have wagered. This part of the card is called the stub, which has a number on the stub, e.g., 23654. This number is also on the top portion of the card. This is a way of determining who bet on this card. The bettor keeps the top portion of the card as a record of which teams he bet on. The bottom portion of the card is removed and is turned in to the person that gave you the card. He is known as the runner. All the stubs have to be turned in to the runner before the first games are played on Saturday, which is usually at 12:00 PM. It is common knowledge that the cards turn up in schools, offices, factories, taverns, barbershops. Some were even delivered hidden in daily newspapers. They are a very popular way to bet football games for a small amount of money. The cards are given free to the bettors. If the bettor gets lucky and has a winning card, the runner will pay him off the following week when he gives him the new cards.

The runner has a good job. He only has to handle the cards when he distributes them on Tuesday, when he collects the cards either on Friday night or Saturday morning and when he turns them in to the bookmaker. The runner collects 25 percent of whatever he books, regardless of who wins or loses. I ran into a runner that was booking $2,000 a week, which means he was making $500 clear without any worries.

The weird thing about parlay cards is that they are not illegal to print because the same information that is on the parlay cards is listed in the newspapers every week. Of course, everyone knows what they are used for, but technically they aren't illegal until the teams are circled and the amount of money bet on the card is marked on the stub. Usually the printer only prints the cards, and the stubs are nowhere near the printer. Whenever we tracked down the printing press, we would get a search warrant and give it to the state attorney for his approval. Then we'd present it to a judge for his approval. I never had a warrant turned down by the state attorney or a judge.

I recall an investigation that my partner Jim Hanrahan and I got involved in that turned into a major operation. The investigation began with a guy we observed playing a parlay card. From him, we managed to find the runner. We tailed the runner until we found out which bookmaker he turned in his cards to. The bookmaker then had to be tailed the next week to find out who he got his load of cards from. This, of course, could be a Sunday night, Monday morning, or any time until Tuesday night.

The bookmaker we found met a distributor in a parking lot on the North Side of Chicago. This took us many hours of tracking and trailing the bookmaker before we could identify the distributor. Our undercover vehicles used for this type of work were not very good, so on occasion; we had to use our personal cars to get the job done without heating it up. Our distributor was a big man who walked slightly bent over. His name was Anthony Verlick who resided at 6051 North Maplewood Avenue, Chicago, Illinois.

Our investigation revealed that Verlick controlled thousands of parlay cards he personally distributed throughout the Chicago area. Now all we had to do was try and track him on a Sunday night, Monday, or Tuesday to try and locate where he was picking up the parlay cards from the printer. I learned the hard way that the printer may meet the distributor on the street to deliver the cards to him; that way, he didn't have to reveal the location of his printing press. In this case, Verlick drove to the printer where he picked up the cards. The printer happened to be in North Chicago about forty miles away.

Eventually, after many hours of watching Verlick, we found that he would leave his residence on Maplewood Avenue early on Monday morning and drive to downtown Chicago where he would meet a man by the name of Sam Minkus in the Conrad Hilton Hotel. To accomplish this feat, it took a lot of luck and some crazy driving in downtown Chicago without losing Verlick in heavy traffic. We observed Minkus give Verlick the point spreads for the coming week's game. So far, so good; but because there were only two of us tracking Verlick, we had to keep him under surveillance and also set up on his car so that we would be in a position to tail him when he left the hotel.

Verlick had parked his car on Van Buren Street, so we decided that both of us should keep his car under surveillance instead of trying to watch him walk around the loop. After about an hour, he returned to his vehicle, drove to the expressway and, headed north toward the Kennedy Expressway. We had to keep him in sight. We managed to stay with him when he looked like he was going to go west on the Kennedy Expressway. He cut over to the entrance of the Edens Expressway and headed north toward Milwaukee.

Now was the moment of truth. We knew for sure that he was going to meet his source for the cards or he was headed directly to the printing press. We sure as hell were not going to lose him now after all this aggravation. Without getting into a lot of details about what we had to do to follow Verlick to the press, I'll get to the point. We tailed him to North Chicago at 2421 Green Bay Road, which has a two-story building. When we saw a sign on the building that said Vogue Printing Co., we were very happy, to say the least.

The only problem we had was that we were a little bit out of our jurisdiction, but we would worry about that later. Now we had to get in a position to see if anyone except Verlick showed up at the printer to get the cards. The first car we saw parked in front was driven by a navy chief petty officer who entered the building. Another vehicle arrived about 3:00 PM, and a man also entered the building. His license checked to a Leslie Sugarman, of 2805 West Hollywood Avenue, Chicago. Several other vehicles parked at the printers; each person came out carrying large boxes and put them in their vehicles and left. Verlick also came out carrying several large boxes and put them in his vehicle and left. We decided to leave the area about 8:30 PM and call it a day and night.

The next day, we reported to our lieutenant of what we had uncovered and that the printing press was in North Chicago, Lake County, Illinois. But we told him that we could handle the situation with a friendly state attorney and judge. His answer was "Forget about it, I'm going to call the FBI. You can give it to them, they've got jurisdiction."

We met the FBI at the Avenue Restaurant at Twelfth and Michigan on October 28, 1968. Our lieutenant had told them that we would cooperate with them and give them the facts of what our investigation had uncovered. Jim and I were not too happy about giving away our work to the FBI because we had heard about the FBI not sharing information with the police. When and if any raids would be made by them, they would take all the credit and not even mention the work done by the police.

Surveillanc, Tracking and Trailing – Common Sense

On any surveillance, it is best not to have two men sitting in any kind of vehicle, especially in three-piece suits. I understand that the former director of the FBI liked his agents to be neat. Always be prepared to be in a fixed position for hours. If need be, have a utensil with you in case you have to relieve yourself. Never park in a place where the suspect may drive by you. If you're covering the rear of the location in a surveillance van in the winter months, do not leave your motor running for obvious reasons. Just wear warmer clothes, or just tail people in the summer.

Position your vehicle facing the same way as the suspect when he leaves, unless you have the eye and other vehicles can take up the chase when you direct them as to the direction the suspect is headed. Of course, you must check your gas supply before starting this endeavor.

When speaking on a walkie-talkie, do not hold it up to your mouth. You would be surprised how many police officers I have worked with on surveillances should know better but do just that.

When we gave the FBI a thorough report on what and who we observed at the Vogue Printing, which, of course, included the chief petty officer that was probably stationed at nearby Great Lakes Naval Training Center. I didn't think they would interview him while conducting their undercover investigation. Forget about it.

I found out later that they interviewed him shortly after we gave them the information, and it seemed that he was working part-time at the printers. The FBI told him that we knew what they were doing in the printers and that if he didn't cooperate with them, they would see that he was sent to Vietnam. In my opinion, I think they were wrong in revealing the ongoing investigation, but then they did have the petty officer by the short hairs, so he agreed to be an informant for them.

In reality, all he could tell them was what we already had told them. He did agree to inform the FBI if there were any changes during the printing of the cards or if Verlick changed his shorts or whatever. I was notified that the FBI was having a problem tailing Leslie Sugarman from the printers to wherever he was going with his load of cards. They told me that when they would follow him, he would suddenly park on the side of the road on Route 41 (Edens Expressway), probably checking for a tail. The next week, I gave it a try. All I did was wait for Sugarman to show up at the entrance to the expressway. That eliminated Sugarman seeing anyone following him from the printers (common sense). In my opinion, I think Ray Charles could have followed Sugarman; it wasn't that difficult. He drove directly home to 2805 West Hollywood Avenue, Chicago. He parked in front of his apartment and unloaded two large boxes and entered the first-floor apartment.

I positioned myself to be ready to tail Sugarman in case he would leave with the cards. I stayed there from 4:10 PM to 6:00 PM. During this time, I left my car on several occasions to get some of the license numbers of ten vehicles that parked by his apartment and to keep track of whose drivers entered the building. Sugarman had left his shades slightly ajar, so I was able to see some of the men that entered his apartment, got a package from Sugarman and then left the building and drove away. The good news was all this was taking place in Chicago; we didn't need the FBI for this.

Things Not to Do

When an undercover investigation is ongoing, it's not a good idea to interview people that are connected to the main target. The FBI did interview the petty officer, which was stupid on their part in my opinion. It was lucky there was a war going on, so they used that as a hammer to get the guy to cooperate with them. But it could have gone the other way as well, and they would have blown all our tracking and trailing for nothing. We did tell the FBI that Verlick hung around the LaSalle Street Railroad Station at 139 West Van Buren Street during the week and knew a lot of people in the building; probably a lot of them were handling the parlay cards for him. Verlick hung around the third floor almost every day. Now wouldn't you think if the FBI started to interview them about Verlick, maybe one of them just might tell him that the FBI had been asking questions about him? (Common sense.) Now if I would have done that, the FBI would probably accuse me of warning Verlick that he was the target of an investigation and would have indicted me for stupidity. Well, that's exactly what they did; of course, they warned Verlick that the FBI had been asking about him. Only Verlick didn't know that we knew where the press was.

Surprise, surprise, guess what? The chief petty officer contacted the FBI and told them that he had been advised by the owner that they were discontinuing the printing of football cards due to excess heat from the FBI. The last batch would be done in a couple of hours. The FBI had to scurry around to get a search warrant signed by an FBI agent assigned to the case. The warrant had to be signed by a judge from the Nineteenth Judicial Circuit Court of Lake County, Waukegan, Illinois.

Accompanied by the chief of police of North Chicago, the FBI executed the local warrant. They confiscated five hundred thousand parlay cards and other miscellaneous gambling paraphernalia. Whoop de do. Of course, the FBI neglected to notify us about the raid. I happened to read about it in the newspapers. This, of course, screwed up the possible raids that we could have made with Sugarman's operation. Now he couldn't get any cards from the Vogue Printing as they were out of business.

FBI Surveillance

I found out that the FBI had rented an apartment across the street from Sugarman's apartment and three agents were keeping his apartment under observation: Bill Roemer, John Bassett, and Robert Alexander. They neglected to inform us of that fact.

A week after the raid at the Vogue Printing, I decided to keep Sugarman's apartment under surveillance for the hell of it. Well, about 4:00 PM, Sugarman arrived home and brought a few large boxes into his apartment. Within two hours, the same vehicles I had seen before showed up and the men entered Sugarman's apartment. They all came out with a familiar bag and drove away. Obviously, Sugarman was back in business and so were we.

I called the FBI the next day and asked them if anything was happening around Sugarman's apartment. The answer from Roemer's surveillance report was "no activity." That's when I told Vince Inserra, the agent in charge, of what I had observed. That the same vehicles that had picked up the cards before were back in business. Inserra said that he would check into it.

The following week was our turn. We had set up all around Sugarman's immediate area within striking distance of apprehending any vehicle that left his apartment with a bag. I had an eye on the apartment and would notify other cars which direction a suspect vehicle was facing. This way he could be apprehended a safe distance away from Sugarman's apartment so that any other bad guy wouldn't get suspicious of police activity when he got near Sugarman's apartment. Everything came off without a hitch. When it was over, we had confiscated ten vehicles and busted twelve guys. They were all in possession of parlay cards, winning stubs from the previous week, and thousands of dollars in cash. I don't recall seeing any FBI agents around the area, but it would have been nice if they would have let us use the apartment they rented across Sugarman's but then maybe the windows were dirty and they couldn't see out of them like the previous week when there wasn't any activity.

Undercover Gambling investigation resulted in the arrest of 4 subjects operating the biggest sports wire-room in Chicago history

Video Poker Machines

Video poker machines are known as the crack cocaine of gambling. They are very addictive and have caused numerous problems with people who lose all their money every week playing them. The machines are legal in Illinois as long as they have a license, but anyone that has poker machines in their place of business pays off on the machines. The only way that the proprietor of the business can be arrested for gambling is when he or she pays off on the machines.

When video poker machines first surfaced in Chicago about 1979, you could play a machine for a quarter. The object would be to accumulate forty units on the machine so that you could win $10 for every forty units. You would notify the person in charge of the business who would then check the units that you accumulated and pay you off in cash.

This activity had to be witnessed by the police before an arrest could be made and the machine or machines could be confiscated. These machines were set up to pay off 60 percent of the time when they first came out, the reason being that the player would continue playing the machines because he or she felt that they could beat the machines. The high payoff was set up to lure the players back to the machines, of course. After a short time, the machine payoff rate was reduced to 50 percent by the operators of the machines. By this time, most players I talked to were addicted to playing the machines and lost their paychecks doing so.

Eventually, the video poker machines were set up where you could bet not only a quarter but a dollar, five dollars, ten dollars, or twenty dollars. One location I knew of had ten machines in the back room of a hamburger joint on Chicago's West Side. The owner told me that his end of the money that was bet through the machines was $10,000 a week. Of course, the Chicago Outfit controlled all the video poker machines in the city and suburbs and would split fifty-fifty with business or locations that had the machines.

The governor of Illinois wants to legalize video poker machines in the state to raise money to rebuild roads, bridges, and schools. The governor wants to have forty-five thousand video poker machines throughout Illinois. I understand that there would be a limit of five machines per location in the state. I'm fully aware that the machines are moneymakers and have kept a lot of businesses from going broke due to the income derived from the illegal gambling from the poker machines.

I have raided hundreds of places that have had poker machines and confiscated hundreds of the machines. When we first became aware of the poker machines springing up all over Chicago, we would witness a payoff from the proprietor to a player in some tavern or grill or wherever they were set up. We would arrest the proprietor and confiscate the machines. We would break into the machines and confiscate all the monies that were in the machine, sometimes totaling thousands of dollars. The outfit decided that it would be better if they gave the proprietor of the business a set of keys so that he could empty the machines daily. In the event of a raid, the police could only confiscate the money from that day's gambling.

In the beginning of the video "joker poker" machines, the "house" had to have a large amount of $10 quarter rolls, which were stacked under the cash register in a back room or even in the refrigerator. A dead giveaway that the establishment was doing a land-office business was the accumulation of quarter wrappers in the waste container or on the floor. In some locations, the machines were so filled with quarters that the machine coin feeder would not accept any more coins. It was a blessing for the outfit and the establishment when the machines were set up to accept currency. To avoid problems with law enforcement, almost every machine had a sign For Amusement Only, which was a joke of course.

In court, we ran into a problem as to what is a payoff and how is it done. Money does not have to physically change hands to constitute a payoff, but for a successful gambling prosecution, it is recommended. On video poker machines, players receive units of play for all winning combinations. This unit or credit is equal to one quarter. The longer the player plays the game, he will either accumulate more credits or lose whatever credits he has; and at that point, he will have to insert more money in the machine to be able to continue playing. Usually the payoff is made when the player who has accumulated more than forty credits will inform the operator of the business that he wants to be paid off. The operator would then check the machine and record the credits that he is paying out. Some of the machines were equipped with knock-off meters and knock-off switches. A knock-off meter may be a mechanical meter or an electronic meter, which appears on the video screen. A knock-off switch is usually found on the back of the machine and is usually a switch or button. The best device I found was a handheld radio frequency transmitter that resembles a garage door opener. Both devices are used during a payoff on the machines.

The vendor is usually responsible for the maintenance of the machines, as well as accounting for the revenue generated by the machines. There were two companies that exclusively supplied machines to certain areas. Zenith Vending at 3516 North Knox Avenue, Chicago, owns Apex Vending at 1985 Anson, Melrose Park, Illinois. This company also supplies cigarette machines, jukeboxes, and pool tables and is associated with two alleged mobsters: Salvatore Bastone with FBI #369832M8, who lives at 50 Cody Lane, Deerfield, Illinois, and Marco D'Amico with FBI #484765LB, who lives at 20 Liberty Drive, South Barrington, Illinois. Another company is J&R Amusement located at 6226 Ogden Avenue, Berwyn, Illinois. This company supplies the majority of video poker machines in the Berwyn area.

After a few years, the manufacturing companies such as Williams Electronics Inc. and Merit Industries began making countertop video poker machines. I, for one, was glad to see this because the large video poker machines weighed five times as much as the tabletop machines.

The towns where this type of gambling became popular are Stone Park, Melrose Park, Berwyn, Cicero, McCook, Summit, Chicago, Addison, Elmwood Park, Stickney, and Lyons. I found out that the more these places get raided, the operators become smarter and smarter. For instance, we raided a restaurant at Kedzie and Irving Park Road where we found five machines being played in open view and the players that won being paid off in front of everybody in the restaurant. Obviously, this was not a very difficult investigation to determine if gambling was taking place, so being trained investigators, we arrested the proprietor and confiscated the five machines. About a week later, we received information that there was gambling taking place in the same location we had just raided. I found this hard to believe, so I made another visit to the restaurant. Lo and behold, I found that five more machines were in operation, only they were now in a rear room where they were almost out of sight from the public. Needless to say, we made another raid and seized the five machines again. We arrested the manager who told me that if it wasn't for the machines, they would have to close the restaurant for lack of business. A week later, the restaurant was closed and out of business.

After I had retired from the Chicago Police Department in 1992, I began working for the sheriff of Cook County, Mike Sheahan. I ran my own unit called Vice Detection, with an office in the Third District Courthouse in Rolling Meadows, Illinois. Our main objective was to bust up mob-controlled gambling operations in the county, mainly wire rooms. On occasion, we would raid places that had video poker machines in Chicago. Of course, when we executed a search warrant in Chicago, I always invited some of my old crew from the gambling unit to join us on the raid.

This one particular grill in the 3900 block of West Irving Park had been raided before when I was with Chicago PD. We would confiscate five poker machines at 10:00 AM, but by 2:00 PM, they had five more machines back in the grill. This pissed me off, so I thought it was my turn to piss them off. We executed the warrant about 11:00 AM and seized five poker machines and arrested the manager of the grill. Only this time, I had one of my crew, who was not with us on the raid, hang around the grill to see if they were up to their old tricks and got some more machines. Sure as hell, my undercover guy, Phil, called me in the office and told me they just got five more machines in. I told him to hang around the grill and see if they paid off anyone playing the machines. I told him we were on the way back to the grill.

Sure as hell, the five machines were as busy as ever. There were even a few guys waiting in line to play the machines. We raided the grill again and confiscated the five machines. The grill man was kind of shocked to see us back on the same day. He even volunteered to give me other locations where they were paying off on their machines and asked why we didn't raid their places as well. I told the guy that if he got any more poker machines in, I would be back "like the Terminator." The grill closed up about a week later, so I guess he believed me.

Most of the bars and restaurants that had poker machines began to build small rooms or hung drapes around their machines to prevent law enforcement from seeing them. If an undercover cop played the machines and won, the proprietor probably would not pay the guy off if he didn't know him. He would have to spend a lot of time and money to get the guy's confidence where he would get paid off if he won. Video poker machines have been declared legal in the state of West Virginia. It has been reported that the state accrued over $210 million from the machines.

A few problems exist with the legalization of video poker machines. Two casinos, the Empress and Harrah's, reportedly have one thousand machines between them. Would forty-five thousand other machines throughout the state affect the casinos' business? Is the Illinois Gaming Board prepared to regulate so many machines in so many locations? The law does say that communities can ban video poker by local referendum. Governor Quinn stated that this was a protection for people who don't want poker machines in their neighborhood bars.

Recently, a former Chicago bar owner pleaded guilty in federal court to running a video poker gambling business involving about thirty taverns and restaurants in the Chicago area. David Leader, seventy, admitted the illegal gambling business generated about $400,000 for him in 1998 and 1999. As part of his plea agreement, Leader agreed to forfeit $250,000. Leader faces up to fourteen months in prison. Leader admitted that he paid the bar and restaurant owners between $2,000 and $5,000 each to place Cherry Masters poker machines in their establishments. Jesse Yale made collections from the machines weekly, reimbursed bar owners for winning wagers, and then gave the owners 60 percent of the profits. Leader pocketed the remaining 40 percent.

This may sound silly, but as I recall, when we were really cracking down on places that had video poker machines, we confiscated hundreds of the machines. They were inventoried and then kept in a warehouse on the South Side of Chicago. So many machines were seized that the warehouse where they were kept was filled to capacity. The city of Chicago didn't want to lease another building to store the confiscated machines that we would confiscate in the future, so we were ordered to stop seizing the machines. I guess that was good news for the amusement companies.

If and when forty-five thousand video poker machines become a fact in Illinois, there will be a problem with law enforcement policing the establishments that have the machines. For example, in New York City, they have in excess of 4,300 offtrack-betting locations, which are all legal. From what I have been told by reliable sources in New York, the betting locations have all been uniform in style and resemble each other. I have also been informed that the crime syndicate has set up their own offtrack-betting locations in New York, which are not legal but they look like the legal offtrack-betting locations.

They, of course, are taking bets on horse races, sports events, and the illegal lottery. The only way they can get caught operating an illegal book joint is for the police to check out every offtrack betting location in New York.

In my opinion, I think the outfit can do the same thing in Illinois with video poker machines. They can put them wherever they want without any connection to the state of Illinois. Again law enforcement would have to check out every establishment in the state that has poker machines to see if they are legal. To my knowledge, the Chicago Police Department only has one man assigned to the gambling unit at this time. The Cook County Sheriff's Police only have a handful of vice detectives that would handle this type of investigation. The Illinois State Police rarely get involved in gambling operations of this kind.

Poker Machines

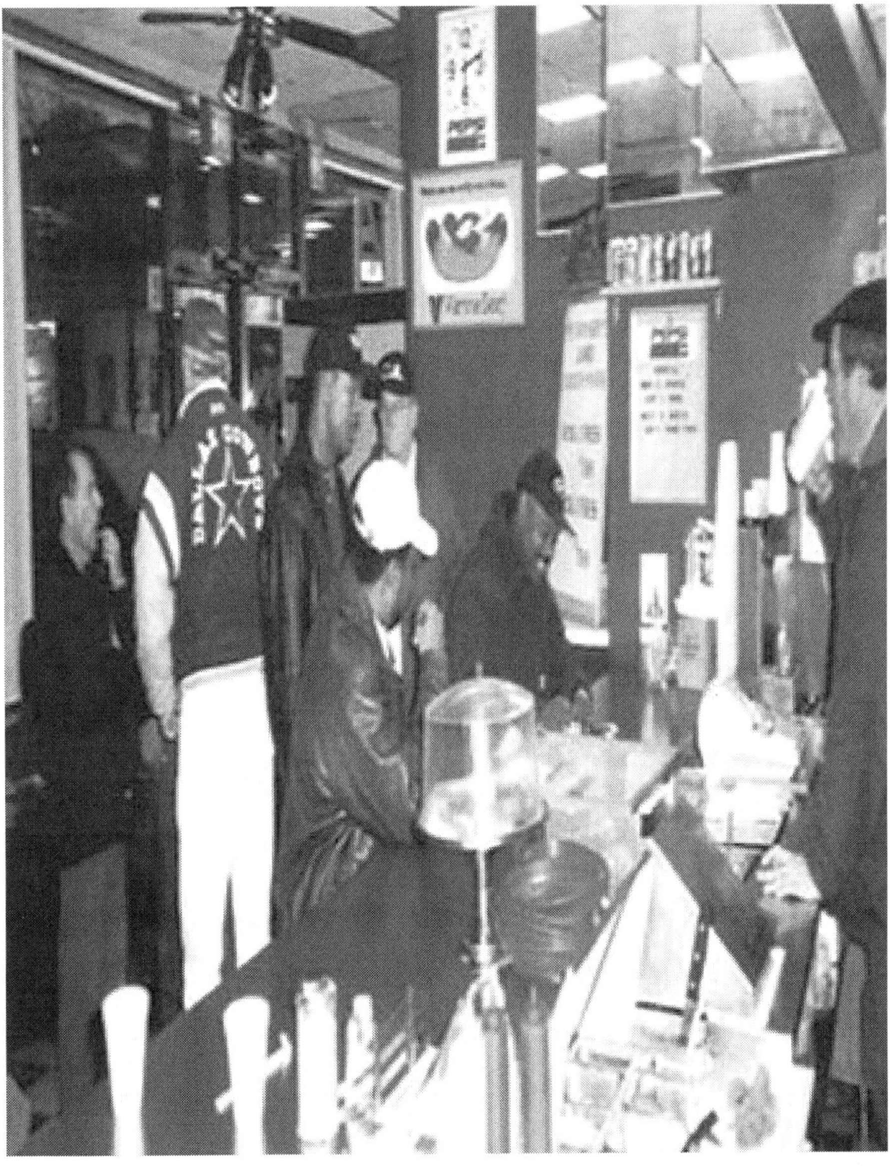

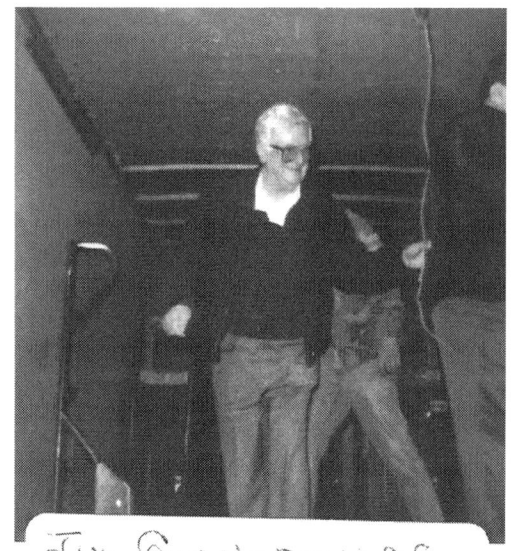

Jim Giangopoulas unloading poker machines

Chicago court hearing reference video gambling machines – 1930

Director Don Herion, Cook County Sheriff's Vice Unit aided by Chicago Police raid a Video Poker machine headquarters in a restaurant in Chicago

The Chicago Dungeon

When we first ran into Lenny Palumbo, he tried to come off as a real Mafia bad guy; he dressed the part of Joe Pesci in the movie *GoodFellas* and had a smart mouth on him as well. To be honest with you, when we tried to stop Lenny, we really had no reason to except for what I would call profile driving. He looked like a gangster to me and drove with his left hand on the wheel and his right hand on top of the passenger seat. Besides that, he gave us a dirty look when he sped past us. As I explained in *Pay, Quit, or Die*, we had a small car chase with Lenny up and down side streets until he hit a dead-end street. We boxed him in and the chase was over. We told him to get out of the car with his hands up while we pointed our guns at him. He appeared to be shaking.

It was 3:00 AM, and there wasn't much traffic or people on the street when we stopped him. We got him out of his car and noticed that he had urinated on himself. He was dressed like a wise guy with the gold chains, an open white sports shirt so we could see a few hairs on his chest, and a black sports coat. He identified himself as Lenny Palumbo and requested to call his attorney. I asked him why he sneered at us and then proceeded to drive past us in an erratic manner. Lenny then explained that he thought we were robbers or carjackers and were after his Cadillac. I felt I had to explain to him that robbers or carjackers rarely use flashing lights or a siren when they want to steal a car. I asked him if he had spilled something on himself because his pants were wet.

I wanted to give him an excuse to tell us why his pants were wet. He said that he spilled some coffee when we were chasing him.

At this point, Lenny told us he wanted us to read him his rights. I explained, "We only read rights to people we arrest. We were only going to give you a couple of traffic tickets, but now we're going to bust you for being dumb, a bad dresser, and for pissing on the public way. But first, we're going to tow your car to a place where it will be safe, while you sit in the shithouse with a few brothers who I'm sure will admire your fine jewelry." Lenny then began whining and sniveling and apologizing for making faces at us and not stopping when he told him to.

We instructed him to remove his pants because we were not about to transport him in a police vehicle with pants that were soaked in urine. When we searched his car, we found some sports schedules and blank soluble paper, which were not illegal to possess. When I read Lenny his rights, he began to piss all over himself again, and he begged us not to tow his car and that he could help us if we would give him a break. I asked him about the sports schedule and soluble paper. Lenny then told us about a three-story building at 1210 West Grand Avenue that had been newly remodeled and was being used by the outfit for prostitution and gambling. We had heard about this place and had been watching it from time to time. It belonged to the Grand Avenue street crew, which of course was controlled by Joey "the Clown" Lombardo. It was down the street from Rose's Sandwich Shop where Richard Cain was murdered years ago.

Lenny gave us the phone numbers to the place and admitted that he had been making bets with a guy named Tony who ran the place. He then begged us to never reveal to anyone that he told us about the place or he would be butchered for sure. I explained to our new informant that if we raided the place and there wasn't anything there, we would hunt him down and throw him in the river. Only kidding, of course. We gave Lenny back his pants and his car and told him that this incident never happened and sent him on his way. Lenny shook our hands and raced out the back door, putting on his urine-soaked pants as fast as he could.

The building at 1210 West Grand Avenue had a camera above a door on the east side of the building. This door led upstairs to the second and third floors. A door on the east side of the building led into the first floor. A camera covered this door and white shades covered all the windows on the first floor. It so happened that I had already checked out this location for bookmaking by posing as a gas company employee to get inside. All I found were an ugly receptionist and remnants of a few torn-up bet slips in a garbage can, which weren't enough for a search warrant. On further investigation, we learned that "Tony" was Tony Vaughn, an ex-con who ran the place for Jimmy Inendino, a mob guy we had busted for loan-sharking. Inendino was also part of Harry Aleman and Butch Petrocelli's crew. Aleman was a stone killer and was doing life in prison; Petrocelli was found murdered and dumped in his car on the West Side of Chicago. With our new informant, I decided to get a search warrant for 1210 West Grand Avenue. We found a friendly judge whose gambler brother had his legs broken by some bad guys. We executed the warrant, and after gaining entrance to the front door with necessary force, we found the same receptionist. She was sitting at her desk writing in a ledger and watching a monitor with a view of the front door, which was of no help to her now. Tony Vaughn came running out of the back office when he heard the commotion we made. We identified ourselves as police and gave him a copy of the search warrant. Tony was a big dude, six foot six, 240 pounds, and mean looking. We escorted him back to his office where he also had a monitor with a view of the front door, two cell phones, sports schedules, and sports wagers. We placed Vaughn under arrest and asked him where the other two doors on the floor led to. He said he didn't know, so we informed him that we would have to break them down. At this point, he gave us keys that he retrieved from under his desk so we wouldn't have to break the doors.

Signs were tacked inside the doors, identifying the place as Chicago Dungeon. The signs were a warning that a group of transsexuals had entered the Chicago area and were offering domination services. Some of these transsexuals are *HIV-positive*. Also it had been proven that some of them were filming their clients without their knowledge and using the films to *blackmail* them for money. And at certain places, clients were getting mugged going back to their cars. Then they bragged about having sterilized rooms, equipment and toys after each session, and other goofy things.

When we checked the place out, we found that it had been in business for eight years. In the basement, we found several rooms set up. One was like a jail cell with leather garments hanging on the wall, with handcuffs, a few whips, even a police-type uniform with assorted masks. The whole place looked like an amusement park for fags. Another room had a small stage with mirrors and wigs hanging on the wall along with women's clothes. I wish we would have hit this place on Halloween night; no telling what we would have found.

On the second and third floor, we found more gadgets, a big six-foot wheel that someone could be strapped to with whips in the room. I guess you spin the wheel, and somebody whips the hell out of you while you're naked and getting dizzy. In another room, we found a female sitting on a pink chair staring at the wall. She was twenty-five to thirty, brunette, had a thin build, wearing a black dress and black leather boots. I was pretty sure she was a female. I asked her what she was doing there with all these whips, chains, straps, nooses, and other leather garments. She told me that she was waiting for her girlfriend who was applying for a job as a waitress. She wanted to know if that was illegal. Just another smart-ass bimbo.

We took her upstairs to the third floor where we found her girlfriend sitting on a bed in the dark next to this red-headed guy who had a silly look on his face. He was in his forties, wore glasses, stood five foot nine, weighed about 200 pounds, and was fully clothed. The female appeared to be Spanish, was about thirty, five foot four, 145 pounds.

She was also fully dressed in a black blouse and black slacks. The room was well equipped with more leather gadgets. In a closet, there was a red light that looked like it came off an ambulance and then more wigs in any color you desired. There was a used condom wrapper on the floor. I asked our guy who said his name was Fred if he had any knowledge of the wrapper lying at his feet. Fred just looked at me like a deer in the headlights and shook his head no very rapidly.

Another goofy room was set up like a hospital room with medical equipment and nurse's uniforms. Somebody was playing doctor and patient, I guess. Then we found a room with a rack-type bench where someone stretched you out and beat you. Other rooms had more of the same crap.

I checked the ledger the receptionist was writing in when we made our entrance to the Chicago Dungeon. Their clients only had first names or code numbers, and each one specified what they liked to do or have done to them. A guy named Sam liked to injure himself while he was dressed like the Wicked Witch of the West. Bill had a panty hose fetish. John liked to be spit on, slapped, and kicked. Jim, "call me Jeanette," is a cross-dresser. Terry sometimes would bring girlfriends or boyfriends and would wear leather stockings while he was put on a wooden rack. The rack had a hole for his head and holes for his hands; someone would then give him a golden shower. I immediately thought about our new friend Lenny, the wannabe mob guy, who could be a real star here. He was always pissing in his pants anyway. It might be a good side job for him. Another guy, who used a code to identify himself, was really weird. He wanted to hang upside down while someone sprayed him with whipped cream and poured chocolate on his genitals. I don't want to describe the rest of the procedure he requested.

By the way, the cheapest price for any of the requests was $200; the highest I saw was $400, depending on how many other guests you bring with you. We had a camera with us, so I took some pictures of some of the rooms and their setups, which will accompany this story about the Chicago Dungeon. We busted Tony Vaughn for syndicated gambling, transmitting wagers, and acting as keeper of gambling. I wish there was a charge for operating a madhouse without a license.

3/00 **BE WARE CAUTION**

ITS BEEN CONFIRMED THAT THERE IS A GROUP OF TRANSEXUALS THAT HAVE ENTERED THE CHICAGO AREA THAT ARE OFFERING DOMINATION SERVICES. SOME OF THESE TRANSEXUALS ARE H.I.V. POSITIVE. PLEASE BECAREFUL THE STATS ON PEOPLE THAT SEE TRANSEXUALS ARE ONE OUT OF TEN ARE INFECTED WITH THE AIDS VIRUS IT ALSO HAS BEEN PROVEN THAT SOME OF THEM ARE FILMING THERE CLIENTS WITHOUT THEIR KNOWLEGE AND USING THE FILMS TO BLACKMAIL THEM FOR MONEY AS WELL AS CERTAIN PLACES CLIENTS ARE GETTING MUGGED GOING BACK TO THERE CARS. WE PRIDE OURSELVES IN OFFERING FIRE CLIENTS SAFE + SANE FANTASY ROLEPLAY FOR THE LAST EIGHT YEARS. AS WELL WE STERILIZE ARE ROOMS EQUIPMENT + TOYS AFTER EACH SESSION ALWAY REMEMBER SAFE PLAY IS FUN PLAY PLEASE BECAREFUL WHERE YOU PLAY.

SINCERLY
CHICAGO DUNGEON

CHICAGO DUNGEON
1210 W. Grand Ave
Chicago, Ill

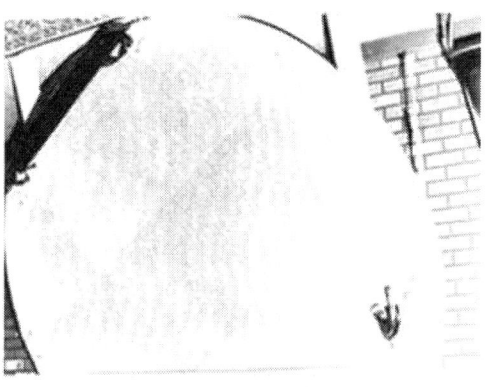

Torture wheel

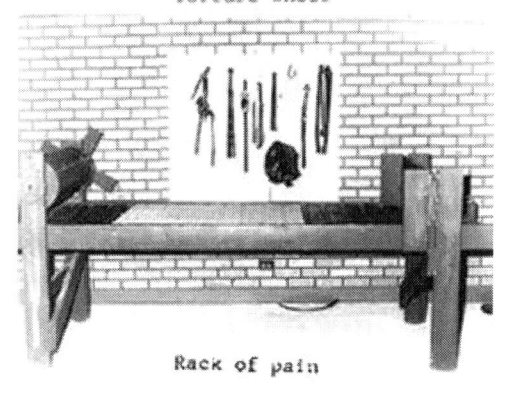

Rack of pain

JAIL

The above items are used for weird things.

The Corporation

This large-scale gambling operation known as the Corporation has a chairman of the board driving this expanding organization by means of violence. It also has accommodation with the Mafia to corner a large segment of the numbers racket in the New York City and New Jersey areas. The chairman of the board, who controls this nationwide Cuban organized crime operation, is Jose Miguel Battle Sr., also known as the Godfather. Jose Miguel Battle Sr. was born in Cuba on September 4, 1929, and is also known as Jose Miguel Battle-Vargas (the name he used in Cuba). Battle, a former Havana vice cop who also served in Batista's army, was a member of Brigade 2506, the Bay of Pigs landing group. During Batista's reign, Cuban gambling casinos were influenced by U.S. underworld figures including Meyer Lansky and Santo Trafficante, head of the La Cosa Nostra family in Tampa. After the failure of the invasion force, Battle was made a lieutenant in the U.S. Army by an act of Congress then returned to the Miami area and became deeply involved in the establishment of this country's first Cuban-controlled gambling operation.

His organization has grown steadily with the migration of the Cubans to other areas of the country, including Chicago. Battle is known for his organizational genius and toughness, but his empire expanded initially through police and political corruption. Battle moved to Union City, New Jersey, in the late '60s and established his gambling operation in the Northeast with the help of organized crime members, such as Joseph "Bayonne Joe" Ziccarelli and Santo Trafficante. Battle soon became the Cuban Godfather mainly by taking over existing numbers operations by means of homicide and arsons.

It is believed in the early 1970s that the Battle gambling operation established a strong foothold in the New York City area. Numbers operations sprung up in almost every Cuban or Spanish bar or bodega. The success of the Cuban gambling operations did not go unnoticed by elements of the Mafia operating in New Jersey. The result was a kind of mutual assistance pact between the Corporation and the La Cosa Nostra whereby the Corporation paid a percentage of the action and laid off some bets with the Mafia. Ziccarelli and James Napoli, identified by the New York City Police Department as capos in the Genovese crime family, were instrumental in negotiating this alliance.

Major legal problems confronted Battle as early as 1970, when he was indicted by a federal grand jury for interstate and foreign travel in aid of a racketeering enterprise. Battle pled guilty and, after being sentenced to eighteen months on these charges, fled the country and resettled in Madrid, Spain, under an assumed name. While in Madrid, Battle lived in luxurious circumstances and was seen at social events at the Venezuelan embassy. Although in hiding, Battle continued to control his numbers operation by employing a secret courier service, which entered the United States via Miami or Canada.

When he attempted to return to the United States in September 1972 by way of Costa Rica, Battle was arrested by the FBI at the Miami airport on the outstanding fugitive warrant and eventually was to serve thirteen of the eighteen-month sentence previously imposed. In December 1974, Battle was arrested again, this time by the Union City Police Department, for carrying a concealed weapon. This time, there were serious corruption allegations concerning this department. The Union City mayor at that time was William Musto who was later convicted on federal charges. Battle's weapons case was transferred to the federal court system.

The federal gun charges against Battle were put on hold several times, pending the outcome of a Florida State indictment charging Battle with first-degree murder and conspiracy to commit murder. These charges stemmed from the Miami homicide of Ernest Torres, a former trusted ally of Battle. On December 16, 1977, Battle was found guilty by a jury of murder and conspiracy to commit murder and sentenced to thirty years in jail, but the conviction was reversed by appeal. On June 19, 1978, after serving eighteen months, Battle was tried in federal court on the weapon charge, found guilty, and sentenced to an additional four years in prison to run concurrent with the state time. Battle then pleaded guilty to conspiracy to commit murder, was given credit for time served, and placed on thirty-three months of probation.

The Corporation has evolved to the point that it has a firm foothold in legitimate businesses. Although Battle himself had a conservative amount of property in his own name, he controls a criminal enterprise, whereby he was able to steer the course of millions of dollars in disclosed as well as hidden assets. The Corporation must be conservatively valued at an estimated several hundred million dollars with an endless cash inflow. Battle owns the Union Management and Mortgage Company Inc., the Union Finance Company, the Union Financial Research Company Inc., Union Travel and Tours, and El Zapotal Realty Inc., all in South Florida. The Corporation owns or controls interests in domestic and foreign financial institutions and has large real estate holdings.

Several key members of the Corporation moved to Florida in 1982. Battle and his associate Abraham Rydz applied for Florida driver's licenses one day apart on April 2-22, 1982. During the seven-month period from August 31, 1982, through March 30, 1983, Battle and his wife, son, and Rydz purchased various real estate for $1,115,000, of which $805,000 was paid in cash.

An undercover investigation of the Corporation's courier system revealed on at least two documented occasions shipments of monies intended for Battle in Florida, which were seized by law enforcement. On April 8, 1983, Jose Battle Jr. and Abraham Rydz were detained by the New York Port Authority Police after resisting the search of carry-on baggage while boarding a flight for Miami. After some resistance, both individuals submitted their luggage for inspection, wherein U.S $439,000 was found wrapped in gift boxes. Both Battle and Rydz denied ownership of the currency and only would indicate that they were vice presidents of the Union Financial Research Inc. in Miami, Florida.

On another occasion on December 3, 1984, the British Customs authorities detained several key Corporation associates including Humberto Davila Torres at London Heathrow Airport. They were found to be in possession of U.S. $450,000. Their itinerary included

Nassau, Bahamas; Geneva, Switzerland; Malaga and Madrid, Spain; with a return to Miami.

Personal property, businesses, and cash seized from members and associates of the Corporation totaling approximately $43 million gave small measure of the economic power of the Corporation. The Corporation has laundered millions of dollars in illegal revenues through financial institutions and the Puerto Rican lottery. The laundering of illegal funds is facilitated by the complex web created by the Corporation's financial holdings in mortgage and lending companies and through real estate ventures. Also, records of the Department of Agriculture disclosed that redemptions of food stamps from bodegas in New Jersey by Battle's financial institution was the largest in the United States, in excess of $10 million in one year. In contrast, Citibank, with 250 branches in New York City, collected $7-8 million in food stamp redemption in one year.

The Corporation used an apparent, unique technique in its continued attempt to launder monies. The technique involved the utilization of the Puerto Rican lottery. Basically, the Corporation would let it be known that they would be willing to purchase winning Puerto Rican lottery tickets for an amount greater than the amount provided by the winning ticket. This technique surfaced in a government undercover operation relating to federal money-laundering offenses called Operation Greenback – Puerto Rico. This was a cooperative effort by the Internal Revenue Service, U.S. Customs Service, the Chicago Police Vice Control Division Gambling Unit, and Drug Enforcement Administration.

On May 10, 1984, at the Palace Hotel, Isla Verde, Puerto Rico, a special agent was introduced by another IRS undercover agent to Guillerino Rivera Guerrero, who was a branch manager of the Western Federal Savings Bank. He was from New Mexico and was in Puerto Rico to launder drug money for various narcotics trafficking. Guerrero described other members of the bank's money-laundering clientele – one of which was known as the Padrino or Godfather. Guerrero explained to the undercover agent that he worked with two or three numbers racketeers that were involved in illegal sports betting and horse racing. According to Guerrero, one of his clients was a *padrino* in the numbers racket who also dealt in drugs and traveled a lot to New York and Chicago. The Padrino laundered his money in Puerto Rico and took it to Costa Rica.

Guerrero, who apparently liked to talk a lot about his job, explained to the undercover agent how to launder money through the Puerto Rican lottery. He stated the first step in laundering through the Puerto Rican lottery was to buy a winning ticket with the main objective being to move the money. Guerrero explained that he had a friend named Ramon who had several lottery agencies. On June 10, 1984, Guerrero told Ramon, the insider man, that he wanted to buy a winning ticket worth over $100,000.

From information received from various law enforcement agencies, evidence was uncovered that the same type of system was going on in other parts of the country. For instance, in Illinois, Texas, Oregon, and Florida, there have been instances where the Corporation has been documented to have purchased winning lottery tickets, so far in excess of their winning value. This technique is used to provide a legitimate source of income for Corporation members, who in turn redeem the purchased ticket. These individuals, who have no other means of legitimate income, are happy to pay the federal tax on their winnings simply to legitimize their expenditures.

A reliable informant revealed that all Puerto Rico lottery tickets sold in the United States are controlled by an organized crime group known to the Cuban community as the Corporation. At one time, the lottery tickets were transported from Puerto Rico to Miami via commercial airlines. However, in recent years, the tickets have been transported by a special plane that leaves Puerto Rico for Miami on a weekly basis loaded with a large volume of tickets. The Corporation makes approximately $14 million per week from the lottery sales. The lottery tickets are sold primarily in the cities of Chicago, Miami, New York, and Los Angeles. However, other cities such as Houston and Tampa also have access to the tickets.

When you become a distributor for lottery tickets for the Corporation, the Corporation gives you detailed instructions as to what to do if you have a large winner. For example, if a bettor from the Tampa area should win a $125,000 prize, the Tampa distributor is to immediately notify the Corporation. The Corporation would then contact the individual and offer the individual $150,000 for the ticket. The winner is told that if he travels to Puerto Rico to collect the $125,000, then reports will have to be made to the Internal Revenue Service and the individual will only get a small portion of the winning ticket. The winners always take the $150,000 offer. The Corporation then takes the ticket to Puerto Rico, cashes the ticket, and pays the IRS the full amount of tax due. The Corporation has so much money that its members are willing to pay twice as much in illegal money in order to obtain legitimate money.

Storefront gambling operations do business openly. In contrast, narcotics traffickers operate in secret and feed a large market, which is open to all comers. If there is any competition, it is eliminated by violence. The lack of law enforcement pressure nationwide permitted the expansion of the Corporation's business under centralized control. Reliable and quick communication, so essential to the success of any gambling operation, has created the need for centralized intelligence concerning operations like the Corporation in order to eliminate this illegal enterprise nationwide.

In New York alone, there are 4,355 OTB parlor-type-gambling storefront locations that have been in operation for years. They operate without a front of any kind. They have Plexiglas put up to guard themselves against theft and problems. They have slots to pass money and numbers back and forth. They have odds posted all over the building. It is only used for gambling.

Chicago did have OTB storefronts that were set up for accepting horse bets from local racetracks. They would charge a bettor 10 percent of the bet he made that they claimed they would place the bets at the racetrack. Of course, the bets would never get to the track; the bookmaker would hold the bets and book them himself. They had different names such as Finish Line Express, Mercury Messenger, daily double, and numerous others. They, of course, were all run by organized crime. We raided every one of them, a lot of them more than once. Actually, it was quite easy to bust them; we made bets with some of them ten minutes before the race was going to be run. We would watch the location to see if anyone would leave and go to the racetrack; of course, no one did. This was the biggest scam the outfit ever set up. Not only would they take the bets but would also make 10 percent on every bet they took in.

Eventually, we got the FBI involved in this scam, and we indicted a lot of mobsters who were behind the operation, like John Spilotro, Dominick Cortina, Bernard "Pepe" Posner, Jimmy Inendino, and a lot of other individuals associated with the outfit. By arresting these individuals and disrupting their gambling operations, we eventually were able to shut them down and put them out of business.

The Puerto Rico lottery was big business in Chicago and surrounding states and was controlled by the Chicago Outfit. Gambling boss Ken "Tokyo Joe" Eto was put in charge of this operation. To my knowledge, Eto set up the multimillion-dollar bolita racket. He also organized and set up a mob-controlled high-stakes game of Monte, a blackjack-like card game. There were some grocery stores, bars, gas stations, and other small businesses that sold bolita tickets and runners who took bets all over Chicago and suburbs as well. Everything connected to the illegal bolita operations was very secretive and not as open as the OTBs in New York.

Eto, who had been arrested numerous times, had worked directly for North Side crime syndicate boss Vince Solano. Solano became nervous for fear that Eto would turn informer after Eto was convicted of gambling charges in 1983. After conferring with other members of the Chicago Outfit about Eto's future in the mob, it was decided that he be killed. Two hit men, Jasper Campise and John Gattuso, were given the job. On February 10, 1983, Eto, accompanied by Gattuso and Campise, drove to a parking lot behind a restaurant at Grand Avenue and Harlem where Gattuso shot Eto three times in the back of the head. They then left the scene, assuming Eto was dead; they were wrong. Eto survived the shooting and then he turned informant against the Chicago Outfit. Gattuso and Campise were arrested for attempted murder and released on bail. That was a mistake; they were both tortured and murdered and stuffed in the trunk of Campises's Volvo that was parked in a shopping mall in Naperville, Illinois. Eto joined the government witness program.

Jose M. Battle Sr., head of the "Corporation" listens to testimony.

JOSE M. BATTLE
"THE CORPORATION"

WEEKLY GROSS PER RETRIEVED "SPREADSHEET"	$2,100,000
PROFIT RATIO (ESTIMATED FROM CONFIDENTIAL INSIDER)	× 43%
ESTIMATED WEEKLY NET PROFIT	$903,000
CONVERSION TO ESTIMATED YEARLY NET PROFIT	× 52
ESTIMATED YEARLY NET PROFIT	$46,900,000

'Cuban mafia' chieftain sentenced in Miami

Published on Saturday, March 17, 2007   Email To Friend   Print Versi(

MIAMI, USA (Reuters): A leader of a "Cuban mafia" organized crime syndicate called The Corporation was sentenced on Friday to nearly 16 years in prison for racketeering and ordered to forfeit $642 million.

Jose Miguel Battle Jr. was convicted last year on various racketeering conspiracy charges including murder, gambling, arson and money laundering.

Battle Jr. is the son and namesake of the "Godfather" of a 40-year-old organization prosecutors likened to a Cuban mafia, and substituted as head of the crime family when his father was out of the country or in jail.

The elder Battle built the syndicate on illegal gambling in New York in the early 1960s after leaving Cuba, prosecutors said. It later branched out to south Florida -- a Cuban population center from those who fled the Cuba revolution -- and into drugs, contract killing, arson and money launderin(

Battle Sr. was sentenced in January to 20 years in prison after pleading guilty to racketeering conspiracy last year.

Prosecutors said The Corporation was responsible for numerous murders including those of a 3-year-old child killed in a fire and an ex-hit man wh was gunned down in the 1970s after leaving the syndicate.

The younger Battle, who was sentenced to 15 years and eight months in prison, oversaw sophisticated money laundering operations in the Cayma Islands, the Dominican Republic, Panama, Spain and other locations,

Mario "Motts" Tonelli— American Hero

I got a phone call from a friend of mine who asked me if I would meet with a friend of his who wanted to give me some information. He suspected that the mob was running a phony gambling scam involving bingo. I told him that bingo was legal and they probably had a state license, but I would be glad to talk to his friend and find out just what was bothering him. My friend told me that the man's name was Mario Tonelli and he lived in Skokie, Illinois. Then he told me that Mr. Tonelli had been a star football player at the University of Notre Dame in the '30s, played for the Chicago Cardinals before the war, and was a survivor of the Bataan Death March in World War II. I called Mr. Tonelli and made arrangements to meet him at his house the next day. When I parked near his house, I noticed that the car parked by his house had POW license plates, which meant that the owner of the car had been a prisoner of war. Mr. Tonelli met me at the front door, we shook hands, and we began talking about our mutual friend and other small talk.

Mr. Tonelli appeared to be in his eighties, five foot eleven, 190 pounds, with gray hair and a friendly smile. When I called him Mr. Tonelli, he said that he had another name he was known by; it was Motts, and I could call him that. I had noticed a variety of items around the house that had the name Notre Dame University on them. Then he told me that being a member of the Italian American War Veterans, he knew of a veteran's hall in Northlake that ran bingo games and he was sure that they were running the hall illegally. They were using the name of the Italian American War Veterans as a front. He then said he had heard that the mob was connected to the bingo hall called the Grand Palace Bingo Hall at 121 East Grand Avenue, Northlake, Illinois.

I asked Motts if he knew any names that were involved in the bingo hall or had any idea of how they were operating illegally. He told me that he had heard from several sources that belonged to the Italian American War Veterans organization that the operators were skimming money and running pull tabs and raffles illegally. The pull tabs and raffles were supposed to be strictly regulated by the operators, but they weren't. I told Motts that I would check out the Grand Palace and see what I could find out.

I then couldn't resist asking Motts about his football career as our mutual friend had told me that he had played at Notre Dame University and the Chicago Cardinals as a fullback. Motts then told me that he played at Notre Dame in the late '30s and then for the Cardinals in 1940. That's when he enlisted in the U.S. Army for a year in March 1941. He had also met a beautiful girl named Mary at a dance. After a brief courtship, they married. He said that he wanted to get his time in the military over with as we weren't at war yet, and then he could concentrate on his pro football career with the Chicago Cardinals.

When Mott's orders came through, he learned that he was going to a place he knew nothing about, somewhere off the island of Luzon called Bataan. The place was filled with green foliage, mosquitoes, monkeys, iguanas, and jungle. Every day was kind of boring with cleaning weapons, drills, marches here and there. The months dragged on. Mott's thoughts were of the coming football season. He wondered how the team was doing, but then in a few weeks, he would be leaving Bataan and be a free man again. Other than the fact that the Cardinals were playing the Bears, Motts and the rest of the men at Clark Field didn't expect that December 7, 1941, would be much different from any other day. But that ended at 5:00 AM when the sirens began to blare and the camp came to life.

Motts and everyone else then found out that the Japs had bombed Pearl Harbor and the United States was at war with Japan. They were then told that Clark Field would probably be bombed next, with the possibility of Japanese paratroopers invading the field. Nothing happened until early afternoon when the sound of approaching planes was heard. They bombed the parked planes first. Men were diving under barracks and tables, and bodies were flying everywhere. Scores lay dead, maimed, heads blown off; arms and legs lay everywhere. Motts picked up a Springfield and fired at anything that passed close. For what seemed like hours, the planes came; but when Motts looked at his watch, it had only been two hours.

The planes returned day after day, bombing, strafing, killing. Rumors kept coming that help was on the way, but help never came. By April, the Americans were in terrible shape; they had little food or medicine left and were racked with dysentery and malaria. It seemed unthinkable, but they were ready to give up and they did. Motts explained that their ammunition had been expended, men were starving, and it was mass confusion. Motts and ten thousand other U.S. troops were now prisoners of war. It was the beginning of a nightmare. The Japanese wanted to clear the area so they could attack nearby Corregidor. They decided that they would march the prisoners out. Motts and the other men thought that they would be marched to some nearby prison camp where they could rest, get medical attention, and be given food and water. Shortly after they began marching out down the dusty road, Motts saw something that made him realize how wrong he was.

He saw something that bobbed in the air. As the object came closer, he realized that the object he saw was a human head on a pole. It was an American soldier's head that was swarming with black blowflies. Motts described the tropical sun as unbearable and the dust from the road made breathing almost impossible. The brutality of the Japanese became apparent as soon as the first soldiers fell. Those that collapsed were bayoneted, shot, or beheaded. Sometimes they were run over by Japanese trucks. Mile after mile, they were beaten and tortured without any food or water in the searing heat and humidity.

Motts described an incident to me that was unbelievable. He saw a Filipino woman who appeared to be about eight months pregnant, standing by the side of the road with a canteen of water that she handed to one of the prisoners who had staggered near her. A Japanese soldier grabbed the water from the prisoner and bayoneted the woman in the stomach. He then cut the baby from the woman's stomach and stuck the baby on a pole next to the road as a warning to other Filipinos not to help the marching prisoners. Some Filipinos that ignored this warning were staked and burned.

When the prisoners were finally stopped, it was because the Japanese wanted to rob the Americans of jewelry, lighters, ballpoint pens, and even pictures of loved ones. If the Japs found Japanese money on anyone, the men were shot and killed on the spot. As Motts watched, he noticed a soldier staring at his hand. Jabbing him with a bayonet, the soldier pointed to Motts's Notre Dame graduation ring gleaming in the sun. Motts said he didn't move until his fellow soldier told him that if he didn't give him the ring, the soldier would kill him. Motts took it off and gave it to the soldier. Motts watched the soldier walk away smiling while looking at the ring. A few moments later, he saw an officer grab the soldier and ask him something. Then the officer walked up to Motts and asked him in perfect English, "Did one of my soldiers take something from you?" "Yes," Motts said. "My graduation ring from Notre Dame." Motts told me he was in total shock that this Japanese officer spoke to him in perfect English while they were on a death march in the Philippines. The officer reached in his pocket and produced the ring. He gave it back to Motts and told him to hide it. The officer then told Motts that he graduated from Southern California the same year Motts graduated from Notre Dame. The officer told him he was at the game when Motts ran for seventy-seven yards on a single play and then five yards to score the winning touchdown for the national championship. The officer then told Motts that he was a hell of a player and wished him luck. Needless to say, Motts was in shock.

Motts said that it was really weird that he had to find the one officer who was present when Notre Dame beat his team. Apparently, the officer was not seeking revenge from Motts. He never saw him again. Motts then changed the subject; I could see that he didn't want to talk about his experiences any longer. He asked me if I would let him know if I found anything out about the bingo hall. I told him no problem, give me a few days, and I would get back to him. I could imagine how he felt that some mob guys were using Italian American War Veterans organization to rip off real veterans. The odds were that none of them were ever in the service; they were probably in prison.

I checked out the Grand Palace Bingo Hall that night. The hall held a lot of patrons. Most of them were little old ladies sitting around tables until they leap to their feet to yell "Bingo." But there was a sprinkling of elderly men as well; they played pull tabs and raffles that were also available. It was a good thing that I had a hat on and found a seat at the very rear of the hall because that's when I observed a man I had busted before – Phil Cozzo He was the son of mob gambling boss Jimmy Cozzo who was busted for operating a large-scale sports wire room in an armored vault that was equipped with an ADT burglar alarm system, a television, four telephones, heat, air conditioning, and soluble paper. His partner at the time was George Columbus whom I had the pleasure of busting before in a barricaded wire room on Central Avenue in Chicago. Both were members of the mob's Grand Avenue crew.

The raid took place on December 15, 1980, in an abandoned warehouse at 517 North Racine Avenue, Chicago, Illinois. The odd thing about that raid was I had checked with Illinois Bell security for any telephones listed to the building at 517 North Racine Avenue and their answer was "There aren't any telephones listed to that building." Without a telephone number, we couldn't get a search warrant, so I decided to do what had to be done – violate their rights! After we got in the building and found the armored vault they were using as a wire room, we also found four working telephones, imagine that. Cozzo and a man named Frank – male, white, forty-five – seemed to be in charge of the proceedings, operating a raffle and pull tabs as well as the bingo games.

While I was playing bingo, I kept my eyes open for any other bad guys I might recognize, when I observed two other guys sitting directly in front of me. They were playing bingo, but they only had one card apiece and appeared to be watching this guy named Frank. I spotted a pair of handcuffs under one of their jackets – another undercover superstar in action. I hoped no one else noticed this because it could only cause some heat and make the bad guys nervous.

The next day, I called the Department of Revenue about the Grand Palace and spoke to a friend of mine whom I had worked with in the past on some black bookmakers that were booking the Illinois Lottery. When I mentioned the Grand Palace Bingo Hall, he knew all about it and told me that there was an ongoing federal investigation. He told me that the feds had been trying to link the money being siphoned off by Phil Cozzo, the son of Chicago mobster Jimmy Cozzo, for a luxury hotel-casino he was operating on the Caribbean island of Curacao. My friend told me that when the Grand Palace opened in 1994, they lured players away from areas like churches and VFW halls that cut into their profits, which were used for the church's elementary school.

I called Motts the following day and told him that I had some news for him. We met at a restaurant near his house. I told him what I had observed at the Grand Palace Bingo Hall and that I wasn't the only person from law enforcement investigating the hall. I told him that he was right on the money when he said that the mob was involved in the Grand Palace Bingo Hall. I explained that there was a federal investigation going on. I also explained that the government operates very slowly, but they'll get the job done.

Motts was very happy to hear the news and thanked me for my help. I told him it was a pleasure, and we shook hands. That's when I noticed the ring on his hand; it was gold and had a diamond in the middle and some initials on the sides, which were worn-out. I asked him if that was his Notre Dame graduation ring. He said, "Yes, that's it, kind of beat-up now, but I've still got it." He then took it off his finger and said, "Here, try it on if you want." When I put the ring on, Motts said, "How does it fit?" I told him it was a little big but it felt great. I took it off and gave it back to him. He was smiling at me; he knew that I really got a kick out of it.

An amazing story appeared on a Sunday, February 3, 2002, in the *Chicago Sun-Times*. Motts was on the front page – a photo of him in a POW uniform and a photo of him carrying a football for the Chicago Cardinals football team. The story read in large letters: HELL AND GLORY. Motts Tonelli's life in football and in war. The first seven pages were about Motts's life story. I was anxious to learn more about Motts so I read the whole article. Here is a summary:

He grew up the son of Italian immigrants on Chicago's North Side and became a star fullback at Notre Dame in the 1930s before playing for the Chicago Cardinals in the National Football League in 1940. After one season, Tonelli enlisted in the U.S. Army and eventually survived the infamous Bataan Death March in World War II and forty-two months of brutal treatment in three Japanese prison camps. Tonelli's weight went from 212 pounds to 92 at liberation.

Finally, at the end of the march, he made it to San Fernando, but then he and his fellow prisoners were loaded into freight cars for a journey to Camp O'Donnell where they would stay. They were packed in the steel freight cars so tight they could barely move their arms. The heat was so intense that many died standing up. Still deprived of food and water and suffering from various illnesses, men would throw up and relieve themselves, giving in to their bloated bowels.

Occasionally the train would stop, and the dead men were dragged off the train. The train would start again and chug off into the dust. When they arrived at Camp O'Donnell, they were allowed to fill their canteens with water from one spigot. It took ten hours in line to fill his canteen. They were put into squads of ten. Their captors made it clear that if one man escaped, the other nine would be executed.

Motts said that he had malaria, beriberi, uncontrollable spasms of diarrhea, and blinding headaches. He had also picked up a parasite from snails while digging in the rice paddies with mud up to his knees. He said that he still have problems from the parasite that caused him stomach and back pains to this day. Motts also dug latrine trenches. Men had dysentery and had to go to the latrine frequently. Many collapsed and slept near the latrine, too weak to make it back to their tents; some fell in and were discovered there in the morning, dead. After many months, the men were informed that they were going to be moved off the island. Unbeknownst to them, they were going on the most horrible journey yet. Hell Ships, as they became to be known. They were packed into the holds of these ships, hundreds of men packed as tightly as slaves on a galley. Vomit and diarrhea slicked the floors and mingled with the sickening smell of the dead. Buckets would be lowered on ropes for use as toilets then rinsed and filled with rice for meals. Motts was on this hell ship for sixty-seven days before docking in Japan. Hundreds more had died during the trip. Motts learned that three other hell ships loaded with prisoners had been sunk unwittingly by American bombers. The ships had not been marked as prison transports.

Motts and the other prisoners that were left were sent to Lasang prison for two months and then to Toyama until the war ended, and Motts still had his graduation ring. Of the ten thousand Americans taken prisoner in the Philippines, only four thousand returned.

I was pleased to get a call one day from my friend in the Department of Revenue who told me that a federal grand jury got around to indicting ten men whom the government contended were responsible for skimming more than $3.2 million in profits from the bingo operation.

I, of course, called Motts and gave him the good news. He said, "That's great, come on over, and I'll buy you a cup of coffee. I'd like to hear more about it." When I got to his house, he said that he had been sitting outside on his porch when a car doubled-parked in front of his house. He said that a man got out with a piece of paper in his hand and asked Motts if he knew where Western Avenue was. Motts said that the man was Japanese and had a familiar accent. His answer to the man was as follows: "I don't know why the hell can't you find Western Avenue, you didn't have any problem finding Pearl Harbor." Motts said the guy jumped back in his car and got the hell out of there.

I am proud to say that Mario "Motts" Tonelli was a friend of mine and a true American hero. Motts passed away on January 7, 2003. I had the honor of being a pallbearer at his funeral. My son Tom is a member of the Pipes and Drums of the Emerald Society Chicago Police. They played the "Notre Dame Victory March" and "Amazing Grace" at the Lady of Lourdes Church. Motts is at peace at Memorial Park Cemetery.

"Motts" Tonelli weighing in at less than a hundred pounds at the end of his captivity in a Japanese prison camp near the end of the war in 1945.

Mario "Motts" Tonelli at Comiskey Park after the war wearing his old Notre Dame number 58. He was coincidentally given the same number in Japanese prison camp.

"Motts" Tonelli wearing his Notre Dame ring at his home in Skokie, Illinois.

To Don / What a guy ? Regards + Best Wishes
Mario "Motts" Tonelli

Mario "Motts" Tonelli.

Mario "Motts" Tonelli
University of Notre Dame
Survivor of Bataan Death March WWII

Ronald W. Jarrett—
Kill and Be Killed

Ronald W. Jarrett was selected by the mob bosses to get whacked. The day of the hit was December 23, 1999, at about 10:15 AM. When Jarrett came out of his house and walked toward his car to attend a wake on the South Side of Chicago, a yellow rental Ryder truck came down Lowe Avenue. The man on the passenger side got out of the truck with a gun in his hand, walked up to Jarrett, and shot him numerous times in the head, shoulders, and arms. The man then calmly returned to the truck and left the scene. The truck drove to a nearby alley where the assassins splashed gasoline in the truck and set it on fire. They were seen getting into a Lincoln and driving away.

I have heard from a reliable source that the first person on the scene of the shooting was an FBI agent. I don't know if he was on a case in the neighborhood or just happened to be driving by when he heard shots, Maybe he was even a witness to the shooting. Jarrett was taken to the Cook County Hospital for emergency care. He was kept alive under armed guard until he passed away as a result of his wounds on January 25, 2000.

When I was a director of a Vice Detection Unit for Mike Sheahan, the sheriff of Cook County, my partner Phil DiPasquale and I came across some information on another case we were working. It involved Ronnie Jarrett in a bookmaking operation along with his two sons, Ronnie Jr. and Anthony. Jarrett lived at 3004 South Lowe Avenue, which so happens to be a very difficult area to set up surveillance. It seems every neighbor knows every other neighbor that lives in the area, so any suspicious vehicle that passes by is immediately looked at as the police.

Jarrett was a well-known professional criminal and a member of the mob's Twenty-sixth Street crew of thieves, burglars, robbers, juice collectors and now big-time bookmaking for Angelo "the Hook" LaPietra, a South Side mob boss. Jarrett had been busted about sixty times in his criminal career. He spent time in prison for the first time in 1965 for auto theft and burglary.

In 1978, the FBI and Chicago Strike Force began an investigation named Burgmurs, which involved a number of burglaries and the murders of burglars associated with organized crime. Jarrett was a suspect in this investigation. He appeared before the special grand jury established for the Burgmurs investigation and refused to answer questions relating to the Burgmurs investigation on the basis of his Fifth Amendment privilege against self-incrimination.

Burgmurs, of course, was the investigation of the Harry Levinson jewelry store burglary on North Clark Street in Chicago. The burglars stole over $1 million of Levinson's best jewelry. He had installed the very best burglar alarm system, and his windows were in public view. There was no doubt that this was a professional crew of thieves. The only problem was, Levinson happened to be a personal friend of mob boss Tony Accardo. The biggest bookmaker in town had introduced them to each other a year ago. Levinson contacted Accardo and met him at a restaurant on Rush Street and told him what had happened. Accardo told Levinson not to worry and he would look into the matter and get back to him. A couple of days later, Levinson got a phone call requesting his presence in his store. That afternoon, $1 million worth of jewelry was returned to him. He was a happy man.

Information has it that Tony Spilotro, who was in Las Vegas and a jewel thief himself, suggested that there was only one man that could have circumvented the burglar alarm system in Levinson's jewelry store and that was John Mendell. Apparently, he was right as the jewelry had been returned.

Then an unbelievable thing happened. While Tony Accardo was with his wife in Palm Springs, California, his house was burglarized. He had a very high-line burglar alarm system installed in his house, which was supposed to be burglarproof. These thieves might have been high-line burglars, but they were just as stupid. Before it was over, there were bodies found all over town; they were beaten, strangled, stabbed, and had their throats cut. Reliable informant information revealed that Ronald Jarrett had lured John Mendell, "his friend," to his death. The killers were Frank Calabrese Sr., Nick Calabrese, Jarrett, and hit man Frank Saladino.

In June 1979, it was learned that Jarrett had participated in the robbery of the Orange Blossom jewelry store in Chicago, Illinois, on December 15, 1977. Two men that had participated in the robbery with Jarrett, Ronald Brown and David Willis, were given immunity in exchange for their testimony concerning Jarrett's role in the Orange Blossom jewelry robbery. In October 1980, Jarrett was indicted for his participation in the armed robbery of the Orange Blossom jewelry store. Jarrett was convicted of the robbery and appealed the conviction. The appeal failed, and Jarrett was sentenced to prison for twelve years. He was paroled in 1993 and apparently rejoined his mob associates.

Phil DiPasquale and I, along with my old crew from the Chicago Police gambling unit, obtained a search warrant for Ron Jarrett's house at 3004 South Lowe Avenue. We executed the warrant on November 16, 1998. Ron Jarrett Sr. was not at home, but his son Ron Jarrett Jr. was. We recovered gambling paraphernalia from Jarrett Jr., but like his father, he refused to tell us where his father was or make any statement about gambling. He was charged with gambling violations.

On December 19, 1998, we again obtained a search warrant to Ron Jarrett's home and executed the warrant when we found Jarrett's sons Ronald J. Jarrett and Anthony Jarrett at home. While we were in the process of searching the house, Ron Jarrett Sr. returned home. He was searched for any illegal paraphernalia, but he was clean. Apparently, he was aware of our presence in his house and got rid of any incriminating evidence before he came home.

During the Chicago mob's Family Secrets trial, Ronald J. Jarrett Jr. testified in court that his father told him that he was working for Frank Calabrese Sr. He was giving money to Frank Calabrese's wife Diane every month from his bookmaking operation while Frank Calabrese

Sr. was in prison. He also said that his father did not like working for John "Johnny Apes" Monteleone, who was giving him orders while Frank Calabrese Sr. was away.

Ronald J. Jarrett Jr. also made a statement that he had been told by a reliable source in the outfit that his father was killed by orders of John "Johnny Apes" Monteleone.

Ronald W. Jarrett

Ronald W. Jarrett Sr.

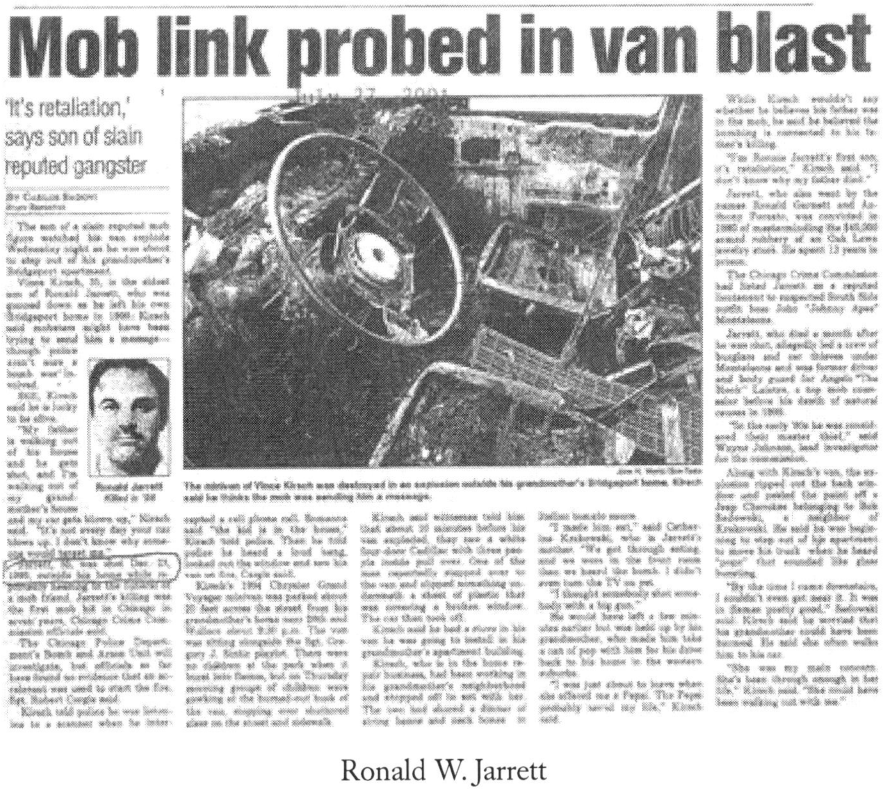

Mob link probed in van blast

'It's retaliation,' says son of slain reputed gangster

Ronald W. Jarrett

PHONE (312) 443-6444

SHERIFF'S OFFICE OF COOK COUNTY, ILLINOIS
RICHARD J. DALEY CENTER, CHICAGO, IL 60602
MICHAEL F. SHEAHAN
SHERIFF

To: Joseph M. Shaughnessy - Inspector General

From: Don Herion - Director Vice Detection

Subject: Attempt murder of Ronald Jarrett-Bookmaker

    1.   The above named person was the target of an organized crime assassination on December 23, 1999 at 1018hrs. This action took place at 3004 S. Lowe Ave. Chicago, Illinois in front of the subjects home. A witness stated that an unknown black male exited a Yellow Ryder truck, walked to the rear of the truck and fired four shots at the victim striking him four times. The offender then got back into the truck and fled S/B on Lowe to 3222 S. Normal Ave. in the alley where the truck was set on fire.

    2.   Jarrett was taken to Cook County hospital by fire ambulance in critical condition. At this time the victim is still alive but in serious condition and has moved to an other hospital for treatment.

    3.   Ronald Jarrett has been the target of the vice detection unit for the past 18 months, and two gambling raids have been effected at his home at 3004 S. Lowe Avenue where both of his sons have been arrested for operating a sports wireroom Anthony Jarrett M/W 26yrs was arrested by this unit with assistance from the Chicago police gambling unit on 16-Nov-98. Ronald Jarrett Jr. was arrested at 3004 S. Lowe also on 16-June-99, also for operating a sports wireroom with two mobile telephones. Ronald Jarrett was the subscriber to the two mobile telephones that Jarrett was using in there gambling operation.

    4.   At the time of the two raids Ronald Jarrett Sr. was not on the premi at the time of the raids. On the first raid Ronald Jarrett Sr. became aware of our presence and refused to come home. Gambling records were recovered from Jarretts bedr as well as his two sons bedrooms. On 16-June-99, Jarrett Sr. did come home and we interviewed him regarding his gambling operation, he denied being involved in any gambling activity and added that he wouldn't tell us anything if he was. He stated that he did a lot of hard time in the penitentiary for not talking, and he certainly wasnt going to talk to us.

    5.   Jarrett has been a member of the Chinatown outfit crew for many year and has been involved in numerous arrests for burglary as well as other crimes, and was an underling to the LaPietra crew. We have learned that Jarrett had been involved in a large scale bookmaking operation in the Chinatown area and had recently quarreled with Frank Caruso AKA"Tootsie Babe" because of his position with the outfit. Allegedl Jarrett expected to be put in charge of the gambling operations in the chinatown area but was told that another mob associate was in charge. His name is Richard Catezone AKA "The Cat" 2716 S. Wells St. Chicago, Il. Catezone is an associate of organized crime figures, Donald Angelini, Ray Tominello and recently deceased Dominick Cortina.

The Gambler

I have been dealing with gambling for over forty years, every type you can think of, both legal and illegal. Gambling consists of risking something one possesses in the hope of obtaining something better. Gamblers risk their money on games of chance, games of skill, and games that combine both chance and skill. For the average person, the most popular form of gambling include lotteries, raffles, wheel of fortune, bingo, policy, bolita, and most dice games. Games of chance and skill include games played with cards: poker, bridge, blackjack, gin rummy, pinochle, and others. Betting on sports such as horses, football, basketball, and baseball is also included in this category. The following story is about a degenerate gambler that got himself into the world of shit and is lucky he didn't wind up in a trunk.

I received a phone call one day while I was sitting in my office in the Vice Detection Unit at the Third District Court House in Rolling Meadows, Illinois. At the time, I was working for the Cook County Sheriff's Police, busting up gambling operations in the county. A guy by the name of Adam asked for Don Herion; I, of course, informed him that he was talking to him. He went on to say that he had gotten my name from somebody that told him that I could be trusted as he wanted to give some information about a big bookmaking operation in the suburbs. He requested to meet me somewhere so that he could explain the illegal sports gambling operation to me. I agreed to meet him at a McDonald's at Touhy and Central Avenue in Skokie, Illinois.

I asked him what he was driving so that I would know who he was when he got there. He described an expensive sports car to me, and the meet was set.

When someone wants to voluntarily give you some information about a gambling operation, there's always a catch, and I wondered what his was. I got to McDonald's ahead of him, and when a sports car pulled in the lot, I knew it had to be him. He was in his twenties, six foot one, 210 pounds, and looked like he came from money. I introduced myself, and we sat down in McDonald's. He kept looking around like he was afraid of being seen with me. He went on to explain that he had been betting on sports with a big-time bookmaker and had been doing very well until recently. He went into a losing streak, and now he owed the bookmaker. I asked him how much he would bet on any given game. His reply was two to five dimes a game. A dime is $1,000. I must admit that I was kind of shocked that a young guy in his twenties would make those kinds of bets. "OK," I said. "Just how much do you owe this guy?" His answer was just over $100,000. I asked him how much he had won in the past from this guy. He said about $150,000, give or take a few dimes. "All right," I said, "You're up $50,000, why don't you just pay the guy?" "That's the problem," he said, "I blew it all playing blackjack at the riverboats."

"Just who is this big-time bookmaker that you're betting with?" I asked. "He's a young guy really, his name is Demitri Stavropoulos," he said. "Some people call him Jimmy." Adam then gave me his cell phone numbers and the car he drove. I then told him that I knew Jimmy very well and have busted him a couple of times in the past. I asked him if he had ever heard of a guy connected to Jimmy by the name of Roger Riccio. Adam, who was getting very nervous by this time, asked me if Jimmy or Roger Riccio would beat him up or kill him if he couldn't pay them. I told him that I had no idea what they would do, but that I knew some outfit guys that would break your legs if you didn't pay them the $100 you owed them.

I explained to Adam, who had now turned very pale, that I would buy him some time. However, he would have to do what I told him. I asked him where he's supposed to pay the $100,000. He said that Jimmy was available anytime to meet him; all he had to do was call him on his cell phone. "The money was due to be paid two days ago," he said. He told Jimmy that his wife was sick and he had to take care of her until her mother from out of town arrived.

I explained my plan to Adam and told him to set up a meet with Jimmy around Oak and State streets. "Tell him that you have the money, and tell him to make the time of the meet." I explained. I told him that I would give him a brown paper bag that would be filled with paper so that it would look like a bag full of money. He would have to sit in his car with the doors unlocked, and when Jimmy showed up, he would probably get in his car. I explained that there would be four undercover cops covering him and when Jimmy got in his car, they would grab them both and the bag before Jimmy could look in it. They would both be spread-eagled and searched for weapons or other illegal items. One of the cops would look in the bag and look very surprised when he saw all the U.S. currency. If Jimmy had any gambling paraphernalia or other illegal items on him, he would be busted and taken to Maxwell Street gambling unit for processing. The police, of course, would confiscate the money bag for evidence. Adam would, of course, act very embarrassed by the whole situation and demand to be released because he did nothing wrong.

As things turned out, we couldn't find any incriminating evidence on Jimmy except a sports schedule, which of course is legal to possess. I had my two ace detectives, Bob Gricus and Rico Lloyd, bring Jimmy into Maxwell Street for interrogation while I told Adam to get the hell out of town for a few days. I gave him a warning that what just happened was only going to give him some more time to straighten out his problem with Jimmy. I also reminded him that he now owed me big-time, and I expected a lot of information from him about other bookmakers he knew about. Adam thanked me over and over and said that he was working on some other bookmakers he knew about and would call me as he was indebted to me forever.

Adam gave me other tips and clues about other bookmakers and introduced me to a friend of his who was also a degenerate gambler and, of course, got himself into the same situation that Adam was in. I can't use his name, but I gave him a number, 003, and he helped me out quite a bit about a large bookmaking ring operating in the Board of Trade in downtown Chicago. I really believe 003 liked being an informant and somehow related it to the CIA. He called me one day and wanted to meet with me because he had something really hot. I told him to meet me on the second floor of a parking garage on North Clark Street. I arrived first and could see the street and the entrance to the garage when I observed a man walking across Clark

Street, heading toward the garage. The guy had a baseball hat on and shoulder-length orange hair, which was part of the hat, and sunglasses. Sure as hell, it was my undercover guy 003. I asked him why he was wearing the hat and wig. He looked at me, kind of insulted, and said, "I thought it would be better if no one recognized me especially talking to you, Sarge."

As things turned out, 003 gave me information about a dope ring operating in the Board of Trade as well as gambling. He also gave me information about a large sports-bookmaking operation that began in Berwyn, Illinois, and was connected to Costa Rica. All this information proved to be reliable, and we busted a few mopes in Berwyn and Cicero and turned over evidence we recovered to the IRS Organized Crime Unit. After I left the Cook County Sheriff's Vice Detection Unit in August of 2000, the sheriff disbanded the unit. He still had his vice unit in Maywood to take care of vice conditions.

I hadn't seen Adam or 003 after I retired, but I did hear rumors about Adam getting in some trouble at the riverboats. Then there was some talk about him losing millions of dollars that he got from a South Side bank. On Sunday, August 6, a program called *Dateline NBC* ran a story bout a high roller who had won and lost millions at the riverboats; his name was Adam Resnick. Adam was at the blackjack table, betting $30,000 a hand, two hands at a time. He seemed incapable of losing, and he'd already won millions. He was asked by a correspondent how he felt standing beside that table with all that money in front of him. Adam answered, "Just like I could gamble forever. When I was in action, I didn't know anything else was going on." Gambling in America is an apparently unquenchable thirst – some would say lust. The belief among many people is that anybody can beat the odds. Certainly, Adam was at the brink somewhere between Nirvana and criminal self-destruction. Resnick said, "I knew what I was doing was wrong."

Adam Resnick grew up well-off in Milwaukee, Wisconsin, and said that his parents took him to his first casino when he was six. At fourteen, he said he got his first real gambler's rush while on a family cruise. Playing blackjack at the ship's casino, he turned a $500 holiday gift into nearly $8,000. That became a legendary story on the ship. In high school, he would bet anytime, anywhere, and on anything. He became a regular at the dog track. He managed to finish high school and went off to college in Tucson, Arizona. When he was asked why he decided to go to the University of Arizona, Adam replied, "Close to Vegas." He went to Vegas several times a month. In three semesters, he went to Vegas thirty-seven times.

He admitted that he gambled a lot of money, everything he could get his hands on, such as his tuition money and student loans. He lost it all – tens of thousands of dollars. Then he vowed to quit gambling and returned to his home state school, the University of Wisconsin – Madison. He was asked how long it was before he went to the casino. Answer: about twenty-four hours.

Between casino visits, he met the love of his life, Meredith. They were both students. Meredith attended class, and Adam attended the Ho Chunk Casino. It didn't take long for her to see how serious his problem was. On their second date, she took him to Gamblers Anonymous. After about ninety seconds, he turned to her and said, "I'm not hanging out here with all these losers."

Meredith graduated from Wisconsin. Adam dropped out, but he did get his act together. He claims he made his first million at age twenty-two, and it wasn't from gambling but from selling mechanical equipment in Chicago. They got married in 1998. She didn't know that Adam was still gambling all the time. Only now, he lied all the time too. Adam continued to make serious six-figure money in business, but his gambling losses piled up. The first time Adam and I met he owed one bookmaker $100,000. On one weekend, he admitted to losing hundreds of thousands of dollars. Adam also likens bookies to drug pushers. He also claims the day his son was born, a bookmaker tracked him down inside the delivery room. When he looked up, the guy made a gesture (like he was going to kill him). Adam knew that the guy wasn't going to kill him because he wouldn't have gotten his money. Banks came after him as well for bouncing bad checks. That is when the story takes a sharp turn. So far, Adam has been like hundreds of thousands of other Americans whose gambling is quite frankly out of control. But now in Adam's case, a friend stepped in, an accountant whose family just happened to run a small bank in Chicago. He told Adam that his mother was the CEO and his sister was the COO.

Adam didn't realize it at the time, but this out-of-control gambler was about to gain access to a huge cache of money that wasn't his. His accountant friend, Terry Navarro, told Adam that he could use a company account, which would not be a problem because the bank was operated by Terry's mom and sister. Terry basically let Adam become an insider at his family bank.

Adam said he deposited several hundred thousand dollars at the bank, which, of course, he gambled, and soon found himself withdrawing the account. Incredibly, his friend's sister, the bank's chief operating officer, cleared Adam's bad checks. So now Adam could bounce a check anytime he wanted. He said that it wasn't her intention, but that's what ultimately happened. Adam did take care of the banker with a BMW, front-row tickets to Cubs games, and trips to Las Vegas. He called that consulting fees.

Adam said that he did try to cover the bad checks by depositing winnings back into the account. But the losses were overwhelming. To hide them, he wrote one bad check after another, 138 in all. He said that he wrote checks for over $200 million. His banking friends were treating him like a prince; the casinos were treating him like a king as long as he kept gambling. One casino even flew Adam and some friends on a private jet to a Mike Tyson – Lennox Lewis boxing match. He bet $300,000 on Tyson and lost.

In his gambling heaven, he did have some big wins on occasion, like the $2 million sports payout he flew to Las Vegas to collect. But even when he lost, within hours, he gambled the $2 million away. Then in June 2002, he said that there was an ominous phone call from a bank lawyer. The lawyer told Adam that there was a problem with the account. If he got $3 million into the bank, they would make this a civil matter. If he didn't, it was out of their hands.

The moment of truth had arrived, so Adam reacted accordingly. He drove to Binion's Horseshoe Casino in Hammond, Indiana. He arrived around 10:00 AM with a million dollars. And betting $60,000 at a time, he said he reached his $3 million goal by noon and kept on winning as never before. By midafternoon, he said he hit the $7 million mark, eventually hit a peak of $8.6 million. He was on top of the world. Then of course, he stopped, right? Went home, paid off the bank, and spent the rest of his fortune on his family. *Forget about it.* That's right, Adam Resnick kept playing. His stack of chips began to dwindle. He played through the night and into the next morning. By 4:30 AM, he said he was down to $2 million. By 10:00 AM, he laid his last chip on the table.

He knew that his life, as he knew it, was over. He drove home to break the news to his still unsuspecting wife, Meredith. He just rambled on the truth to her. He was now burned out. The small bank that he used collapsed with $10 million in losses.

In July, Adam Resnick pleaded guilty in federal court to wire fraud. He also agreed to pay a $10 million restitution. His accountant friend pleaded guilty to bank fraud and is awaiting sentencing. Adam's plea agreement calls for three and a half years behind bars.

Gambling addiction has become a big problem in America. Most compulsive gamblers relapse. Adam is playing sports these days, not betting on them. We'll see.

Anthony "Tony the Hatch" Chiaramonti

The killing of a Chicago mob boss is no big deal in Chicagoland. We have had over 1,100 of them for one reason or another. The hit of Tony "the Hatch" was believed by police to be another squabble over control of some turf involving gambling, juice collections, or some other mob enterprise. The murder of Chiaramonti, sixty-seven, who climbed the mob's ranks as a violent street enforcer and debt collector, was the second in less than two years. The last one was Ronald W. Jarrett who was shot December 23, 1999, and died in January 2000. Both men were involved with South Side rackets and were trusted members of the Chicago Outfit.

Chiaramonti was gunned down in the vestibule of a Brown's Chicken & Pasta restaurant in Lyons, Illinois, in November 2001. It seems that he was trying to expand his muscle in territory that belonged to some other mob boss. Reliable information revealed that "the Hatch" or "Hatchet," as some people call him, made arrangements to meet Donald "Captain D" DiFazio, a bookmaker who was employed by Connie's Pizza on Archer Avenue in Chicago. A Twenty-sixth Street mobster, Joe "Shorty" LaMantia, had orders to deliver DiFazio to the meeting that was to take place across the street from Connie's Pizza. DiFazio told Chiaramonti that he was paying street tax of $500 a month to Frank Calabrese and asked why he was going to be squeezed from both ends.

Chiaramonti heard rumors about a Connie's Pizza that was going to open in Lyons, Illinois. He explained that he had interests in other restaurants in Lyons and didn't need any competition and if a Connie's Pizza opened in Lyons, someone was going to get hurt.

Police were of the opinion that Chiaramonti's murder might be part of a struggle for control of lucrative South Side rackets once controlled by John "Johnny Apes" Monteleone, who died of natural causes in January 2001. Monteleone was one of the top mob bosses that controlled the rackets in the south suburbs, Cicero, the Twenty-sixth Street crew, and Chinatown. The outfit's most lucrative enterprises included sports bookmaking, loan-sharking, and labor racketeering. I was aware that Monteleone had taken control of the video poker machine racket. Several informants of mine verified that Monteleone's collectors spoke freely of his takeover of this lucrative gambling operation. After Monteleone's death, police believed Chiaramonti assumed that he was next in line to control their operations. It was unclear whether street crew bosses, who were under Chiaramonti's jurisdiction, ever acknowledged his authority. Apparently, someone didn't approve of his takeover.

The South Side operation was crippled by the 1993 racketeering convictions of its bosses, including Chiaramonti. He was released from prison in 1998; Chiaramonti was the first of the old leaders to be back on the streets. He ran loan-sharking operations for Sam "Wings" Carlisi who had also passed away. Chiaramonti once bragged to his friends about stabbing a guy in the neck with a fork and putting another guy who owed him money on a hot griddle.

Reliable informant information revealed that Chiaramonti was murdered by Anthony C. Calabrese, forty-seven, who was the leader of a South Side robbery gang, and his accomplice Robert Cooper. He admitted that he drove the getaway van from the chicken restaurant parking lot. Anthony C. Calabrese was not related to Frank Calabrese in any way, although he would let people think that he was. Cooper testified that he and Anthony C. Calabrese beat a suspected informer and kicked him with steel-toed boots to get him to admit that he was an informer. The victim, Edmund Frank, actually was an informant but knew if he admitted it, he would be a dead man. He was wearing a wire when he was searched by Calabrese, but he failed to find it.

The beating was taped and played in federal court at Calabrese's trial. Testimony revealed that Calabrese had ordered one of his crew to use a hammer to break both hands of the owner of a tattoo parlor that had tattooed the underage daughter of a Chicago mob boss. Calabrese was charged in a series of suburban robberies in Morton Grove, Lockport, and Maywood, Illinois. He was found guilty and sentenced to sixty-two years in prison. He has never been charged with the murder of Anthony "the Hatchet" Calabrese. Robert Cooper admitted that he was Calabrese's partner in the murder of Tony "the Hatch" and is now serving time in prison for driving the getaway vehicle.

Reliable informant information had reported that Tony C. Calabrese was taking orders from James "Jimmy" Inendino. Inendino was a former partner of Mafia hit man Harry Aleman and murdered mob boss William "Butch" Petrocelli. All three of these rascals had been arrested for running large-scale gambling operations on the South and West sides of Chicago. Inendino is considered a leader in the mob's Twenty-sixth Street crew.

Nov 22, 2001

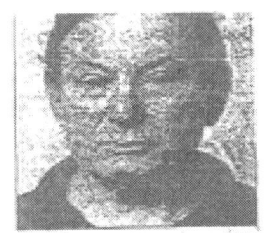

Photo courtesy of WGN
The killing Tuesday of Anthony "Tony the Hatch" Chiaramonti, is seen as a classic mob hit.

Mob boss gunned down in Lyons

Target of hit ran rackets operation, police believe

By Cam Simpson
and Matthew Walberg
Tribune staff reporters

A reputed Chicago mob boss, believed by authorities to be at the center of a struggle for control of the Outfit's most lucrative turf, was gunned down Tuesday night in the vestibule of a west suburban chicken restaurant.

The murder of Anthony Chiaramonti, 67, who climbed the mob's ranks as a violent street enforcer and debt collector, is the second in less than two years of a top figure in the Outfit's South Side rackets, authorities said. The killings follow what had been a long lull in the murder of organized crime fig-

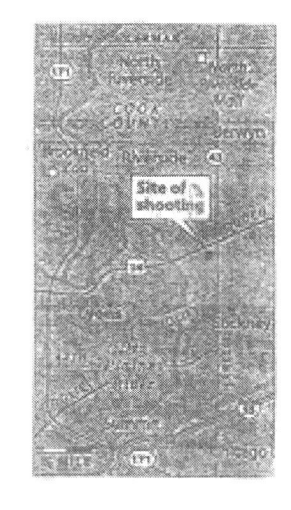

Execution of Mob Hitman
Nov 2001

Joseph "Jerry" Scalise

Jerry Scalise (a.k.a. One-Armed Jerry) became famous when he and Arthur "the Brain" Rachel robbed the famous Marlborough diamond in London, England, in September 1980. Of course, they became famous because they screwed up and got caught. They pulled the robbery off in broad daylight in the exclusive Knightsbridge section of London at the Graff jewelers.

The two Chicago stickup men had cased out the store before they pulled it off in less than a minute with masks, a gun, and an alleged hand grenade. Witnesses reported that they knew exactly what they were looking for. The Marlborough diamond had a retail value of nine hundred and sixty thousand dollars. But that wasn't all they took; they grabbed two pendants and twelve other jewels as well. The two robbers were described as two well-dressed white men with mustaches. There were five store employees and two customers in the store, as well as a uniformed guard. They were all taken by surprise and told to lie on the floor and not move. The robbers quickly grabbed the jewels they wanted and left the store.

A witness revealed to Scotland Yard, which handled the case, that he was walking past the jewelry store when the two robbers were entering the store. He noticed that one of the men had a false beard detached from his face and that both were putting on gloves when they entered the store. The witness remained outside the store because he knew that something was not kosher. When the robbers left the store, the witness followed them to a car they had rented, wrote down the license plate number and called the police. This information was given to the police who traced the license number on a Fiat to a Hertz rental agency in London. This is remarkable to me because whenever I checked a license number on a rental car, it took at least two days before I was able to find out where the car had been rented from. In any case, they did get the information they needed almost immediately, which is outstanding.

Scotland Yard was then able to get the names of whoever rented the Fiat. I find it hard to believe that these two slick robbers used their own names when they rented the Fiat. And then it gets worse. They didn't even use aliases when they registered at the hotel they were staying at, and for damn sure didn't have to name the real hotel they were staying at. I think they could have named another hotel in London instead of the Mount Royal where they had been staying since September 4. The robbery took place on September 11. They registered as J. J. Scalise and Arthur Rachel of 1020 Ardmore Avenue, Chicago, Illinois. How about using Mickey Mouse and Donald Duck when they registered?

This robbery and escape plan is amazing to me. I have worked on cases with some of the dumbest mob bookmakers in Chicago, but at least they used phony license plates on their cars, the phones they were using were registered to a vacant lot, and if they rented an apartment, they sure as hell didn't use their real names on the lease. I only wish they didn't lie and cheat and were honest as Scalise and Rachel. They would get busted every other day. Scotland Yard, which had been given all this information, figured out that just maybe, the two slick robbers might just be headed out of the country because they were from the USA, especially Chicago. So they checked the airplane manifests at Heathrow airport. Sure as hell, our two slicksters were listed under their real names to fly out of London on British Airways flight 298 departing London at 2:15 PM. The flight was to arrive at O'Hare field at 4:45 PM Chicago time. Scotland Yard contacted the FBI in Chicago, and when the plane landed, the FBI welcomed our two master criminals back home.

I would like to add that the FBI did a great job apprehending these two felons, but I think that if Scotland Yard would have notified the Salvation Army, they would have made the capture as well. Of course, everyone was happy that the two slicksters were nabbed and in custody. They were searched, as well as their luggage, but they found nothing that would link them to the diamond robbery. Scalise and Rachel thought they had gotten away with the robbery because they had no idea that witnesses in London could identify them as the robbers. The two suspects fought extradition back to London, England, where they would go on trial for the robbery, but all efforts failed. They were tried and convicted in 1984 and were sentenced to serve fifteen years in a British prison.

But there was still the mystery of the stolen diamonds. Scotland Yard learned that the rented Fiat they drove was abandoned and the robbers finally used their heads and took a taxi to the airport. The taxi driver had remembered our two slicksters and remembered that they made a request to stop at a post office on the way to the airport. A clerk at the post office recalled that Scalise mailed a package, and thought that it was being sent to New York. Scalise and Rachel never did admit to the robbery, let alone what happened to the jewels. So the jewels are still missing. One thing for sure is that the Chicago mob would have to give their OK for them to pull off a heist like they did. Furthermore, you better believe they got the jewels and their end of the proceeds. If they didn't, they would have interrogated the two boys to fnd out where the jewels were stashed. I'm sure they would have cooperated or they wouldn't be here today. Scalise was paroled from prison in December 1992, and Rachel was released in January 1993. Following their imprisonmnent, they returned to the States.

REPUTED MOBSTER GETS 9-YEAR TERM

Chicago Tribune - Thursday, September 2, 1999

A reputed Chicago mob figure who did prison time in England for stealing the 45-carat Marlborough diamond in 1980, was sentenced Wednesday to 9 years in prison for conspiring to deliver several kilograms of cocaine and heroin.

Joseph J. Scalise, 61, who pleaded guilty in May to the federal drug charge, cooperated with law enforcement authorities in other drug investigations as well as against the leader of the drug ring for which he worked, Assistant U.S. Atty. John Scully said in court.

Scalise was primarily responsible for delivering money to buy cocaine for further distribution in the Chicago area, authorities said.

He was arrested in Los Angeles last year.

Scalise was released from a British prison in 1993 after serving 13 years for the daylight theft of the Marlborough diamond and other gems from a London jewelry store.

Edition: CHICAGO SPORTS FINAL
Section: METRO CHICAGO
Page: 8
Index Terms: FEDERAL ; COURT ; SENTENCE ; DRUG ; DATE ; ROBBERY BRITAIN
Record Number: CTR9909020246
Copyright 1999, Chicago Tribune

Joseph J. Scalise arrested for stealing 45-Carat Diamond in London England – 1980

Five are indicted in cocaine sting - Alleged mob jewel thief arrested

Chicago Sun-Times - Friday, July 10, 1998
Author: CAM SIMPSON

Reputed Chicago mobster Joseph "Jerry" Scalise, jailed 18 years ago for the theft of the famed 45-carat Marlborough diamond, was indicted Thursday with four others for an alleged cocaine conspiracy.

Also charged were Andrew Theodorou, 61, a former Taft High School chemistry teacher and millionaire who in 1980 was charged with running a drug ring that imported 7.5 tons of marijuana.

Scalise, Theodorou and the others were allegedly caught in a government sting. According to the indictment, they attempted to buy 20 kilograms of cocaine from a government informant operating out of Los Angeles.

Scalise, 60, of the 3100 block of South Morgan, was arrested after paying $269,000 to the informant on May 1 in Los Angeles, authorities said Thursday.

An underling of reputed South Side mob boss John Monteleone, Scalise made his name in the 1970s and 1980s as a top jewel thief.

He was arrested at O'Hare Airport on Sept. 12, 1980, as he left an airliner from London. A day earlier, a gang stole British gems that were, at the time, valued at more than $3.6 million.

Among the gems was the Marlborough diamond, which has never been recovered. After his arrest, Scalise was extradited at the request of British authorities and spent more than 12 years in prison.

Scalise is in federal custody, authorities said Thursday.

Theodorou, whose last known residence was in Park Ridge, is a fugitive, authorities said. He received a seven-year prison sentence in 1981 after pleading guilty to drug and tax charges.

The three others indicted Thursday are Ronald DeWayne Waddy, 47, of Calumet City; Harvey Woods, 36, of the 6000 block of South Cottage Grove, and an unidentified man residing in Colombia known only to authorities as "Danielo." Waddy also remains in federal custody, while Woods is free on bond.

Edition: LATE SPORTS FINAL
Section: NEWS
Page: 12
Index Terms: indictments ; cocaine ; conspiracy ; charges ; sting ; CRIME ; DRUGS ; LEGAL
Record Number: CST07100050
Copyright 1998 Chicago Sun-Times, Inc.

Joseph J. Scalise arrested on Cocaine Sting

John Scalise and Albert Anselmi (center and right) were infamous hit men who murdered Chicago gangster and Capone rival Dean O'Banion in his flower shop on State Street on November 10, 1924. They murdered Frankie Yale in 1927 and victims of the St. Valentine's Day Massacre in 1929. Scalise was about to be indicted for the massacre when he and Anselmi turned up dead. It is suspected that Capone believed the two were going to turn on him.

Don Herion - Warden - Jerry Scalise
Stateville Prison - Public Enemies

Public Enemies— Technical Advisor

In the fall of 2007, I got a phone call from Mr. Bryan Carroll who identified himself as a movie producer and asked me if I would be interested in being a technical advisor on a movie that was going to be filmed in Chicago. He said that the name of the movie was *Public Enemies* and that it took place in the early 1930s. The movie was about the bank robbers John Dillinger, Baby Face Nelson, Homer Van Meter, Pretty Boy Floyd, and other Depression-era gangsters. Mr. Carroll went on to explain that the movie was going to be directed by Michael Mann, and Johnny Depp was going to play Dillinger. Christian Bale was signed up to play FBI Agent Melvin Purvis whose job was to kill or capture John Dillinger.

Needless to say, I thought about this for about two seconds and told Mr. Carroll that I would be happy to help them out with *Public Enemies*. Mr. Carroll then asked me if I could help Michael Mann's daughter Ami Mann who was writing a screenplay about bookmakers and mob guys. I said, "I would be glad to help her; have her call me."

The production office was going to be set up at 1436 West Randolph Street in Chicago. They planned to start their setup schedule in February. They had location managers in Wisconsin, Indiana, and

Florida where scenes were going to be filmed. This was going to be a big-budget movie, that's for sure.

Johnny Depp was once in a movie called *Donnie Brasco*, a New York mob guy. He played Brasco and really did a great job. Al Pacino played his mentor and got whacked at the end of the movie. Brasco, of course, was really an FBI agent working undercover who infiltrated the mob. After I met Johnny Depp, who is a great guy by the way, I asked him how he liked playing a mob guy. He told me that during the day, he hung around with FBI agents to get an idea how they acted in certain situations, which helped him in his role. Then at night, he palled around with some real mob guys so he could watch them and learn their habits as wise guys. In my opinion, he nailed it and came across as a real wise guy when he had to be.

Depp has been in a lot of movies. He has played a variety of characters, and has done a great job in all the roles he played. I really liked him in the *Pirates of the Caribbean* movies where he played Captain Jack. I met Michael Mann who, of course, was the director, producer, and writer of *Public Enemies*. He is a great director and has filmed movies like the *Thief* with James Cann, which was filmed in Chicago. It was about a jewel thief. There were a lot of Chicago actors in the movie including Chicago cops and authentic burglars. One of them was a thief and con man by the name of John Santucci (a.k.a. Schavoni) who was incidentally hired as a technical advisor for the movie. Santucci was a real mobster and safecracker who did time in a Texas prison years ago until he became an FBI informant for the Chicago office. I'll explain his story later.

Christian Bale, "Batman," was playing FBI crime fighter Melvin Purvis; he played the part really good and was a nice guy as well. It seems that FBI Director Hoover was very fond of Purvis and considered Purvis as his favorite agent. He made Purvis the SAC in the Chicago office. Allegedly when Purvis arrived in Chicago, he brought his own horse and stabled it in Lincoln Park and rode on weekends. He also brought a manservant; a black man named President who chauffeured Purvis around Chicago in a shiny Pierce-Arrow.

After eight months as the SAC, Purvis still had no idea about gangland Chicago. He made a mistake when he began associating with the chief investigator of the state prosecutor's office, a former Chicago cop named Dan "Tubbo" Gilbert. Purvis worked with Gilbert to crack the strange kidnapping case of John "Jake the Barber" Factor. Factor had been trying to evade extradition to face criminal charges in Great Britain. Many people in law enforcement believed the kidnapping to be a sham when it was reported. Factor was well-known as a syndicate con man. Purvis believed that the kidnapping was genuine; it was his first major kidnapping case. Dan "Tubbo" Gilbert announced to the press that Jake Factor had probably been kidnapped by an Irish gangster named Roger Touhy whose suburban bootlegging operation was a rival to Al Capone. Capone had been sent to prison on tax evasion charges, so the outfit was being run by Frank Nitti. He was locked in a struggle with Touhy to take control of several Chicago unions.

Gilbert claimed he had evidence that Touhy had kidnapped a man named Hamm as well. Purvis made no independent investigation of the Hamm or Factor kidnappings. As far as he was concerned, Gilbert's word was enough for the bureau.

William Hamm and several eyewitnesses to the kidnapping were brought to Chicago to identify Hamm's kidnappers. Looking through a one-way mirror, Hamm wasn't at all sure they were his kidnappers and said so to reporters. But one eyewitness, a cabdriver, was sure, and that was all Purvis needed. He emerged from his office to announce to reporters that the bureau had assembled an ironclad case against Touhy for the Hamm kidnapping. "We have positive identification of all four of the prisoners," Purvis said. "The government men worked carefully and thoroughly on this case, and we are sure of ourselves."

In Washington, Hoover was thrilled and sent Purvis a message praising him and his entire staff. Actually, it was far from the truth. In fact, Purvis was fooled into arresting the wrong men by a corrupt investigator in cahoots with the Chicago mob, a fact that would be confirmed twenty years later by a federal court. Roger Touhy would ultimately be also convicted of the false kidnapping of Jake Factor. Only after two decades in prison was he able to convince a judge he had been framed. In 1954, Judge John Barnes, in an opinion that led to Touhy's release, noted that the Illinois state prosecutors, which he found to be dominated by Tubbo Gilbert, had never brought charges against a single member of the Chicago Outfit. Judge Barnes found that motives by Dan "Tubbo" Gilbert and the politico-criminal syndicate wanted to remove Touhy permanently from the scene. With Purvis as an unwitting ally, the judge found Gilbert and the FBI worked in concert to convict Touhy of something.

Touhy's luck was going to get worse. On December 16, 1959, on a cold Chicago night, I happened to be working in uniform in a squad car with my partner Bob Peters when we heard what sounded like gunshots. When we arrived in the area where we thought we heard the shots – 125 North Pine Avenue, a two-flat building – we found two white men lying on the front porch. They had both been shot. Roger Touhy was one of them along with his bodyguard Walter Miller. I asked the older man (Touhy) what happened. He just kept saying, "Those fucking dagos, they never forget." Both men were taken to the hospital where Touhy died from loss of blood from gunshot wounds. Walter Miller survived to live another day.

After I did some research on *Public Enemies*, I learned that the movie was really about the beginning of the FBI. The Kansas City massacre was the killing of five lawmen and wounding of two others by machine-gun fire. This was the beginning of the war on crime in this country. It transformed the FBI into the country's first federal police force. The attorney general Homer Cummings composed the new War on Crime – the hiring of a special prosecutor, Joseph Keenan. It became a legislative package that would, among other things, make it a federal crime to kill a federal agent, and the formation of "special squads" inside the bureau to take on major cases. Thus, a little-known bureau of the Department of Justice became a cutting edge of President Roosevelt's New Deal policies. If Hoover and his neophyte agents could defeat "name brand" gangsters, it would be immediate and tangible evidence of the New Deal's worth.

Thus, the war on Bonnie and Clyde, Baby Face Nelson, Pretty Boy Floyd, Ma Barker Alvin Karpis, Machine Gun Kelly, Eddie Bentz, Harvey Bailey, Frank Nash, Homer Van Meter, and last but not least, John Dillinger and his gang had begun.

I met the unit production manager, Julie Herris. She was in charge of all the problems that might come up while filming the movie. I also met the property master, Kris Peck, and his assistant, Brad Good. They took care of anything that was needed in the movie. The armorer was an expert on all kinds of weapons; his name was Harry Lu, and he really knew his business. The set decorator was Rosemary Brandenburg The tactics and weapons technical advisor was Mick Gould. The key grip, Mike Lewis, did everything. The FBI technical advisor was a local agent, Dale Shelton.

Bryan Carroll, the producer, asked me if I was aware of a special unit the Chicago Police had back in 1933-34 called the Dillinger Squad. If they had one, I had never heard of it, but I would check it out. I went through some Chicago Police archives and even checked some newspapers from that era to find out about this special squad and if it really existed. After spending many hours checking on this Dillinger Squad that seemed to be a big secret, I finally found a newspaper article from 1934 that mentioned the Dillinger Squad. The Dillinger Squad was formed to hunt down and kill or capture John Dillinger. They would not be given any other assignments.

The Dillinger Gang's good times came to a halt on December 14 when a Chicago police detective received a tip that one of Dillinger's Auburns was being serviced at a garage on Broadway Avenue. John Hamilton appeared at the garage that afternoon. He was approached by Detective William Shanley. Hamilton panicked and drew his gun and shot Shanley dead. Hamilton fled the scene and escaped. If I had been Shanley, I would have had my gun out and shot Hamilton before he shot me. But that's Monday-morning quarterbacking. The killing of Detective Shanley made front-page news and, two days later, was the main reason the Chicago Police Department formed the Dillinger Squad.

The following named police officers were members of the Dillinger Squad: Capt. John Stege; Sgt. Frank Reynolds; Sgt. John Howe; Det. Thomas Curtin; and Patrolman. Lawrence Maize, Frank Czech, Peter Hepp, James Shields, John McLaughlin, Harry Gleason, John Fitzgerald, Harry Bingham, John Dawe, Francis Kearns, John Osterman, Harry Neuman, Louis Glen, Herbert Hine, Arthur Marason, John Daly, Thomas Stapleton, James Sweeney, and Walter Fergus.

There is a great scene in *Public Enemies* where Dillinger gives a lift to Anna Sage's girlfriend, Polly Hamilton, who has to pick up a license at police headquarters at 1121 South State Street. When Dillinger drops her off, he has a notion to enter the lobby of the building. That's when he observes the building directory. When he sees the name Detective Division: fifth floor, he gets a twinkle in his eye, gets in an elevator and gets off at the fifth floor. We have to remember that he is public enemy number 1 in the country. He walks down a hallway toward a door that has a sign on it: DILLINGER SQUAD.

Of course, we see him enter the door, which is a large L-shaped office with desks, chairs, typewriters and walls covered with wanted posters, most of which are of him and other villains who are terrorizing the country. Dillinger, of course, looks the posters over and smiles. Up to this point, there doesn't seem to be any detectives in the office; but when he turns a corner, he begins to hear a broadcast of a Chicago White Sox baseball game. Then he sees about six detectives seated around a desk listening to the ball game. Most of them have their backs to him. Dillinger then asks what the score is. One detective turns around, looks at Dillinger, and tells him the score of the game. Dillinger smiles and then nonchalantly walks back the way he came in. I don't think this really happened, but that's show business. On the other hand, if it did happen, the detectives that were sitting around the desk should have all been put back in uniform, and transferred to the identification section where they could study wanted posters.

The beginning of *Public Enemies* is very exciting. It takes place in the Indiana State Prison where convicts, who are working in the shirt factory, open a box marked Thread. Under spools of thread are four Colt .45 automatics with loaded magazines. Among the men is Harry "Pete" Pierpont, thirty-two, a violent man who hates all authority; Charles Makley, forty-four, a certified nutcase; and Homer Van Meter, twenty-seven, an unemotional killer. He would continue to ridicule guards even when it would cost him months in the hole.

At the same time, Red Hamilton, thirty-four, looks at his watch; it's 7:00AM. He drives an unmarked police squad car up to the Indiana State Prison gatehouse. John Dillinger is in the backseat with his hands handcuffed behind him. Hamilton is wearing a star. He drags Dillinger out of the car and shoves him to the door where the turnkey opens the door. Pierpont, Makley and Van Meter, and another con (Walter Dietrich, in his fifties) all have the .45s, have taken over the shirt factory and subdued the guards. Dillinger (his handcuffs removed now), is armed with a Thompson submachine gun. Hamilton, with a sawed-off shotgun, take over the guard station where five guards are playing poker.

The guards are told to take their uniforms off. A guard gives a convict a dirty look. The convict batters the guard's head with a metal pipe, and it caves in his head. Another guard grabs for Van Meter's .45. Van Meter shoots the guard. Of course, the shot alerts other prison guards and the siren goes off. The convicts run for the car. Bullets are flying all over the place. The guard towers are firing at the prisoners. Dillinger is firing his Thompson at the guard tower, as is Makley and

Van Meter. And so on and so on. Of course, Dillinger, Makley, Pierpont, and Hamilton escape.

Actually, the exterior of the prison break was filmed outside of the Stateville Penitentiary near Joliet, Illinois. Between scenes, I had a long conversation with Johnny Depp and some of the other actors who played convicts. I had a photo taken with Johnny standing outside the prison wall. I asked him how he liked firing the Thompson submachine gun. He thought it was a great weapon and was sure it came in handy on bank robberies.

Michael Mann thought he needed an authentic bank robber to get an idea of what was in a bank robber's psyche. Mann wanted to know the feeling one would get before the robbery occurred, how the robbery was planned, and after you make the score, what is the feeling like. You won't believe who he hired. Michael asked for Jerry "One-Armed" Scalise and his partner Art Rachel. They are the two I wrote about earlier who got caught stealing the Marlborough diamond. They reported, "You feel like a king when you are involved in a robbery; there's no high like it. The whole thing is like a thrill. You want it again and again.".

When Hamilton, who belongs to Dillinger's gang, got involved in the shooting of a Chicago police officer, it created a lot of heat in the city. The Chicago Outfit was very upset with Dillinger for causing all this heat. Al Capone's replacement, Frank Nitti, was running the outfit now and met with Dillinger in a wire room that was being remodeled on the second floor of a cigar store near Wrigley Field. Nitti's lieutenant, Phil D'Andrea, and four of his goons along with the Guzik brothers, set up the wire room to take horse and sports bets on sixteen telephones in the room. Some of the phones were being answered by clerks wearing shades, while other technicians were installing other phones.

I, of course, had to help them set up this wire room. They didn't have a clue how this type of gambling operation was set up back in the '30s. Well, to be honest, I had never actually been in a wire room as big as the one they wanted in the script, so I did a little research and interviewed a few old friends. I talked with George Mitsos, a veteran horse enthusiast who knew more about horses than any jockeys did.

I had to find out which racetracks were in operation in the country and what months they were open for racing. The background in the wire room had the names of the racetracks and the names of horses with the odds on every race. Michael Mann, the director, was a very particular person and wanted everything to be authentic when the scene was filmed.

Dillinger and Hamilton walk up to the second floor. They are both armed. Two goons attempt to search them. Dillinger pulls out two .45s, and Hamilton displays two Thompsons concealed on shoulder straps under his coat. D'Andrea smoothes everything down and everybody relaxes. D'Andrea tells Dillinger that the syndicate has a new policy and says, "Guys like you, Karpis, and Van Meter are not going to launder your money or bonds no more. Stay away from our whorehouses. No armorers. No doctors. No nothing, get it? You've caused nothing but heat in this city, it's over. This is strictly business, that's all it is. The real money is operating places like this, not robbing banks. You robbed a bank in Greencastle, Indiana, and got $74,802. Split five ways, that's $14, 960.40. You thought that was a big score. These phones make that much in one day." Dillinger responds by saying, "Unless the cops come through the door." "They won't because we pay them not to, unless you're here. You're bad for business." says D'Andrea. Dillinger and Hamilton just smile at D'Andrea and walk out.

Needless to say, I had a great time working on this movie and meeting Johnny Depp, Christian Bale, Bryan Carroll, Michael Mann, and all the other people it took to make a great movie like *Public Enemies*.

Indiana Sheriff Lillian Holley's car, Stolen By Dillinger, Found on North Side of Chicago 3-5-1934

Original movie theatre where John Dillinger was killed

Don Herion as Technical Advisor during production of PUBLIC ENEMIES
Starring Johnny Depp & Christian Bale – Filmed in Chicago 2008

Johnny Depp at the world premiere of *Public Enemies* in Chicago.

Christian Bale at the world premiere of *Public Enemies* in Chicago.

MICHAEL SNEED
sneed@suntimes.com

Sister wades in

The Blago beat . . .

Psssst! The sister of swamp-sodden **Patti Blagojevich** is heading to the rescue . . . via Facebook!

◆ To wit: State Rep. **Deb Mell**, Patti's younger sister, is not only pulling for Patti to win "I'm a Celebrity . . . Get Me Out of Here!" — which is being televised from the bug-infested jungles of Costa Rica — but she's encouraging folks on her Facebook page to: "Vote for Patti 1-877-553-3707. You can vote 10 times."

◆ Buckshot: Patti survived Thursday's ouster of two celebrities from the jungle.

The Blago agenda?

A top Sneed City Hall source chirped Wednesday: "After watching Patti's performance on the survival show, it's pretty obvious she is trying to address prospective jurors in her husband's upcoming trial."

Deep Depp . . .

Deep dirt: Sneed hears infamous jewel thief **Jerry Scalise**, 71, who spent 16 years in a British prison for stealing $3.6 million in gems — including the famed 45-carat Marlborough diamond — was hired to help out with filming prison sequences in the Chicago-based film "Public Enemies." The film, starring actors **Johnny Depp** and **Christian Bale**, had its Chicago premiere Thursday night.

◆ Backshot: Scalise "knows a lot about jails — he also did time for narcotics," said a Sneed source, who claims Scalise always keeps his left hand, which only has four fingers, in his pocket.

◆ Foreshot: Sneed is told Scalise, who is from Chicago, now lives in the west suburbs. "He served lots of prison time. He's got quite a record."

Deep Depp II . . .

Former Chicago cop **Don Herion**, a mob fighter for 46 years until his retirement from police work a decade ago, also served as an adviser on "Public Enemies."

◆ Bet 'em: Herion, who has written *Pay, Quit or Die*, an inside look at organized crime in Chicago, helped transform the second floor of a Wrigleyville antiques store into "an old-time wire [betting] room."

◆ Describe 'em: Herion tells Sneed that Depp learned how to handle a tommy gun at a State Police gun range, was protected by an Irish bodyguard named Jerry, and was "a guy who talked to you like anybody else would" . . . unlike actor **Tommy Lee Jones** on the set of "U.S. Marshals," where Herion had

Deborah Mell

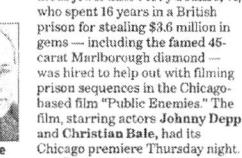

Tommy Lee Jones

Wesley Snipes

Paula Abdul

Lionel Richie

Don Herion with Johnny Depp

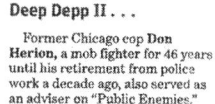

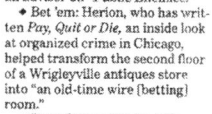

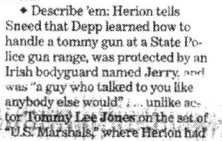

a small role. "He'd [Jones] walk right by you, not even look at you. He thinks he's better than you."

◆ Swamp 'em: Herion claims actor **Wesley Snipes**, who also appeared in "U.S. Marshals," refused to shoot a scene in a swamp. So, they had to shoot in a swimming pool disguised as a swamp."

I spy . . .

White Sox outfielder **Brian Anderson** having a drink at the new Rockit Bar & Grill across from Wrigley Field Wednesday . . . Cub **Alfonso Soriano** dining at Sunda Wednesday night and leaving in a white Rolls-Royce convertible that was kept parked out front . . . Rapper **Kanye West** lunching at the Original Pancake House on the Gold Coast Thursday.

Please note . . .

Condolences to the family of **Ingrid LoGuidice**, whose beloved father, Dr. **Gissur Brynjolfsson**, passed away this week. No father had a better daughter . . . Congrats to police Capt. **Edward Griffin**, who retired Friday after 36 years of service with Chicago's finest . . . and Sheriff **Tom Dart** and wife **Patricia** on the birth of their daughter **Shannon Patricia** . . . and congrats to **Patricia Cox**, named chairwoman-elect of the Goodman Theatre board of trustees.

MICHAEL SNEED
sneed@suntimes.com

Got him covered

$$$$$$ . . .

Good luck/bad fortune: Sneed is told the wife of a Cicero cop charged with stealing $70,000 from the Police Benevolent Association fund won a $2 million Illinois lottery prize last March.

♦ Bond 'em: Cicero officer **Gerald Bossolono**, who was charged Wednesday with one count of felony theft by the Cook County state's attorney's office, was ordered held on $250,000 bond Thursday.

♦ The buckshot: Bossolono, treasurer of the fund aiding families of deceased officers, allegedly wrote 39 fraudulent checks from the fund during 2007-2008, according to prosecutors.

Dennis Farina

The Bob job . . .

Now comes word Ald. **Bob Fioretti** is also a Mr. Fixit. A Sneed source claims Fioretti drives around the 2nd Ward calling 311 to fix neighborhood problems — but has been known to get paint cans out of his truck and paint over graffiti problems! There ya go.

Frost 'em . . .

Pssst! Former President **Bill Clinton** is set to be interviewed by renowned TV host **David Frost** later this year in London.

♦ Hmmm. As you may recall, Frost put former President **Richard Nixon** on a spit, which was chronicled in the movie "Frost/Nixon." But this interview reportedly is supposed to be fun.

Phil Spector

Phil swill . . .

Jam 'em! Now comes word via the L.A. press that convicted musician/murderer **Phil Spector**, 69, who is serving 19 years for killing actress **Lana Clarkson**, is permitted to have musical instruments in his cell. Good grief.

John Kerry

Say Whaaaa?

♦ Brutally honest? Consider this quote by former presidential contender **John Kerry** in the new issue of Men's Journal: "When I'm flying, I usually take

Joy Behar

[Headline News], so I don't have to get married anymore," she joked.

Cops & robbers . . .

Actor **Dennis Farina**, a former Chicago cop, got a kick out of bumping into an old "suspect" at the Chicago premiere of "Public Enemies" last week.

♦ Translation: Farina bumped into jewel thief **Jerry Scalise**, an adviser on the film, who did time in a British prison for stealing the 45-carat Marlborough diamond, which was never recovered.

♦ To wit: Farina told former cop **Don Herion**, who also worked as an adviser on the film, he "tailed Scalise around Chicago one night in 1980 — but lost him." One week later Farina read the headlines about Scalise's diamond heist.

♦ Background: Scalise, who reportedly lives in the western suburbs, has a long arrest record and spent 16 years in a British prison for the jewelry theft.

♦ The endshot: "I tried to get Scalise to hint what happened to the diamond," said Herion. "But he kept saying 'Don't know. Don't know. Don't know.'"

Sneedlings . . .

I spy . . . Counting Crows singer **Adam Duritz** in a Pink Floyd T-shirt at Lux Bar

ADMIT ONE | **ADMIT ONE**

Special Screening

PUBLIC ENEMIES

Thursday, June 18, 2009

7:00 PM

AMC River East 21
322 East Illinois Street
Chicago

No one will be admitted once the screening has begun
THIS TICKET IS ABSOLUTELY NON-TRANSFERABLE

UNIVERSAL

Special Screening

PUBLIC ENEMIES

Thursday, June 18, 2009

7:00 PM

AMC River East 21
322 East Illinois Street
Chicago

No one will be admitted once the screening has begun
THIS TICKET IS ABSOLUTELY NON-TRANSFERABLE

UNIVERSAL

The Execution of Mike Norton

Michael Norton, fifty-five, was a friend of mine; I say *was* because he is no longer among the living. He was executed in his store on May 14, 2009, by two hooded black men. He was found slain in the back of his store, lying facedown with his hands and feet bound. He had been shot once through the back of the head. A witness told the police that two black men entered the store through the front door and then one of the men locked the door behind them. The two men were seen pulling off the masks as they left the building a few minutes later.

Norton's family and neighbors said that he recently kicked out gang members who allegedly were selling drugs out of an apartment above the store. Mike was not one to back away from a fight nor would he turn his back on somebody in need. Mike's father, Jim, had owned the two-story building at 4759 West North Avenue for decades. He was a Chicago police officer who worked at the old Thirty-first District, also known as Cragin, at 4900 West Grand Avenue. I remember running into Jim one day in the father's waiting room at St. Anne's Hospital at 4950 West Thomas Avenue. My wife Gen was having our third child, and Jim told me that his wife Mary was having a miscarriage. I think they had six children at that time.

I lived across the street from Norton's store and knew Jim very well. He encouraged me to join the Chicago Police Department when I got out of the army in 1953. He had a partner; his name was Shoes, a big man with big feet and was maybe the biggest bullshit artist in town. During the early 1940s, when times were tough, I lived with my mother, sister, and grandmother in an apartment building at 4752 West North Avenue. For extra money, we had to rent out a front room that had a Murphy bed that folded into the wall. Shoes was our tenant.

A streetcar barn was located across the street at the southwest corner of North Avenue and Cicero, so a lot of conductors and motormen would visit Norton's store. I believe Shoes was running a handbook on the side as he would visit the car barns frequently and always had a scratch sheet in his pocket.

During WWII, Shoes was never in the military, but if you ever heard him talk about the battles he was in, in the South Pacific, you would think he was Admiral Bull Halsey. I remember one day he was talking to a couple of sailors who were home on leave from the South Pacific. They had been in a few major battles, and Shoes overheard them talking about it. He joined in the conversation and began telling them how he had been torpedoed in the same battle and so on. All I heard then was the two sailors saying "Wow, boy, you were lucky to survive!" They were even slapping him on the back like he was a war hero.

Jim Norton and Shoes were partners for quite a while. Jim and his wife Mary lived at Wabansia and Keating Avenue. Their children went to St. Peter Canisius School at 5000 West North Avenue. When Mike Norton and his brother Pat would take a shortcut to school, they used a gangway next to our apartment building. They were always fighting with each other.

When Shoes died, Jim still had the store, and Mike helped him out on occasion, stocking shelves and other chores around the store. Jim Norton passed away in 1988, and Mike took over the store. Mike ran the store with the stern but passionate grip of a policeman's son.

The neighborhood was changing, and crime was showing its ugly head. Mike began to keep a gun under his counter for protection. In 1991, Norton shot two men who tried to rob him at the store, killing one and wounding another. From that point on, Norton installed safety glass around the entire counter, but wouldn't close the store, as he had too many friends in the neighborhood.

Every now and then, I would stop in and see Mike and we would always wind up talking about the neighborhood and how things have changed. The streetcar barns were gone and replaced by a shopping center. Even my old apartment building was demolished and replaced by a Walgreens Drugstore. There were gangs all over the neighborhood, which, of course, brought narcotics.

Mike had told me that he had a few nasty incidents with gang members and said that he had recently kicked out a woman and other alleged dope dealers from an apartment above his store. I remember one day I paid him a visit and we talked about the shoot-out he had with two stickup guys. He showed me the bullet holes that were still in the walls. I told him that he should write a book about his life experiences in running a store in a dangerous neighborhood. He said that he had thought about it and he might just do it.

Mike was like his father, Jim, who was one tough cop and didn't take any crap from anybody. If anybody threatened Mike, he gave it right back to them. There was no way he could have stayed in the neighborhood as long as he did if he showed any fear. Actually, he was liked by everybody in the area. He was known for always taking care of everyone that needed help. After he was killed, neighborhood people wrote notes on paper about how much they loved him and would miss him. They stuck them in between the scissor gates surrounding the door and front windows.

Mike kept the store open six days a week to accommodate the neighborhood people. I asked him if he got nervous when he closed up and had to walk to his car in the dark. He told me that one time, someone took a shot at him in the alley, but they missed, thank God. I told him he had more guts than I did. I knew that neighborhood very well, and I wouldn't walk back to my car without my gun in my hand.

While writing this story, I have learned that the Chicago Police have arrested two people for the execution of Mike Norton on May 14, 2009. Charged for his death are Elvin Payton, twenty-six, and Beatrice Rosado, twenty-four, both of the 700 block of North Avers Avenue. Another man took part in the murder and is being hunted down. Payton, who has a diamond tattoo near his right eye, is an admitted member of a street gang. Police were able to track down Rosado, who had the apartment lease, because she allegedly had intentionally struck a woman in her black 1992 Chevy Van in Logan Square earlier, records show. Another witness saw the same van with Rosado in it near Mike Norton's store at the time of his murder.

Hopefully, the police will capture the other assailant. Maybe he will resist arrest, which would mean that the police would have to use necessary force to take him into custody. Hopefully, justice will be served. But no matter what happens, nothing will bring back Mike Norton, a great man. He will be missed.

Store owner tied up, fatally shot in business

Michael Norton was known to help the less fortunate and had no tolerance for West Humboldt Park gangs

By Gerry Smith,
Carlos Sadovi
and Angela Rozas
TRIBUNE REPORTERS

Michael Norton was not one to back away from a fight nor would he turn his back on somebody in need.

For decades, Norton's family ran a sweet shop in the West Humboldt Park neighborhood, providing a place for people to grab a soda, chat about the neighborhood's woes or even get help with alcohol addiction.

Norton, known as "Mike" to his friends and customers, took over Norton's Sweet Shop after his father, a Chicago police officer, died in 1966. He ran the place with the stern but compassionate grip of an officer's son, chasing after children who stole candy but then letting them go with a warning rather than calling police.

But he was no pushover. In 1981 Norton shot two men who tried to rob him at the store, killing one and injuring another. Norton installed safety glass around the cashier's counter but wouldn't close up shop. He had too many friends in the neighborhood, his family said.

On Thursday night, Norton, 56, of unincorporated Glen Ellyn, was found shot to death in the rear of his store, his hands bound and a bullet through the back of his head. Police are calling the incident robbery-related. No one was in custody Friday evening.

Residents worry, though, that Norton may have been targeted after standing up to gangs in the neighborhood. Recently, Norton had told gang members allegedly selling drugs to get out of an apartment above his store, family and neighbors said. They in turn threatened to "break his legs" and even take his life, they said.

Last week, someone fired a gun into the North Avenue side of Norton's corner store. Norton, who owned the building, told neighbors that he believed the angry tenants were responsible. On Friday, a bullet hole remained visible in the window behind a metal window gate.

Still, Norton kept to his routine, keeping the shop open six days a week. His perseverance in the face of such threats was a hallmark of his personality, the family said.

"If anybody threatened him, he was in their face right back," said his sister, Margaret Carolan. "You have to know when you're in a changing neighborhood for many years that you have to present a strong front."

As a teenager, Norton wanted to be a stockbroker, but his father needed help at the shop. He began stocking shelves and driving to the bank when he was old enough to drive, Carolan said.

When his father died, Norton was chosen from among eight siblings to take over the store because he had taken college courses, although he never graduated, she said.

"When you're in a large family, you learn to pitch in wherever you're needed and that was that," Carolan said.

Over the years, Norton became known for his generosity, granting credit to those in need and even personal loans. He sponsored several residents for Alcoholics Anonymous after he got sober 30 years ago.

The shop was a neighborhood gathering spot. When the CTA bus barns were located across the street, bus drivers would spend hours in the store playing pinochle, Carolan said.

"It was always more than just a neighborhood store," she said. "A corner store is like the bar 'Cheers.' You have somebody to talk to, to tell your troubles to, to support you when needed."

Norton also raised his 16-year-old daughter, Brittany, by himself because her mother "had medical issues," Carolan said. Once a year, he would take a week off from the store and take his daughter fishing in Wisconsin, often joking that she caught more fish than he did, his sister said. "His life did revolve around her," Carolan said. "She was everything to him."

Rosa Lopez, who runs a travel agency out of another building owned by Norton, said he told her about the 1981 robbery. Norton told her how as the armed men demanded money, he threw a large pile of cash on the counter, causing it to scatter. Distracted, the men took their eyes off Norton for a moment.

"When he saw they dropped their view, he grabbed his gun and fired," Lopez said.

Carolan said a tenant who lived above the store told her that Norton recently threw gang members out of another tenant's apartment and "they said they would break his legs." She said Norton did not carry a gun but kept one in the store.

Terry Sherrod, a neighbor who had known Norton for more than 25 years, said Norton told him that he evicted tenants for allegedly selling drugs in the building.

"He told me they said threats to him like, 'We're going to kill you,'" Sherrod said. "He wasn't afraid. ... He'd been there forever."

gsmith@tribune.com
csadovi@tribune.com
arozas@tribune.com

Some of the Alleged Mob Guys We Busted As Well As Their Associates

The following subjects were arrested for illegal gambling. It does not indicate if they were convicted for these crimes or have affiliations to organized crime. The symbol * denotes busted more than once.

Steve Abarbanell
Bobby Abbinanti
Joseph Accardo
Jeff Adelman*
Anthony Albate
Harry Aleman*
Rich Alesse
Raymond Alyea
Anthony Amari
Frank Amato
Alia Amin*
Bruno Andriacchi
Donald Angelini*
Carmen Antonelli*

Ronald Antos*
Balterzal Argamaso
Anthony Arnieri
Edward Arnold
Paul Aronson*
Varavit Arora
Yithya Arora
William Asher*
Elias Attallah
Frank Aureli*
Hussein Azimi
Selana Badamo*
Mary Bagmell*
Paul Bagwell*

Rosanna Bajrami*
Edward Bak
Roger Baldwin
Richard Balsis
Paul Balzano
Sandra Bandringa
Kenneth Bandusky*
Richard Banea
Richard Bangelowski
Dominick Barbaro*
Thomas Barlas*
Nelson Barnes
Patrick Battaglia
Bruno Barsella

Frank Bartuca*
Anthony Basase
Dominick Basso*
Michael Basso*
Brenetta Bates
Mark Bausone
Delbert Bell*
Robert Bellavia*
Paul Bellos
Louie Belpedio
Joseph Benes*
Isadore Benitivich*
Vincent Berk*
Marilyn Berkowitz*
Harvey Bernstein
Phil Bertucci
E. G. Bicker
Sam Bills
Herb Blitzstein
Michael Blechman*
Mike Bolis
James Bollman
Ronald Borelli
Joe Borsellino
Darryl Bosak
Paul Bowers*
John Bowling*
Rose Bozan
Fred Braun*
Terence Brennan
George Brigham
Terry Britton
Joseph Brown
Raymond Brown
Hugh Buchcanon
John Buckley
Frank Bura
Daniel Byron
Ray Caccamo

Joe Calato*
Joseph Calcagno
John Caldarulo*
Mike Calderone*
Ron Calderone*
Larry Caldrone
Gabe Caliendo
Martin Callary*
Jose Camacho*
John "Haircuts"
  Campanelli
Rocco Campanile
Jasper Campise*
John Capodice
Dan Caponigri
Henry Capra*
Salvatore Caracci
John "Beef" Carracci*
Ralph Carbonari*
Frank Cardascio
Chris Carlson
John Carmody
Chuck Carroll
Andrew Carsello
Larry Carter*
George Caruso*
Morris "Mutt" Caruso
Anthony Carvotta*
Frank Casa
Nick Cataudella
Anthony Catizone*
Richard Catizone*
James "the Bomber"
  Catuara
Arthur Cazzato
Dale Cecola
Terry Cecola
James Cerone
Bobby Cerva*

Vito Cesari
Frank Cesario*
John Chaconis
Harry Chase
Jay Cherim
Geoffrey Chierici
Vuthana Chindamanee
Ben Chokler*
Morris Christensen*
Richard Christifano*
Michael Chud
John Cialoni*
John Cimitili*
Arthur Cioe
Anthony Cipriano
Loy Clark
Charlie CoCo*
Aaron Cohen
George Columbus*
Roy Combs*
Karen Conner*
Mathew Connolly*
Joe Corngold*
Ross Corriero
Dominick Cortina*
Vernon Cotton
Edward Coy
Phil Cozzo
Vincent Cozzo
Agnes Craft
Thomas Culhane
Marco D'Amico*
Louis DeCanio
Anthony DeCore
Jay DeGraff*
Richard DeGrazia*
Sal "Solly D"
  Delaurentis*
Gene Del Guidice

Vincent Del Guidice
Frank DelBlasio*
Raymond C. DeBlasio
Marshall DeFrank
Charles Demke*
Woody Demma*
George Demos
James Dennis
Edward DeRose
Richie DeSantis*
Carmen DeSanto
Renato Desilvestro*
Sam DeStefano
Gregg Devilin
Jeffrey Devine
James DeVito
Charles Dewitt
Loren Diamond
Joe DiConstanzo
Frank DiCostanzo*
William DiDomenico
John DiFilippo
John "No Nose" DiFronzo
Antonio Dionisio*
Joe DiVarco
Benny Dixon
John Doherty
Herbert Don
Richard Donkel
Leonard Donner
John Dore
Anthony Dote
Carl Dote*
Harry Doyle
Frank Bopo
Robert Ducato
Robert Ducek
Jeffrey Ehredt

Nick Elam
Vince Ellano
Anthony Eldorado
Carol Ellison
Alfred Emody*
Joe Eng*
Richard Engalls
Richard Engel*
Mike Englehart*
Dennis Enright
Frank Esposito
Ken "the Jap" Eto*
Frank Falbo*
Anthony Fatigato*
Gary Fazio
Harry Fehl
Allen Fiala
Fredrick Fields
Ed Finck*
Charles Finn*
James Fitzgerald
Kevin Fitzpatrick
Patrick Fitzpatrick*
John Flakus*
Larry Flemming*
Dominic Florio
Paul Flowers*
Thomas Foley
Jack Foreman*
Joel Foreman*
Thomas Frachella
Thomas Francis*
Chuck Frankian*
Joseph Fraser
Linda Frawley
Edward Freeman
Carol Friduss*
Anthony Frieri*
Frank Frisch*

Peter N. Frpstis
Michail Froustis
Michael Fuertsch
Moore Fundukian*
John Gabriel
Augie Galan*
Nick "Keg" Galanos*
Albert Galluppi
Dennis Gancarz
Charles Garafolo
Evelyn Garrett
Robert Garrison
Danny Gasperini*
Bernard Geers
Steve Geisler*
Julius Gelber*
Morton Geller
Angelo Gernardo
Joseph Gianforte
Sam Gianforte
Anthony Giannone
James Gianopoulas*
Salvatore Gibbelina*
Charles Gibe*
Russ Gibe*
Patrick Giemzik
Nick Gio
Anthony Giorango*
Mike Giorango*
Jerry Glickman*
Joel Glickman*
Marvin Goldberg*
Sherman Goldman*
Guillermo Gonzales
Ken Goodman*
Richard Gora*
Danny Gordon*
Edward Gorniak
Peter Grafner*

Michael Gratice
Arthur Greco
John Greene
Lavergne Guerrieri
Gregory "Emmett" Paloian
Gus "Slim" Alex
Eugene Gutierrez
Cosmo Guzaldo
Phil Guzaldo*
Tony Guzaldo*
Villegas Guzman*
Phan Hai Than
Richard Halperin*
Joseph Hamilton
Larry Hanauer
James Hansen
Richard Hansen
Rudolfo Haro
Jack Harris*
Howard Harris
James Hartman
John Heishman
Mark Hellwig
Mathew Hendrich
Paul Herman*
Clarence Hermann*
John Hezinger
Lawrence Hilberger
Robert Hillenbrandt*
Conrad Hillesheim*
Robert Hoffman
Adolph Holiday
Mark Hollendonner*
Thomas Horrell
Steve Hospodar*
Lamont Howard*
Joanne Hucek
Scott Humes

Jack Icanbar
Ronald Ignoffo
Angelo Imparato*
James Inendino*
Ernest "Rocky" Infelise*
George Ivanoff*
William J. McGuire
David Jackson
Walter Jackson
Thomas Jacobowsky
Harris Jacobs*
Jake Jacobs*
James Jacobs
Michael Jacobs
Burt Jacobson*
William Jacobson
Ronald Jaffe
Murry Jans*
Ronnie Jarrett Jr.*
Ronnie Jarrett Sr.
Dan Jarzembowski*
Sam Jaroki
Steven Jasinski
Frank Jerome*
Everette Johnson
Robert Johnson
Mathew Jones*
Darrin Joss
Raymond Kacor
Irv Kahn*
John Kasperek
David Kassmier
Harold Kasten*
Nick Katsis*
Bernard Katz*
Alan Kaye
Sanford Kaye
Kevin Kelly

Thomas Kerrott
Martin Kervin
William Kevil
Kramholl, Traymany
Joseph Kica*
Phil Klosowski*
Morris Klotz*
John Kobylarz*
Louis Kopple
Dave Kopulos*
James Kossar*
Robert Kozik
William Kreznor
Lenny Kucala
Nick LoCoco*
Daniel LaCrosse
Santo LaMantia
Donald Lanacki*
Alan Lang*
Brian Langer
John LaPlaca
John Lardino
Jerry Laurie
George Laurie
Jimmy LaValley
William Lawler
Rose Laws
David Leader*
Leo Leaney
Jerome Leavitt*
Lawrence Lederer
Michael LeDonne
Theodore Lee
Mark Lehman
William Leman
Tore Leno
Donald Lenza*
Gerry Lenza
James LePore*

Jeff Lesniak
Mark Levy
Robert "Bobby" Lewis*
Bobby Likas
Walter Liss
Robert Lobash
Vic Locallo*
Joe "the Clown" Lombardo
Sam London
David Long*
James Loverdi
Michael Loverdi
Steve Lubansky
Dan Lubertozzi*
Eugene "Yudi" Luffman
Terance Lyons
Steven Macatek
Thomas Mackey
Gerald Mader*
Anthony Maggio
Donald Maggio*
Nick Maggio
Orlando Maggio
Ron Magliano
Sygmunt Makas*
Robert Mangiamele
John Mann*
John Manzella*
Louis Manzella
Frank Marasso
Louie Marino
Nick Markese
Marvin Marks*
Roy Marshall
James Maurogeanes
John Marusarz

Ralph Massucci
Nick Matelli
Thomas Matriciano
Louis Matroci*
Dave Mattioli*
James Mavrogeames
Joe Mazzuca
Donald McAvoy
Thomas McCandless
Matt McCarthy
Kevin McCormick*
David McGlennon
Richard J. McGovern
Brian McKinley
David McVey
Anthony Mecca
Dan Meister*
Ken Meister
Michael Melchert
William Melchior
William Melchiore
Willie Messino*
Barry Metrick
George Michals*
Ron Michelon
Robert Milice
Harvey Miller*
Robert Miller*
Terrence Milos
James Minarczyk
Patrick Minaugh
Sam Minkus
James Moccio*
August Monteleone
Ben Moody*
Ronald More*
Scott More
James Morici
Joseph Morici

Dan Morsovillo
Stan Moskal
Harvey Moy*
Charles Mulberg*
Gerald Murphy
James Murphy
Wilbur Murray*
Anthony Nardiello
Joseph Naverro
Thomas Navigato*
Henry Nemirow
James Nicholas*
Nick Nitti*
James Nitz
James Nolan
Anthony Nolfe
Steve Nolfe*
Sultian Noorullah
Mitchell Norton
Max Nuttler
Kevin O'Flynn
Linda Oakes*
John O'Brien
Brett O'Dell
Aaron "Obie" Oberlander
Gary Oliva*
Jack Oliver
James Oliver
Zel Olken
James Olson
Anthony Orlando
Thomas Orlando
John Orsi
Ben Oshansky*
Jerry Otto
Daniel P. Paclke
James Pacini
Joseph Pace

Errol Pacynski*
Billy Pagounis*
Anthony Panico
James Panovich
Charles Parrilli*
Louie Parrilli*
August Parrillo*
Paul Parrillo*
Noli Pascqual
Joe Pascucci*
Edward Pasinski
Eugene Pasinski
Lenny Patrick*
Louie Papelli
Joseph Pawlowski
George Peara
Robert Pedraza
Joseph Pepitone
Sheldon Perlman*
Tony Perozzi
Frank Perrone
Leroy Peterson*
William "Butch" Petrocelli
Anthony Petronella*
Larry Pettit
Proxay Phanthamaly
Jack Phillips
Michael Pignato
Richard Pikarski
Arthur Pilotto
Roman Pinedo*
Anthony Pinto
Bruce Pinto*
Frank Piro
Maureen Pitt*
Ben Polcheri
Ray Polino*
Robert Ponti
Prakarn Poonbunker
Albert Pope
Marshall Portnoy*
Bernard "PP" Posner
Robert Powers
Donald Pozsgay*
Bernie Prestigacomo*
Michael Prestigacomo*
Donald Preston
George Price
James Prignano*
Mark Provenzano
Glenn Prushnick
Nick Psiminas
Larry Pufahl*
David Puhl*
John Puntillo
Renaldo Punzalan
Henry Rabin
John Radtke
Mario Rainone
Sam Ranola
Ernest Rediger*
Gary Reich
Paul Reichel
Susan Reid*
Adam Resnick
Walter Rhodes*
Roger Riccio*
Jacquelin Richardson
Rueben Richardson
Patrick Rattaglia
Kenneth Rigan
James Roberson
Willard Roberts
Ed Robinson
Joseph Rocco
Jimmy Rodich
Thomas Roebuck
John Rogala
William Rogers
Elmer Roman*
Miguel Roman
Harry Rose
Joseph Rosengard*
Julius Rosengard*
Louis Rossi
Leslie Rothenbaum
Michael Rotondo
Darnell Rudd
James Russell
Tim Russell*
Thomas Russell
Steven Ruzich
Bruno Ryndak*
Bradley S. Mrozek
Robert Salerno*
Frank Saletta*
James Sammarco
Clyde Sampson
Melvin Santos*
Ben Saracco*
James Saracco
Chris Saraceno
Natale Saraceno
Joe Sarillo
Joseph Sarillo
Mike Sarno
Jean Saulter
Jean Saulters
Chris Savides*
Dino Savides
John Scala*
Jack Scanlon
Ray Schiersz
Tom Schimick
Howard Schneider
Francis Schutte

Dan Scottie*
Darla Seaberg
Jeff Segretti*
Michael Segretti
James Semla*
Phyllis Senn*
Chris Serritella*
Charles Settino
Norman Shabas*
Al Shamest
Moe Shapiro*
Pat Sheehan*
Phil Sheehan*
Terry Sheldon
Carl Sheppard
Joseph Silva
Arthur Simmons
Louis Sinople
Calvin Sirkin*
Tom Sitarski*
Joseph Skoka
Thomas Sloan
Gerrit Sluyk*
Donald Smith
Hal Smith*
Michael Smith*
Renee Smith
Mike Soleau*
Ralph Solone*
George Sommer*
Greg Sommes
Steve Soupas*
Frank Soverino
Paul Spano
Ray Spencer
Ernest Speranza
Edward Sperka
Anthony Spilotro*
Victor Spilotro

Chris Spina*
Adam Sroki
Basil Stapralis
Alex Starvos*
Ronald Stella*
Anthony Stellato
Marvin Stellman*
Dina Stellwagen
Tex Sterling*
Vicky Stluka
Willie Stokes*
William Stone*
Peter Storino
Robert Strada*
Charles Strange
Willie Strange*
Demitri "Jim"
  Stavropoulos*
Ralph Strocchia*
Lester Sugarman
Hayward Suggs*
Lang Sullivan
Pat Sullivan
Thomas Sullivan
Thomas Sum
James Swider
Robert Szany
Richard Szyc*
Mike Talerico*
Arnold Taradash*
Edward Tarala
Greg Tarala
George Teinbelle
Louie Tenuta*
William Tenuta*
Larry Teske
Jess A. Testa*
Jesse Testa
Ted Thomas*

Anthony Tito
Ray Tominello*
John Torello
Linda Trapp
Linda Tripp*
Alfonso Trobiani
Ralph Trobiani
Alfred Troiani*
Bobby Truppo
Paul Tumlin
Arthur Turgeon
Carl Urbanetti
Frank Urso
Robert Van Houghton
Adam Van Wilzenburg
Randy Vanloon
Vathanasombat
  Vasukri
Anthony Vaughm*
Ted Veesart*
Paul Vehla
Donald Venetucci
Peter Vente
Anthony Verlick*
Lane Vermeyen
Fred Vermeyens
Joseph Vertucci
Albert Vodvarka*
Joe Volpentesta
Daniel Vuletich*
Kurt W. Stein
Robert Wallach
James Walsh
James Wasik
Bruce Wasz
Thomas Weber
Adolph Weis
William Wheatly
William Wheatly Jr.

John Whirity
Andrew White*
David Whitfield
Paul Wicker
Donald Wilson*
Robert Wilson
Tom Wilson
Joe Wing*
Robert Wingertner*
Warren Winkler*
John Wisniewski

Jerry Wojcik
Donald Wren*
Jerry Wright*
Stanley Wysocki
Jesse Yale
James Yama
Frank Yario
James Yario
William Yavitz*
Son Yoeun
Lottie Zagorski*

Oscar Zamora
Victor Zamora
William Zanon
David Zidek
Jim Zindell
Tom Zitzer*
Paul Zivilich
Thomas Zizzo
Glen Zucker
August Zymantas*

Gangland Murders: 1961-1992

Source material for the following murders is from the
Chicago Police Department and Chicago Crime Commission

Date of Death	Deceased	Killer
March 31, 1960	Charles Vaughn	Unknown
October 13	Michael J. Urgo	Unknown
November 15	Michael DeMarte	Unknown
December 6	Lester Belgrad	Unknown
December 12, 1960	Frank DelGuidice	Unknown

1961

February 2, 1961
Deceased: Theodoros Sampaniotis
Killer: Unknown

    Theodoros Sampaniotis, age thirty-three years, body found at 7:30 AM on February 2, 1961, in an abandoned garage at 642 Blue Island Avenue. He had been shot three times in the head and twice in the chest at close range. He had been dead for four to six hours when he was found. Police theorized that Sampaniotis's[1] slayers harbored a personal grudge against him because the body bore marks that indicated it was kicked after he had been shot five times. He was known to be a gambler, and it was therefore believed that he might have cheated an acquaintance or had failed to pay his gambling debts.

March 31
Deceased: John Arthur Powers
Killer: Unknown

At about 1:10 AM on March 31, 1961, thirty-eight-year-old John Arthur Powers was about to enter his basement apartment in Chicago when he was ambushed by gunmen, shot five times, and killed. Only a short time before the shooting, Powers, a bartender at the Velvet Lounge at 3551 West North Avenue in Chicago had left his place of employment. After stopping for something to eat at a restaurant at Crawford and North avenues, he took a taxicab to his residence address. He was shot before he could enter his basement apartment. Powers was a known patron of Cicero gambling joints and was heavily in debt. Shortly before his death, he had confided to friends that he owed $1,800 to the outfit, a name frequently applied to the syndicate.

Powers, an ex-convict, was sentenced to the Illinois State Penitentiary in Joliet for robbery in 1941. Following his parole in 1946, he was returned three times for violation of the terms of his parole. He was discharged from parole in 1956.

While in state prison, Powers became friendly with another inmate, Morris Litberg, who was until 1961 a principal figure in a vending company. Several months before Powers was murdered, Felix "Milwaukee Phil" Alderisio and other syndicate hoodlums became connected with the company. Litberg complained that he was being muscled out of his business, and he sought the aid of his friend John Powers. Powers in turn brought his friend Edward J. McNally into the picture.

May 15, 1961
Deceased: Edward J. McNally
Killer: Unknown

On the night of May 15, 1961, Edward J. McNally, thirty-three years, was ambushed and slain a short time after he left the Velvet Lounge, 3551 West North Avenue in Chicago. He had been shot three times in an alley in the rear of 3441 West Fulton Street in Chicago. The slaying of McNally occurred just six weeks after his friend Powers had been murdered. Like Powers, McNally had frequented Cicero gambling establishments and was in debt to loan sharks. On one occasion, he allegedly participated in the holdup of a Cicero bookie. A few months before they were murdered, Morris Litberg reputedly offered Powers and McNally $15,000 to kill three syndicate hoodlums who had muscled into his vending business. Instead, Powers and McNally reported the offer to the mobsters who gave Litberg a beating, and he fled the Chicago area. Powers and McNally were murdered a short time later.

June 13, 1961
Deceased: L. C. Smith
Killer: Unknown

L. C. Smith, age thirty-nine years. His body was found at 7:15 AM on June 13, 1961, in his parked car in Chicago's Loop. He had been shot five times in the back of the head with a .45-caliber automatic pistol. Four men had forced Smith's car to the curb at 4006 West Sixteenth Street. Two of the men got into Smith's car and forced him to drive off while the other two followed in their car. On July 21, 1961, a Cicero gambler was arrested as he stepped off an elevator in the first-floor corridor of the criminal court building. He was identified by a witness as having been one of the four men who had participated in the kidnap-murder of Smith. The September 1961 Grand Jury Term returned no bill on the charge. It was reported by the press that police were attempting to connect Smith's slaying with underworld loan sharks known as juice men.

June 14, 1961
Deceased: Shelby Faulk
Killer: Unknown

Shelby Faulk, age thirty-six years. Body found on the early morning of June 14, 1961, in Faulk's white 1961 Cadillac, blood spattered in an alley in the rear of 7304 South Union Avenue, Chicago. Faulk was slumped against the right front door, bullet holes over his left ear and in his left chest and chin. Two bullets had been fired through the right front and rear floors. Police stated that robbery might have been the motive since Faulk's wallet and pockets were empty and a valuable ring was missing. When police went to his home, they found a dice game in progress in the basement of the home. Of the forty participants, seventeen were arrested.

Faulk had been convicted of peddling narcotics and was sentenced to two to three years in state prison in 1955. In November 1960, he had been freed on charges of possession and sale of narcotics in the criminal court. He had also served a prison term for manslaughter in his native state, Tennessee. Police information indicated that Faulk was carrying $7,000 to purchase narcotics when he was last seen. While robbery appeared to be the apparent motive, police added that there might have been "a falling-out among thieves."

June 20, 1961
Deceased: Ralph Del Genio
Killer: Unknown

Ralph Del Genio, fifty-seven years of age, of Cicero. At 11:55 AM on June 20, 1961, a traffic policeman ticketed a battered 1954 car parked in front of 626 South Wells Street. His partner believed he had seen the car there the previous day. At 12:40 PM the officer telephoned the police auto pound to order the car towed in. An employee of the pound subsequently drove the car, and when he later lifted a blanket on the rear floor, he found Del Genio's body lying facedown. He had been beaten to death with a blunt instrument. The body was disfigured with angry cuts and bruises and appeared to have been dead for at least two days.

Del Genio was due in U.S. bankruptcy court at 10:00 AM on the day before his body was found, but he failed to appear. A Skokie finance company, which had turned down Del Genio on a loan, reported that Del Genio was indebted to fourteen other firms including several other finance companies. Police theory was that Del Genio was killed because he owed money and was in debt to the juice men.

July 29, 1961
Deceased: Michael Joyce
Killer: Unknown

Michael Joyce, age thirty years. At 2:30 AM on July 29, 1961, a burning car was spotted by police in front of 819 North Harding Avenue, Chicago. When firemen extinguished the blaze, the body of Joyce was found humped over on the floor next to the driver's seat. He had been shot twice in the head. The car had been doused in gasoline. Joyce was a minor hoodlum who had been arrested numerous times as a burglary and narcotics suspect and for traffic violations. He had been arrested as a suspect in the Charles Gross shotgun slaying in 1952.

August 1, 1961
Deceased: Carl Wiltse
Killer: Unknown

Carl Wiltse, age twenty-seven years. Between 11:00 and 11:30 PM on August 1, 1961, Wiltse was slain by shotgun blasts fired in the living room of his four-room apartment as he was watching television. A screen and fan had been removed from the kitchen window, and the slayer or slayers fired through the window or climbed into the apartment. Wiltse was shot in the neck and chest.

He was described by police as a small-time burglar and hoodlum. He served six months in jail for auto larceny. Wiltse's wife reported that two months before, six shots had been fired into the apartment and six more into Wiltse's 1953 car. She added, "He was a loudmouth when he drank, and word got out that he was a fink – a finger man."

August 11, 1961
Deceased: William "Action" Jackson
Killers: Fiore Buccieri, Jack Cerone, Dave Yaras, others

William "Action" Jackson, age thirty years, of Cicero. His almost nude, cut, and bruised body was found stuffed in the trunk of a green two-door 1957 Cadillac, abandoned on the lower level of Wacker Drive between Franklin and Wells streets on the night of August 11, 1961. The car was registered in the name of William Kearney, an alias used by Jackson. It was conjectured that the body had been in the trunk for as long as three days. An autopsy showed that Jackson had been beaten to death after being tortured. His chest was crushed. There were no bullet or stab wounds. Police considered several possible motives for the slaying:

1. He was engaged in hijacking trucks and thus incurred the wrath of syndicate authorized hijackers.
2. He had run afoul of his syndicate bosses by shorting them on the amount of money he was charged with collecting in the vicious juice racket.
3. Top hoodlums might have feared that Jackson would tell too much at his scheduled appearance before federal judge William J. Campbell on September 21 on charges of helping to steal $70,000 worth of electrical appliances from a railroad yard.
4. Burglars, whose stolen goods he disposed of, might have killed him because he reportedly cheated them.
5. He might have ignored syndicate warnings to stop stealing from other thieves.

October 20, 1961
Deceased: John A. Kilpatrick
Killers: Dana Nash, 99-150 years; William Triplett, 14 years

John A. Kilpatrick, fifty-four years, of 5231 South Lawndale Avenue. Body found 9:10 AM on October 20, 1961, by three city forestry workers in his car, which was parked in the rear of 3312 West Sixty-first Street, two blocks from his union headquarters at 3304 West Sixty-third Street. Kilpatrick was international president of the United Industrial Workers of America and president of Local 300 of the UIWA.

Kilpatrick had been shot once under the left ear. Two sticks of dynamite were found wired to the ignition of his car in what investigators said was a previous attempt to kill Kilpatrick. The dynamite failed to explode because of faulty wiring or because the dynamite was wet from rain that had seeped under the hood.

Angelo Inciso was president of Local 286 of the UIWA. A federal jury had found Inciso guilty of milking his union's funds of $420,667, and he was sentenced to ten years in prison. Inciso blamed Kilpatrick for starting the investigation that resulted in the conviction.

November 4, 1961
Deceased: Albert Brown
Killer: Unknown

Albert Brown, age thirty-nine years, of 604 South. May Street. At about 9:15 AM on November 4, 1961, four shots were fired outside the plant of Lonergan Dye Co. at 4615 Arthington Street, Chicago. When a plant foreman went out to investigate, he found Brown dying and lying facedown on the ground beside a car he had borrowed from his brother. He had been shot in the back of the head and through the chest. A 7.65 mm Italian Beretta automatic pistol was found in a clump of weeds about one hundred feet from the body.

On October 31, Brown had been convicted of burglary in the criminal court and had been sentenced to the penitentiary for five to ten years. Brown was at liberty on an appeal bond at the time of his slaying. The police leaned toward the theory he was killed by members of the juice racket.

November 8, 1961
Deceased: Joseph Gentile
Killer: Unknown

Joseph Gentile, age fifty-one years, was shot to death on the early morning of November 8, 1961, as he and two companions were seated in his car, which was parked in front of his home at 1631 West Nineteenth Street, Chicago. Of the six shots fired from a second car, one struck Gentile in the temple. It was theorized that Gentile might have been the victim of the underworld moneylending racket, which had been held responsible for earlier gangland slayings.

November 9, 1961
Deceased: Albert "Transom" Testa
Killer: Unknown

On the morning of November 9, 1961, Albert "Transom" Testa, age forty-eight, of 700 North Monticello Avenue, was found lying in a coma in the alley in the rear of 1031 North Francisco Avenue. He had been shot twice in the head. He died in the county hospital at 1:05 PM the same day.

Testa was very short in stature and weighed less than one hundred pounds. He was given the nickname Transom because he used transoms to enter places of burglaries. Theories advanced the following:

1. An eighteen-year-old striptease dancer, whom Testa had introduced to high-ranking syndicate members, had turned informant.
2. Testa was a longtime friend of William "Action" Jackson.
3. Testa was a handbook operator associated with Charles English, West Side gambling boss for the syndicate.

November 14, 1961
Deceased: Louis DiMeo
Killer: Unknown

The bludgeoned body of Louis DiMeo, age twenty-four years, was found by firemen in the closet of DiMeo's apartment at 1910 Lake Street, Melrose Park, Illinois, on November 14, 1961, at 3:00 PM. Firemen responding to call of fire found the bed and couch blazing and gas jets open on the stove of the apartment. Although weapon was never found, it was believed by Melrose Park Police that DiMeo was beaten to death with a five-pound caulking hammer. It was purchased in a neighborhood hardware store on the morning of the slaying by a man described as being about thirty years old, swarthy, and about five foot six inches tall.

November 16, 1961
Deceased: John Hennigan
Killer: Unknown

John Hennigan, age forty-three years, was shot to death on the early morning of November 16, 1961, as he was seated in his car, which was parked across the street from his home. He had been hit in the groin by the shotgun blast. An empty shotgun shell was found in the street nearby. Two blasts had been fired at him, one missing and the other shattering a car window. Hennigan was an unemployed truck driver. His body was found by his wife, Sophie, when she returned home from her job.

Hennigan, at the time of his slaying, who was free on bail on an armed robbery indictment, returned on March 23, 1961. In a pocket, police found a receipt from a Melrose Park gambling den and other cards with addresses of Cicero gambling houses. Three motives were advanced for the slaying:

1. He was a police informer who had been eliminated because someone talked too freely.
2. He might have been killed by a gang engaged in extorting part of their loot from holdup men and burglars such as Hennigan.
3. He had run up gambling debts or had been involved in gambling house robberies and had been ordered executed.

1962

January 20, 1962
Deceased: August Vivirito
Killer: Unknown

August "Gus" Vivirito, age thirty-five, an alleged police informant, was shot six times on January 5, 1962, near his home and died January 20. Police said he named a Cicero gambler as his assailant, but the grand jury refused to indict him.

February 4, 1962
Deceased: Henry Volanti
Killer: Unknown

Henry Volanti, age twenty-four, of 218 West Twenty-fourth Street, an ex-convict, was found strangled on February 4, 1962. His hands were tied behind his back in the trunk of an auto that had been in the parking lot at 2328 South Dearborn for two weeks.

April 24, 1962
Deceased: Gerald J. Valente
Killer: Unknown

Gerald J. Valente, age fifty-eight, of 3450 Ohio Street, a small-time gambler, was shot and killed on April 24, 1962, in front of Bea's Lounge at 4634 Cermak Road, Cicero.

April 26, 1962
Deceased: PhilipScavo
Killer: Unknown

Philip Scavo, age thirty-eight, of 2554 Rose Street, Franklin Park, with his brother Ronald and Mrs. Lydia Abshire, were shot to death in a car on April 26, 1962, in Elmwood Park. Homicide detectives called it one of the "best-planned executions."

April 26, 1962
Deceased: Ronald J. Scavo
Killer: Unknown

Ronald Scavo, age twenty-eight, of 1444 Ohio Street. (See Phillip Scavo above.)

April 26, 1962
Deceased: Lydia Abshire
Killer: Unknown

Mrs. Lydia Abshire, age twenty-eight, of 2817 North Newland Avenue. (See Phillip Scavo.)

May 8, 1962
Deceased: Michael Raganese
Killer: Unknown

Michael Raganese, age twenty-five, a former bartender and tavern manager who had been rooming in West Side motels, was found shot twice in the head on May 8, 1961, in a car parked in the garage of a building under construction in Stickney Township. He had been sought by the FBI for questioning about a $1.75 million Florida jewel robbery.

May 14, 1962
Deceased: James Roscoe Miraglia
Killer: Tony Spilotro (indicted)

James "Rocco" Miraglia, age twenty-five, of 1845 North Mulligan Avenue. On the night of May 14, 1962, his body and that of William J. McCarthy was found in the trunk of Miraglia's car, which was parked in front of 3855 West Fifty-fifth Place where the car had been since the night of May 3-4. Miraglia had been beaten and strangled. He was last seen on May 3, 1962. They had been scheduled to surrender themselves on May 15 to begin a two-year prison term. It was believed they have been tortured by criminals on the theory that they talked to federal authorities in exchange for light sentences.

May 14, 1962
Deceased: William J. McCarthy
Killer: Tony Spilotro (indicted)

William J. McCarthy, age twenty-five, of 4336 Gladys Avenue (see James Miraglia). McCarthy's body bore marks that indicated his wrists had been tied, and a heavy growth of beard indicated he had lived two or three days after his disappearance on April 30, 1962.

May 20, 1962
Deceased: Peter J. Bludeau
Killer: Unknown

Peter J. Bludeau, age fifty, of 5115 West Thirty-second Street, Cicero. Body found on May 20, 1962, stuffed in the trunk of his car parked in front of 2658 South Christiana Avenue, Chicago. He had been arrested on March 21, 1962, in a gambling raid in Chicago.

May 31, 1962
Deceased: Leo Johnson
Killer: Unknown

Leo Johnson, age twenty-two, was found dead as a result of a bullet wound in his brain on May 31, 1962, in an alley at the rear of 1521 West Harrison Street. He was employed as a car hiker for a beauty shop. He had been arrested for larceny and had spent some time in prison. He is believed to have been connected with the Guido-Yonder gang.

June 18, 1962
Deceased: Herbert Kwate
Killer: Unknown

The body of Herbert Kwate, age twenty-three, was found on June 18, 1962, in a ravine north of Carpentersville, Illinois. It was believed he was gunned down by members of his bandit mob who blamed him for setting up a police trap in which two of his fellow bandits were slain.

June 18, 1962
Deceased: Sidney Frazin
Killer: Unknown

Sidney Frazin, age fifty-two, of 4422 Monroe Street, was shot on June 18, 1962, by two men who chased him into the Community Friends Social Club at 765 Taylor. He was a gambling collector for the syndicate in the Loop. It was believed he was slain for double-crossing the gambling overlords of the crime syndicate. He had been arrested by the police on June 18, 1962, at 845 South Wabash Avenue and charged with being a keeper of a handbook.

August 24, 1962
Deceased: Alex Sorrentino
Killer: Unknown

Alex Sorrentino, age fifty-four years, was shot to death. His body was found in a field at 501 Parnell Avenue, Chicago Heights, Illinois, on August 24, 1962.

1963

February 28, 1963
Deceased: Benjamin F. Lewis
Killer: Unknown

Benjamin Lewis, age fifty-three, of 3949 West Fillmore Street, Chicago. Body found on February 28, 1963, in his office at 3604 West Roosevelt Road, the Twenty-fourth Ward Democratic Headquarters. He was believed to be shot on February 27, 1963. He was alderman of the Twenty-fourth Ward.

May 6, 1963
Deceased: Irving Vine
Killer: Unknown

Irving Vine, age fifty-eight, of Chicago. Body was found on May 6, 1963, at about 9:45 AM in room 507 of the Hotel del Prado at 5307 Hyde Park Boulevard. He was said to be a salesman. Body was found by a maid who noticed his legs were taped and hands tied behind him with a bedsheet over his head. Evidence found in room indicated he was booking horses.

June 7, 1963
Deceased: Kenneth C. Gordon
Killer: Unknown

Kenneth Gordon, age forty-one, of 418 Webster Avenue, Chicago, was found shot in an automobile at 3006 Waterloo Court on June 7, 1963, at about 3:30 AM. He was said to be a salesman of jewelry.

August 24, 1963
Deceased: Mario Liberatore
Killer: Unknown

Mario Liberatore, age thirty-four years. Liberatore's body was found knifed in a car at 2209 South Ridgeway on August 24, 1963.

October 18, 1963
Deceased: Robert Carpenter
Killer: Unknown

Robert O. Carpenter, age thirty-one, of 6541 Peoria, was killed on October 18, 1963, by shotgun pellets fired from a passing car. Auto was parked at 7410 Peoria. He was manager of Jazz Lounge, at 3221 Fifth Avenue.

November 18, 1963
Deceased: Leo S. Foreman
Killer: Unknown

Mario DeStefano was found guilty. Case was reversed, and he died before he was retried. Sam DeStefano and Tony Spilotro were found not guilty in separate trials.

Leo S. Foreman, age forty-two, of 4817 Neva Avenue, Chicago, was found shot and stabbed in the trunk of an automobile parked at 5204 Gladys Avenue on November 18, 1963. He was president of LeFore Insurance Co. and said to be an acquaintance of Sam DeStefano.

1964

January 21, 1964
Deceased: Anthony Moschiano
Killers: Thomas Durso, 100-150 years; Michael Gargano, 100-150 years

Anthony Mosciano, age twenty-six, of 914 Oakley, was stabbed on January 21, 1964, in a garage at 10656 West Twenty-eighth, Westchester, the home of Chicago police officer Thomas N. Durso. Body was found on April 13, 1964 in the Des Plaines River near River Grove. He was an ex-convict and narcotics informer.

March 6, 1964
Deceased: Albert Louis Roman
Killer: Harold Johnson, 40-60 years

Albert Louis Romano, age forty-one, of 209 North Pulaski Road, was found shot to death in alley behind 4137 Grenshaw Street on March 6, 1964. He had been a bodyguard for Al Capone; was an ex-convict who had been found guilty of armed robbery, assault to murder, and extortion; and was a suspected narcotics peddler. He was a son of Louis Romano, a one-time Chicago labor slugger and Capone mob associate.

August 31, 1964
Deceased: Guy Mendola Jr.
Killer: Unknown

Guy Mendola Jr., age thirty-nine, of 1554 North Forty-third Avenue, Stone Park, was killed by shotgun blasts as he parked his automobile in the garage of his home on August 31, 1964. He was a member of the Paul Panczko burglary gang and an associate of Rocco Pranno. At the time of the murder, he was free on bond on federal warrant charging unlawful flight to avoid burglary prosecution.

September 7, 1964
Deceased: Charles William White
Killer: Frank O'Connell, 40-60 years

Charles W. White, age thirty-three, of 4710 Kenmore Avenue, Chicago. Body was found in a ditch along Naperville Road, three miles southeast of Elgin, with two bullet holes in his skull. White was a convicted murderer with a lengthy record of arrests.

1965

March 21, 1965
Deceased: Bertha Mae Bullock
Killer: Unknown

Bertha Mae Bullock, age twenty-seven, on March 21, 1965, was found shot three times sitting in her sports car at Forty-seventh and the Lake. She was a narcotics informer.

April 24, 1965
Deceased: Willie Horn
Killer: Unknown

Willie Horn, age thirty-nine, codefendant in the federal court in Chicago with Americo DePieto, was shot and killed on April 24, 1965, at Seventy-second and Wabash Avenue by an unknown person while sitting in a car with a woman who was wounded at the same time.

September 9, 1965
Deceased: Eddie Mae Harrison and Joan Williams
Killer: Unknown

On September 9, 1965, Joan Williams and Eddie Mae Harrison, eighteen and nineteen years of age, were found shot in the head alongside the Westlawn Cemetery near 4300 North Thatcher Road, south of Norridge, Illinois. Both had eyes and mouth taped with adhesive tape. Both had long police records as prostitutes.

September 11, 1965
Deceased: Manny Skar
Killers: Joe "the Clown" Lombardo, Tony Spilotro

Manny Skar, age forty-one, was shot and killed at the entrance to an apartment building garage at 3800 North Lake Shore Drive, his residence, by two unknown men.

November 24, 1965
Deceased: Angelo J. Boscarino
Killer: Unknown

On November 24, 1965, the body of Angelo John Boscarino, age thirty-three, was found in the street at 4214 West Twenty-fourth Place. His throat was cut, and he had stab wounds and bruises on his face and body. He was a suspect in the $380,000 hijacking of silver bullion.

December 15, 1965
Deceased: Anthony P. Ponzio
Killer: Unknown

On December 15, 1965, a car was parked at O'Hare parking lot; and on January 10, 1966, when the trunk was opened, the body of Anthony P. Ponzio was found strangled. The car was stolen.

1966

February 5, 1966
Deceased: Mitsuri Wakita
Killer: Unknown

On February 5, 1966, Mitsuri Wakita, age forty-three, died from gunshot wounds to the chest after replacing a flat tire on his car in front of 243 West Twenty-eighth Street. He was a brother-in-law of Daniel Escobeda.

February 28, 1966
Deceased: Leonard Centrone
Killer: Unknown

On February 28, 1966, Leonard Centrone, age twenty-nine, was found dead behind a factory building at 2074 George Street, Melrose Park. He was shot eleven times in the head, heart, and groin, probably in his car parked fifty yards away. He had been implicated in a hijacking in which several men went to prison.

February 28, 1966
Deceased: Clarence A. Forrest
Killer: Unknown

On February 28, 1966, the body of Clarence A. Forrest – age twenty-six, of Worth, Illinois – was found in the trunk of his car at

St. John, Indiana, about ten miles south of Hammond. He had been shot twice at close range in the chest and right thigh. He had been a part-time bouncer in three joints allegedly operated by Frank LaPorte. Forrest was suspected of spying on the LaPorte group for a rival mob.

July 20, 1966
Deceased: Van Corbin alias Panveno
Killer: Unknown

On July 20, 1966, Van Corbin, real name Sam Panveno, was shot and killed outside the Country Club Motel at 8303 North Avenue, Melrose Park, Illinois, where he was staying temporarily with his wife and family, by two unknown men using silencers on guns. He was an associate of hoodlums and had been a contractor in the building of the new home of Tony Accardo.

August 30, 1966
Deceased: Louis Pratico
Killer: Unknown

On August 30, 1966, at about 7:00 AM, the body of Louis Pratico – age forty-two, of 42 West Fourteenth Street, Chicago Heights – was found in a ditch at Joe Orr Road and West End Avenue in the outskirts of Chicago Heights. He had been beaten and shot twice in the head. He was alleged to be a front man for Frank LaPorte and had been a Chicago Heights police officer but was dismissed from the force.

November 22, 1966
Deceased: Charles C. Crispino
Killer: Unknown

Charles C. Crispino, fifty-one, of 1738 North Natoma, was shot five times and killed as he got out of his car near his home. He had worked in the office of the Illinois secretary of state.

1967

February 22, 1967
Deceased: Robert T. Hannah
Killer: Unknown

On February 22, 1967, the body of Robert T. Hannah, age thirty-one, of 1058 North Marshfield, was found frozen in a snowbank on Thirty-First Street near the Tri-State Tollway, Lyons Township. He had been shot eight times and was alleged to have been prepared to testify in court against someone in a narcotics case.

February 27, 1967
Deceased: Wesley Funicella
Killer: Unknown

On February 27, 1967, the body of Wesley Funicella – age thirty-nine, of South Holland, Illinois – was found in the trunk of his car parked in Blue Island. He left home at about 5:30 PM on Sunday, February 26, 1967, to "see a man." He is believed to be a victim of juice operators; had borrowed $17,000 in January 1964; and repaid only $4,600. He was beaten and strangled.

March 7, 1967
Deceased: Joseph F. Polito
Killer: Unknown

On March 7, 1967, Joseph F. Polito, age thirty-three, was shotgunned to death in the vicinity of his residence at 4121 North Spaulding. He was an admitted swindler and basketball game fixer. Heavily in debt to mob loan sharks, he had testified in 1965 to sport fixing.

March 17, 1967
Deceased: Alan R. Rosenberg
Killer: Unknown

On March 17, 1967, the body of Alan R. Rosenberg, age thirty-six, was found in the backseat of a rented Cadillac, his hands cuffed in front and shot about seven times. He lived in Skokie, Illinois. He is believed to have been slain between 9:00 AM and 3:00 PM on March 16, 1967. He was an ex-convict and an associate of Phil Alderisio.

July 12, 1967
Deceased: Arthur "Boodie" Cowan
Killer: Unknown

On July 12, 1967, the body of Arthur "Boodie" Cowan – age forty-six, of 7307 Crawford, Lincolnwood – was found in the trunk of his car parked at a curb in front of 418 South Kilpatrick, Chicago. Cowan left home at 8:30 PM on July 5, 1967, for a three-hour meeting on the South Side. The car parked on Kilpatrick was first noticed at 8:30 AM on July 7, 1967, and stayed there until the police department was notified on the evening of July 12, 1967. He was a juice collector and was shot once behind the left ear with a .32-caliber weapon.

1968

No gangland slayings.

1969

December 5, 1969
Deceased: Earl Omer Addlesman
Killer: Unknown

Earl Omer Addlesman, forty-seven years, of Zion, Illinois. Body was found on December 5, 1969, at 11:45 AM on the floor of a 1967 Chevrolet wagon at Fourteenth and Peoria. He had been bound, gagged, and shot in the head with .22-caliber gun. He was heavily in debt and reportedly involved in the juice loan racket.

1970

March 21, 1970
Deceased: Carmen Trotta
Killer: Unknown

On March 21, 1970, Carmen Trotta, age twenty-eight, of Crestwood, was shot twice in the left side by two unknown men in a parking lot in Lyons at about 12:30 PM. He had been convicted of hijacking $138,000 worth of cigars.

A woman motorist told the Lyons police that as she drove by the parking lot, she saw Trotta stagger, clutching his side and screaming, and that two men appeared to be chasing him and one held a pistol. She said that as Trotta fell, a passing male motorist got out of a car and apparently alarmed the first two who leaped into a car with the driver hunched behind the steering wheel and almost collided with a truck as it sped from the scene.

September 28, 1970
Deceased: Mario Sprovieri
Killer: Unknown

Mario Sprovieri was shot and killed at about 5:10 PM in a vacated store used as a social club at 2620 West Huron Street. Five bullets entered the head and face.

In 1965, he was charged with the murder of one Leslie R. Vanna, twenty-five years, of 1949 West Twenty-first Street. After numerous continuances, the case was stricken off call with leave to reinstate by Judge Power. Vanna, a uniformed watchman for a detective agency, had been assigned as a day guard. When found, his ankles and wrists were bound behind him with a tough nylon-reinforced plastic tape, which also had been looped around his head and covered his mouth.

1971

January 7, 1971
Deceased: Rosario "Ross" Corriero
Killer: Unknown

The body of Rosario Corriero, age forty-one, of 19211 South Emerald, was found in the rear of his 1969 station wagon. He was shot once in the head and chest and was found around 10:30 PM by Crete police. The police said hundreds of football parlay cards were found in the car printed by the syndicate gamblers. He was a syndicate gambler.

October 19, 1971
Deceased: Sam "Sambo" Cesario
Killer: Unknown

On October 19, 1971, Sam "Sambo" Cesario – age fifty-three, of 917 South Bishop Street, Chicago – an ex-con and syndicate gambling boss, was clubbed and shot to death by two masked gunmen while he, his wife, and a friend sat on lawn chairs in front of 1071 West Polk Street, a building owned by Sam. He was involved in running the juice loan and gambling in the Maxwell Street area.

1972

March 10, 1972
Deceased: Charles W. Carroll
Killer: Unknown

The body of Charles W. Carroll – age thirty-nine, of Hickory Hills, Illinois – was found on March 10, 1972, stuffed in the trunk of a parked car at 8119 South Ada. He was bound, gagged, and blindfolded. He was shot once in the back of the head. Carroll was a longtime South Side bookmaker lieutenant of Ralph Pierce.

August 8, 1972
Deceased: Guido Fidanzi
Killer: Unknown

Guido Fidanzi – age forty-five, of Chicago Heights, Illinois – an ex-convict and crime syndicate chieftain, was shot to death on August 8, 1972, in the office of a gas station in Chicago Heights, Illinois. The two killers pumped seven shots from two handguns into Fidanzi. One source stated ten shots were fired.

1973

April 14, 1973
Deceased: Sam DeStefano
Killers: Tony Spilotro, Mario DeStefano

Sam DeStefano – age sixty-four, of Chicago, Illinois – was shotgunned to death on April 14, 1973, about 10:30 AM, while cleaning out his garage. DeStefano was an underworld figure for the past forty years and a syndicate chieftain who pioneered the loan shark rackets in the Chicagoland area through terror and torture. Sam was awaiting trial for the murder of Leo Foreman and had been granted a severance from Mario DeStefano (his brother) and Tony Spilotro, codefendants in the same case. Mario DeStefano and Tony Spilotro were found not guilty.

December 20, 1973
Deceased: Richard Cain, alias Scalzetti
Killers: Angelo, James LaPietra, J. Fecarotta, Turk Torello, Joe Aiuppa

Richard Cain, age forty-nine, while conferring with four other men at Rose's Sandwich Shop at 1117 West Grand, two men wearing ski masks and carrying shotgun and pistol entered and lined seven patrons against a wall until a lookout gave an all-clear signal, at which time they fired the shotgun point-blank into Cain's head. He had been in the Chicago Police Department until 1962 then became chief investigator for the Sheriff's Department. In 1964, he revealed he was a double agent for the mob and resigned. Convicted for his part in the Franklin Park bank robbery of 1963, he served three years, was paroled in 1971, fled to Mexico to join Sam Giancana, and had been back in Chicago only about three weeks before he was killed.

1974

January 27, 1974
Deceased: Wayne Cascone
Killer: Unknown

Wayne Cascone, twenty-six or twenty-seven years of age, of 3412 South Bell, was found shot to death on January 27, 1974, in a car parked near 3335 South Western Boulevard. Informant said two men had lured Cascone into a car in an alley near his home; he had boasted to a girlfriend that he had info on the death of Sam Hantis, who was found dead on February 24, 1974. An ex-con friend of Rantis said five deaths were linked to infighting over passing counterfeit money through bolita racket: Cascone, Rantis, Joe Grisafe, Sam Marcello, William Simone. James Irwin, suspected by police of killing Rantis and Cascone, was himself killed on May 1, 1976.

February 24, 1974
Deceased: Socrates "Sam" Rantis
Killer: Unknown

Socrates "Sam" Rantis, age forty-three of 7912 West North Avenue, Elmwood Park. His frozen body was found on February 24, 1974, with puncture wounds on the chest and a slashed throat and was stuffed in the trunk of his wife's Buick at O'Hare during police check of autos with expired plates. He was last seen on December 7, 1973. He owned Albano's – Pizzeria at 1015 South Western and used to own Korner Sandwich Shop at the same address where the bodies of Joe Grisafe and Sam Marcello were found stuffed in fifty-five-gallon drums on July 6, 1974. An ex-con friend of his said his killing was linked to infighting over passing counterfeit money through bolita racket and resulted in the deaths of Grisafe, Marcello, Wayne Cascone, William

Simone, and Rantis. He had owned Motor World West Hotel at 5255 West Forty-seventh, Forest View, which was raided by agents on June 1970, who confiscated counterfeit bills and equipment for which Rantis served eleven months.

April 21, 1974
Deceased: William Simone
Killer: Unknown

William Simone, age twenty-nine, of 2415 North Laramie Avenue, was found by a passerby at about 10:00 AM. He was shot in the head in the back of his parked car in front of 2446 South Kedvale Avenue, with hands bound behind the back and tied to the feet with a heavy rope and surgical gauze taped across the mouth. He was an associate of Sam Marcello and had alleged ties with the Cicero mob and mob boss Fifi Buccieri. Later, his death was believed linked to four killings – Rantis, Marcello, Grisafe, Cascone – that occurred in early 1974, over counterfeit ring.

June 14, 1974
Deceased: Anthony "Tony D" Dichiarinte
Killer: Unknown

Anthony Dichiarinte, age fifty-six, of 6336 North Kolmar, Chicago, was reported missing on May 10 by his wife and had not been seen since leaving in a rented car on April 30. His badly decomposed body was found in the trunk of the rented car late Friday night of June 14, 1974, in a parking lot of the Holiday Inn in Willowbrook where it had been abandoned for eight days. He was involved in the narcotics racket with a record of arrests from hijacking to armed robbery. He was apparently dead for as long as four weeks. ID was in clothing, cause of death unknown.

July 6, 1974
Deceased: Samuel J. Marcello Sr.
Killer: Unknown

Samuel J. Marcello Sr., age fifty-seven, of 6017 North Emerson Street, Rosemont, was found July 6, 1974, along with Joe Grisafe, both badly decomposed and stuffed into fifty-five-gallon oil drums in the rear storage room of the Korner Sandwich Shop at 1015 South Western. He was reported missing by wife on February 5 but last seen November 24, 1973. Chicago Police Department had been tipped to search Korner in April by ex-con friend of Sam Rantis who said five killings grew out of infighting over passing counterfeit money in bolita racket: Rantis, Grisafe, Marcello, Wayne Cascone, and William Simone. John McGee, fifty-two, of 7912 West North, owner of Korner, reported odor in the back room. Korner was formerly owned by Rantis, who was found in the trunk of a car at O'Hare on February 24.

July 6, 1974
Deceased: Joseph "Big Joe" Grisafe
Killer: Unknown

Joseph Grisafe, thirty-four, of 742 West Dempster Street, Mount Prospect, was found on July 6, 1974, along with Sam Marcello, both badly decomposed and stuffed into fifty-five-gallon oil drums in the rear storage room of the Korner Sandwich Shop at 1015 South Western. Marcello was last seen on November 24, 1973. Grisafe, six foot six inches and 240 pounds, had legs severed to fit him into the drum. Korner was formerly owned by Rantis, who was found in the trunk at O'Hare on February 24, 1974.

July 13, 1974
Deceased: Orion Williams
Killer: Unknown

Orion Williams, thirty-eight, was found shot to death at 70 East Thirty-third Street and stuffed in the trunk of his girlfriend's 1972 Chevrolet. Unemployed and involved in hijacking, he was believed to have withheld information from the mob. His federal indictment was pending and set for trial on July 9, 1974, and he possibly might have been cooperating with the police.

September 27, 1974
Deceased: Daniel R. Seifert
Killers: Joe "the Clown" Lombardo, Frank Schweihs

Daniel R. Seifert, twenty-nine, of Bensenville, was shot with a .38-caliber pistol upon entering his Plastic-Matic Products Co. in Bensenville with his wife and child at 8:00 AM. He ran into the neighboring plant where he was blasted with a shotgun at the rear door by a third ski-masked gunman. At the front door, he was shot again, fell to the ground, and dispatched with the shotgun held to his head. Fourth gunman remained in one of the two cars used for getaway. Seifert was partners with Irwin Weiner and Felix Alderisio in International Fiberglass Company in Elk Grove. He was scheduled to be a government witness in the January trial of seven mobsters accused of defrauding Teamsters Pension Fund of $1.4 million in loans to American Pail Company in Deming, New Mexico, that included Weiner, Lombardo, DeAngeles, Dorfman, Sheetz, Matheson, and Tony Spilotro.

September 28, 1974
Deceased: Robert W. Harder
Killer: Unknown

Robert W. Harder, thirty-nine, of Hoffman Estates, was found at about 7:30 AM Saturday, shot in the face in a bean field near Dwight, Illinois, with a 7.65 Walther pistol under the body. His wife's car was nearby. An informant in the killing of Hillside patrolman Anthony Raymond in 1972, he was due to testify against his partner Silas C. Fletcher. The Fletcher-Harder gang was composed of some ten jewel thieves and home burglars. Federal authorities, in the 1978 sentencing of mobster James Inendino, charged that he and hit man Harry Aleman had previously unsuccessfully attempted to kill Harder.

December 27, 1974
Deceased: Richard J. Mazzone
Killer: Unknown

Richard J. Mazzone, forty, of Melrose Park, was gunned down by shotgun blasts in the back and abdomen just after parking his car in his driveway at about 1:10 AM. He claimed to be a self-employed plumber and owner of Mazzone Plumbing, Sewer and Rodding Service.

1975

January 16, 1975
Deceased: Carlo DeVivo
Killer: Unknown

Carlo DeVivo, forty-six, of Nora Avenue, was shot by two gunmen wearing ski masks as he came out of his apartment and walked to the car. He was shot three times to the head and three to the body from a shotgun and a pistol, virtually blowing his head off. The gunmen used a van with a wheelman, and a blocker drove a car in the rear. The van was stolen and abandoned behind a store at 7062 West Belmont. DeVivo was a minor mob muscleman and juicer with record dating back to 1951and was associated with the Torello mob.

April 29, 1975
Deceased: Anthony P. Battaglia
Killer: Unknown

Anthony P. Battaglia, sixty-one, brother of the late crime boss Sam "Teets" Battaglia and himself a mob figure, was accosted and shot under the chin with a .38 caliber in the driveway of his home in LaGrange Park. He owned Cicero Amusement Devices (pinball machines distributor). He might have been a victim of mob tension in Cicero involving four deaths in 1975 among Italians and hillbilly mafia. He operated out of the Annetta Hotel at 2400 block of Laramie and the Silver Spur Lounge at 2100 block of Cicero Avenue.

May 12, 1975
Deceased: Ronald T. Magliano
Killer: Unknown

Ronald T. Magliano – forty-three, of 6232 South Kilpatrick, Chicago, reputed underworld fence scheduled to be sentenced on May 20 for fencing – was found shot by a .25-caliber pistol behind the left ear. With gasoline poured on the floors and windows of his house and ignited to conceal murder, he was blown out from the explosion. He was blindfolded and gagged, and three separate fires ignited.

June 19, 1975
Deceased: Salvatore (Sam, Momo, Cigars) Giancana
Killer: Unknown

Salvatore Giancana, sixty-seven, of Oak Park, was shot seven times with a .22-caliber revolver in the head, mouth, and chin at approximately 10:30 PM in the kitchen basement of his home while preparing a late snack. Police surveillance teams noted that Chuck English, Butch Blasi, and DePalmas had been there and left. Blasi returned; team then left, and in interim, Momo was shot and later discovered by the caretaker, Joe DiPersio, at about midnight. He had returned from Houston Hospital that same day. He had been in exile in Mexico from 1966 to 1974 to escape the heat that hindered his control of the Chicago mob. Motives for the hit were he wanted his old job as boss back, he refused to share profits of foreign operations, or it was feared that he would talk to the congressional committee investigating CIA Castro murder plots that involved the mob.

July 14, 1975
Deceased: Christopher Joseph Cardi, a.k.a. Chris or Richard
Killers: Harry Aleman, William "Butch" Petrocelli

Christopher Cardi, forty-three, of Elmwood Park, was shot eight times in the back and once on the face by two ski-masked gunmen using .45-caliber weapons at 12:11 AM inside Jim's Beef Stand at 1620 North River Road, Melrose Park, as his wife and three of their kids looked on. An employee was wounded. He was sentenced in 1971 to ten years for heroin pushing, was a former cop from 1957 to 1962, and paroled on June 18, 1975. He was the nephew of William "Wee Willie" Messino and also a juicer for Joseph "Gags" Gagliano.

August 28, 1975
Deceased: Frank Goulakos
Killer: Unknown

Frank Goulakos, forty-seven, of Elk Grove Village, was a cook at DiLeo's Restaurant at 5700 North Central.

He reached his car two blocks away at Seminole and Parkside and discovered that the left front tire was flat when a masked man jumped out of a car and fired about six shots, striking him in the head and chest. The killer jumped back into the car, and the wheelman sped away with killer.

August 30, 1975
Deceased: Nick Galanos, a.k.a. Keggie or Kegee
Killer: Unknown

Nick Galanos, forty-eight, of 6801 West Wabansia, was found slain in his home on August 30 although he might have been shot after 10:00 PM, Friday, August 29, nine times with a .45-caliber weapon in the head, back, and chest in the basement recreation room. A city dump foreman who had interest in a Broadview discount store, he had been subpoenaed by ICIC in 1969 and warned by mob gambling bosses not to move his bookmaking operations into Forest Park, which he appeared to ignore. He probably knew his killers as there was no forcible entry and the alarm had not been set off.

October 31, 1975
Deceased: Anthony J. Reitinger
Killers: Harry Aleman, William "Butch" Petrocelli

Anthony J. Reitinger, thirty-four, freelance bookmaker, mostly football, operated out of his home at 5203 North Magnolia Avenue, a two-flat he owned. He was believed killed for defying the mob. He was eating and waiting for a meet at Mama Luna's Restaurant at 4846 West Fullerton on October 31, 1975, Friday night when two gunmen entered, one with a hockey goalie's mask and the other with a ski mask, a shotgun, and a .30-caliber carbine, pushing him back into the booth. They fired two shotgun blasts to his head and four rifle shots into the right side and back. He was said to be doing $30,000 a day business.

December 3, 1975
Deceased: Ned C. Bakes, a.k.a. Ignatius Spacchesi or Ignatius Spechesi
Killer: Unknown

Ned C. Bakes, seventy, of Addison, was found by his daughter in the trunk of his 1975 Chevrolet Caprice parked a half mile from his home at Torch-Lite Restaurant. He was shot twice in the top of the head with a large-caliber handgun and was strangled. His wife reported him missing, and he was last seen leaving at 8:30 AM, Saturday, November 29. As a mob figure from the Capone era, he had served as courier for Paul Ricca in the '40s and '50s when in prison. He served time for tax evasion and paroled in June 1973 on stolen securities convictions. In the '30s, he was county bailiff and in '40s, a deputy sheriff.

1976

January 20, 1976
Deceased: Frank DeLegge Jr.
Killer: Unknown

Frank DeLegge Jr., thirty-eight, of Melrose Park. His frozen body with the throat slashed was found by a youth in the afternoon, just off Roman Road in a ditch near the Tri-State Tollway at Elmhurst. He was reported missing that night. He had been released from prison eighteen months earlier for the Franklin Park bank robbery of 1963 that saw convictions also of DeLegge Sr., Richard Cain, Willie Daddano, and Rocco Montagna. He was also convicted of robbing a Crystal Lake jewelry salesman twice. He was the son-in-law of Nick Palermo and worked at Nick's Mayo Plumbing Co. As a tough guy with solid mob connections, his murder surprised the police.

January 31, 1976
Deceased: Louis DeBartolo
Killer: Unknown

Louis DeBartolo, twenty-nine, of Melrose Park, was found slain in the rear of International Discount Sales at 5945 West North Avenue, where he worked on his prison release program after being convicted for robbing the Columbia National Bank of Chicago. He was reported missing by his wife on January 29. His neck had been punctured four times, apparently with a wooden mop handle found nearby and shot once in the right ear with a small-caliber weapon, and marks indicated someone stood on his arms to hold him down during torture. His papers indicated he was deeply in debt and might have been on juice.

June 24, 1976
Deceased: Paul Haggerty
Killers: Frank Calabrese Sr.; Ron Jarrett; Nick Calabrese; James Torello;
    Frank Saladino; A. LaPietra

Paul Haggerty was a twenty-seven-year-old ex-convict who screwed up by dealing with a mobbed-up jewelry store. Angelo LaPietra and other mob bosses wanted him dead. Haggerty was staying at a halfway house on Indiana Avenue on the South Side. He had a day job to report to, which was part of his release program. Frank Calabrese Sr., Nick Calabrese, Ron Jarrett, and Frank Saladino began staking out the halfway house to see what time he left and how he went to work. After weeks of surveillance, they began to get a pattern of his routine. They followed him on a bus on Michigan Avenue going north then got off and walked to Wabash Avenue to a building known as jewelers row at 5 South Wabash Avenue. Haggerty was followed to a door with the name Marshall Field's department store on it; the crew now knew where he worked. Using walkie-talkies and a police scanner, they made a plan to grab Haggerty on the street.

Nick would walk ahead of Haggerty, and at the opportune time, he would notify the other hit squad to pull up in a car next to Haggerty. Nick would then grab Haggerty while Frank Saladino, a three-hundred-pound man, would assist Nick getting Haggerty into the work car. Haggerty had to be beaten and forced into the backseat of the car. The entire episode took only a few seconds and it was over. Jarrett was driving the work car, an Oldsmobile, and drove to his mother-in-law's garage in Bridgeport. Nick followed in another work car, which he parked two blocks away. By the time Nick got to the garage, Haggerty had already been cuffed. Frank Sr. told Saladino that he was no longer needed and that Nick was to stay with Haggerty whose hands were cuffed and his eyes and mouth were covered with duct tape. Frank Sr. told Nick that Jarrett and he had to leave for a few minutes to get someone and they would be right back. When Frank Sr. returned, he was with James "Turk" Torello and Angelo LaPietra, both mob bosses. Torello removed the tape from Haggerty's mouth and asked him some questions about him selling jewelry to a store in Elmwood Park, Illinois. Haggerty apparently gave him the wrong answers.

Torello retaped his mouth, and he and Angelo LaPietra left the garage. Frank Sr. and Jarrett also left the garage to steal a car to get rid of Haggerty. Haggerty apparently had a sideline of burglary, stealing jewelry, and selling the stuff to a mobbed-up jewelry store. Nick, being a kind soul, allowed Haggerty to relieve himself and also gave him some water. Frank Sr. and Jarrett returned with a vehicle they had stolen from a parking lot by a movie house when the owner entered the movie. They knew that they had some time before the vehicle would be reported stolen. They pulled the Oldsmobile out of the garage and parked it nearby then pulled the stolen car into the garage. They popped the trunk with a hammer and screwdriver. Haggerty's time had come. Frank Sr. took a rope and put it around Haggerty's neck and pulled as hard as he could. Haggerty, still cuffed, was unable to resist. It was soon over. Frank Sr. then put a plastic bag on Haggerty's head and cut his throat with a knife, catching as much blood as he could. Haggerty was dumped into the trunk of the stolen car, and Jarrett and Frank Sr. parked the car on Ashland Avenue. They then returned to the garage, got Nick, and drove to a meeting with Angelo LaPietra at a Chinatown restaurant. LaPietra had to be notified that the Haggerty problem was over.

May 1, 1976
Deceased: James Erwin
Killer: Unknown

James Erwin, twenty-eight years old, of 1937 West Thirty-third Street, was wounded thirteen times in the abdomen, back, and shoulder by a shotgun and .45-caliber handgun as he stepped out of his car at 1873 North Halsted Street.

October 5, 1976
Deceased: Steven H. Ostrowsky
Killer: Unknown

Steven H. Ostrowsky, thirty-four, of Flossmoor, was shot and killed by five .30-caliber rifle bullets fired from a van that pulled alongside his Cadillac as he parked it across the street from his South Chicago Auto Parts Inc. at 7370 South Chicago Avenue at 10:00 AM. Convicted in 1973 for interstate auto theft along with William E. Dauber, he was a reputed hit man for Jimmy "the Bomber" Catuara and served one year. Two former partners were also murdered: Harry Holzer (June 5, 1975) and Harry D. Carlson (August 6, 1969). Believed to be the mastermind of an interstate stolen auto parts ring, he might have been a victim of mob war over this lucrative racket.

1977

February 12, 1977
Deceased: James Villerreal
Killer: Unknown

James Villerreal, twenty-four, of 1364 West Ohio Street, was found stabbed to death in an alley behind 1439 Augusta Boulevard.

He allegedly went into a tavern with a sawed-off shotgun and forced five people against the wall, demanding to know the whereabouts of Henry J. Cosentino, a minor hoodlum who disappeared on January 24 and showed up dead in a car trunk on March 15, 1977. That same night on February 12, a friend of Villerreal, Sam Rivera, and his wife were shot in a tavern at 1326 West Grand Avenue. He died.

February 12, 1977
Deceased: Sam Rivera
Killer: Unknown

Sam Rivera, twenty-seven, of 1649 West Ohio Street, was fatally shot, and his wife was wounded in a tavern on West Grand. Earlier that same day, their friend James Villerreal (news spells it Villareal) was stabbed to death, allegedly after entering a tavern with a sawed-off shotgun and demanding to know the whereabouts of Henry J. Cosentino. Consentino disappeared on January 24 and was found dead in a car trunk on March 15 1977.

March 4, 1977
Deceased: Patrick J. Marusarz
Killer: Unknown

Patrick J. Marusarz, twenty-one, of West Huron, was shot five times with an automatic pistol in the face, chest, and knee at about 4:00 AM.

Marusarz was playing cards with Philip Cozzo and Arthur Bravieri and a possible fourth killer wearing a rubber gorilla mask, who entered through a side door for which he probably had a key. Police speculated there might have been a link to a mob takeover of betting services or juice loan.

March 15, 1977
Deceased: Henry J. Cosentino
Killer: Frank Calabrese Sr.

Henry J. Cosentino, fifty-two, of 5726 North St. Louis Avenue. His partially decomposed body was found at 7:20 AM by a civilian employee at the Chicago Police Department Auto Pound 5, making a routine check before turning the auto over to a wrecking firm. It had been towed there on February 18, eleven days after it was tagged abandoned at 2963 North Wisner Avenue. Cosentino's wife reported him missing on January 24. His body was bound, gagged in the trunk; death was caused by a blunt instrument forced through his neck. His record dated back to 1948 for burglary, cartage theft, bad checks, and he served one year for interstate theft. He was the brother-in-law of Jimmy Cozzo, part owner of Flash Messenger Service at 543 North Ogden, where Henry's friend Patrick Marusarz was gunned down on March 4, 1977. James also co-owned Rose's Sandwich Shop with his father, Sam, where Richard Cain was gunned down on December 1973. Motive may be mob war over messenger service or loan-sharking.

March 29, 1977
Deceased: Charles "Chuck" Nicoletti
Killer: Unknown

Charles Nicoletti, sixty, of 1638 North Nineteenth Avenue, Melrose Park, received three .38-caliber shots in rapid succession in the back of his head late Tuesday night while sitting in the front seat of his Olds auto parked in a lot at Golden Horns Restaurant at 409 East North Avenue, Northlake. He died on Wednesday, about six hours later, at Northlake Community Hospital. The engine of the auto caught fire, apparently from overheating. He was a top hit man.

April 4, 1977
Deceased: John D. Lourgos
Killer: Unknown

John D. Lourgos, age fifty-three, was shot to death early in the front of his home at 8501 South Springfield. He was gunned down with a 12-gauge shotgun by one of the two men who had tailed him home from his South Halsted Street restaurant in a silver Camaro. (Business: Lorenzo's Pizza & Gyros, 315 South Halsted Street.) Attackers wearing ski masks shot four times and struck the victim three times. Motive not known.

June 13, 1977
Deceased: Richard Ferraro
Killer: Unknown

Richard Ferraro – thirty-six, of Oak Lawn, owner of Statewide Auto Wrecking Co. Inc. at 630 State Street, Calumet City – last seen at night at Thirteenth at Condesa del Mar in Alsip, was reported missing by his wife on June 14. His '77 Lincoln was found empty in his junkyard. He was an associate of Joseph F. Theo, a robber found shotgunned on June 15, and of Joseph Scalise, Theo's partner, who recently was employed at Statewide.

June 14, 1977
Deceased: Thomas McCarthy
Killer: William "Butch" Petrocelli

Thomas McCarthy, thirty-seven, of 10217 West Belden Avenue in Leyden Township, was found shot once in the base of his skull with a .38 caliber in the trunk of his own '74 Cadillac parked in the O'Hare Airport garage. After the sheriff's investigator called the airport to check if his car was there, he was partially decomposed. He was last seen on June 4 leaving home at 10:30 AM. Under FBI investigation for cartage theft, he had an arrest record back in '69 for burglary. The car was first listed at the garage on June 7. His cousin John W. McCarthy's body was found in the trunk in southwest Chicago in '62. Thomas's wife reported him missing on June 6.

June 15, 1977
Deceased: Joseph Frank Theo
Killer: Unknown

Joseph Frank Theo, thirty-three, of 665 West Diversey Parkway, was found shot to death twice in the head in the backseat of an auto by a passerby at 1700 North Cleveland Avenue on a Wednesday morning while the car was parked across the street from closed-down Pegasus Co. track betting office at 1720 Cleveland. His arrest recorded back to '61, and he was a member of a burglary ring that often used disguises and were arrested in '71 for the burglary of Carriage House Apartment Hotel at 215 East Chicago Avenue year before. He was a friend of Richie Ferraro, a car parts dealer, who disappeared on June 13 and who employed Theo's burglary partner, Joe Scalise, at his junkyard. It is speculated his death might have resulted from a dispute over loot or from stolen auto parts mob warfare.

July 3, 1977
Deceased: John R. Schneider
Killer: Unknown
John R. Schneider, twenty-seven, of 1030 North State Street.

His partially decomposed body was found shot once in the head with a .25 caliber, wrapped in plastic, and stuffed in the trunk of a rented Chevrolet Caprice parked in the O'Hare Airport garage. He was found about 1:15 PM, Sunday, when a patrolling officer noticed foul odor. The car was rented by John Sochacz, his roommate. Schneider was a part-time real estate salesman last seen by Sochacz on Wednesday, June 29. He had credit problems and was reputed to be a friend of Sam Annerino, the mobster killed on July 25, 1977. But no definite motive was established although it definitely was not robbery.

July 12, 1977
Deceased: Earl S. Abercrombie Jr.
Killer: Unknown

Earl S. Abercrombie Jr., thirty-four, of Chicago Ridge. His nude, decomposed body shot twice in the head was found in the trunk of his auto parked at O'Hare Airport late Tuesday, July 12, 1977. His mother said he disappeared on July 7 en route to his job as baker. The car was there about a week before attendants noticed the odor. He had an arrest record back in '67 and was believed to have been into auto theft and narcotics pushing. A Mississippian, he was known to have peddled stolen cars there. Police speculated he could have been killed in a "chop shop" stolen car parts war over drugs or burglary loot.

July 13, 1977 Deceased:
Morris Saletko, a.k.a. Maurice, Maishe Baer
Killer: Unknown

Morris Saletko, sixty-three, of 4255 Chase Avenue, Lincolnwood, was found dead Wednesday night. He was shot in the left side of the face and head in the trunk of his V77 Olds parked in the Brickyard Shopping Center at Narragansett and Diversey. He was probably shot Wednesday afternoon and driven to the lot. A previous attempt to kill him and George Weinberg occurred in May 1975, shortly after his parole on a $1 million silver hijacking conviction that involved a host of mob figures. A well-known First Ward loan shark, he was speculated by police to have been killed for short changing mob bosses.

July 22, 1977
Deceased: Mark C. Thanasouras
Killer: Unknown

Mark C. Thanasouras, forty-nine, of 9601 South Southwest Highway, Oak Lawn, was slain about 5:15 AM, Friday, by shotgun blasts to the head and abdomen in front of 5507 North Campbell, as he was walking a woman friend to her residence there. From '66 to '70, he was Austin District Police commander. He was later convicted and sent to prison for eighteen months for tavern shakedowns. He got an early release in '75 for testifying against four CPD captains who were acquitted. He was working as a bartender at L&L Club No. 2, Buckley Road, Lake Bluff. Police speculated he might have been killed by mob loan sharks or due to unrest in the Greek restaurant community or for being a government witness.

July 25, 1977
Deceased: Samuel J. Annerino
Killer: William "Butch" Petrocelli

Samuel J. Annerino, thirty-four, of 9520 South Mayfield, Oak Lawn, was slain at 4:20 PM, Monday, by a masked gunman who fired five shotgun blasts into him as he left the Mirabelli Furniture & Appliances

Ltd. at 10550 South Cicero Avenue in Oak Lawn. The killer fled in a red car driven by another man. Speculation was he was a lieutenant of Jimmy "the Bomber" Catuara and was slain as part of an apparent mob war over stolen car chop shop racket, which might have claimed six victims in last ten months and at least twelve in all.

August 25, 1977
Deceased: James A. Palaggi
Killer: Unknown

James A. Palaggi, forty-six, of trailer camp 4700 block South Harlem Avenue, Lyons, was found partially decomposed and shot by a .32 caliber and wrapped in furniture-moving pads in the rear of his van parked near 3221 North Keating Avenue. Neighbors called the police due to the odor. He was last seen Friday, August 19. His wife reported him missing on Saturday. He was believed to have been forced out of his Kankakee New Era junk business three months previous, which he ran with Richie Ferraro who vanished on June 13, 1977. He left for Las Vegas and returned about two months later before joining at least a dozen persons in stolen auto parts racket believed to be slain in the last two years. He and Richie were associated with Sam Annerino (killed July 25, 1977), reputed lieutenant of Jimmy "the Bomber" Catuara, believed to be at war with Albert Tocco over auto parts racket. Palaggi was imprisoned in '71 for interstate cartage theft.

December 13, 1977
Deceased: Leo Frank Filippi
Killer: Unknown

Leo Frank Filippi, forty-three, of Cicero was shot three times in the forehead and once in each shoulder with a .22 or .32 caliber. He was laid out on the backseat floor of a '77 Chevy parked in front of 4730 West Forty-sixth near Keating on the southwest side, after neighbors reported a suspicious car. A sheet covered the body. Filippi was last seen Wednesday, December 7, leaving Zorba's Lounge, a disco at 5807 West Roosevelt, Cicero, where he worked. He had served four months for income tax evasion in 1975-76.

1978

January 20, 1978
Deceased: Bernard F. Ryan
Killer: Unknown

Bernard F. Ryan, thirty-four, of 2727 West 111th Street. His body was shot three or four times in the head, discovered slumped behind the wheel of a '76 Lincoln Continental registered to his brother, John, which was snow covered and parked for several days. He had a scanner radio in his hand (used to intercept police calls). Residents reported the car there at 1657 South Forty-fourth Avenue, Stone Park. He was apparently shot by someone in the backseat. Victim had served time on three burglaries and one federal securities forgery convictions. Police felt his death might be linked to four other murders (Mendell, Moretti, Renno, and Garcia) of possible members of a burglary ring being disciplined by the mob. All four were likely killed at the same time.

February 2, 1978
Deceased: Steven Robert Garcia
Killer: Unknown

Steven Robert Garcia, twenty-nine, of 5615 North Cumberland, was discovered late Thursday at the Sheraton O'Hare Motor Hotel parking lot at 6810 North Mannheim Road, Rosemont, with his throat cut and stab wounds in the upper torso and was stuffed in the trunk of a rented white 1977 Ford Granada. He was missing for over two weeks. Police suspected he was murdered after discovering his burglary ring partner Bernie Ryan's body on January 20. The search continued for other members of the ring until by February 20, five bodies in all were found, including Moretti, Renno, and Mendell. Police theorized the mob killed them for failure to follow the rules. A known jewel thief, he and the others were suspects in over $1 million theft of jewels and furs.

February 4, 1978
Deceased: Vincent Moretti
Killers: William "Butch" Petrocelli, John "Apes" Monteleone, Joe Ferriola, Frank Calabrese Sr.

Vincent Moretti, fifty-one, of Elmwood Park, was discovered Saturday with the throat cut and badly beaten and wedged alongside the body of Donald R. Renno in the backseat of Renno's Cadillac parked in the lot of Esther's Place at 5009 South Central Avenue, Stickney. Police believed he was the leader of the ring of burglars, five of whom were killed between January 20 and February 20. Members of the ring were suspects in over $1 million theft of jewels and furs on December 19, 1977. Vince's twin brother, Salvatore, was murdered on April 17, 1957, and another brother, Michael, was convicted of killing two youths in 1951. All three brothers had been policemen.

February 4, 1978
Deceased: Donald R. Renno, a.k.a. Donald Swanson
Killers: William "Butch" Petrocelli, John "Apes" Monteleone, Joe Ferriola, Frank Calabrese Sr.

Donald R. Renno, thirty-one, of 2554 North Neva, was discovered with the throat cut and wedged alongside the body of Vincent Moretti in the backseat of Renno's Cadillac parked in the lot of Esther's Place at 5009 South Central Avenue, Stickney. One of five burglars murdered between January 20 and February 20, Renno, who changed his name from Donald Swanson, was least known and might have been a victim because he was with Moretti, whom police thought had been fencing a loot in Las Vegas against the mob's wishes. Members of the ring were suspects in over $1 million theft on December 19, 1977, of jewels and furs.

February 20, 1978
Deceased: John Mendell
Killers: Frank Calabrese Sr., Ron Jarrett, Frank Saladino

John Mendell, thirty-one, of Lincolnwood, was discovered with his throat cut, signs of torture and stuffed in the trunk of his '71 Olds parked at 6304 South Campbell since January 17, a day after he was last seen alive. Police had been searching for him since January 20 when the body of Bernie Ryan was discovered. Since then, Garcia, Moretti, Renno, and Mendell were found murdered. Mendell was an electronics expert of the burglary ring, suspected to have stolen over $1 million in jewels and furs. Police theorized the mob killed the five for failing to cut them in on the action.

March 17, 1978
Deceased: Dino J. Valente
Killer: Unknown

Dino J. Valente, forty-one, of 954 East 171st Place, South Holland, was shot four times with a 12-gauge shotgun on March 16, 1978, near his '77 Continental in the lot next to Rukavina's Restaurant at 645 Torrence Avenue, Calumet City. He died early Friday in St. Margaret Mercy Hospital, Hammond. He was long associated with a music company in Chicago Heights (founded in part by mobster Frank Laporte). Valente also operated a jukebox and billiard business out of his home. Police theorized these activities probably prompted his slaying.

April 3, 1978
Deceased: Frank J. Smith Jr.
Killer: Unknown

Frank J. Smith Jr., sixty-three, of 1247 Ashland Avenue, River Forest, was shot twice in the temple and chest about 1:30 PM Monday in a residential alley behind 4149 North St. Louis. Frank still ran F&M Vending Co. at 1112 West Westgate, Oak Park, and was on collection rounds when shot. Police speculated he and another vendor, Dino J. Valente (shot March 16, 1978), might be victims of a takeover war in vending rackets and Frank's missing car might have contained important records.

April 6, 1978
Deceased: Robert A. Hertogs ← FAMILY OF COMMERCIAL BURGLARS
Killer: Unknown

Robert A. Hertogs, twenty-two, of 2119 West Iowa St., was found shot in the head and was clad only in shorts in the trunk of a '72 Olds parked in Jewel parking lot at 3552 West Grand Avenue. The car was reported stolen previously on Thursday, March 30, when victim was last seen alive. A professional burglar, his associate Patrick Marusarz was gunned down on March 4, 1977, at the Flash Messenger Service owned by James Cozzo whose brother-in-law Henry J. Cosentino was found in a trunk on March 15, 1977, tortured to death by a blunt instrument through his neck, similar to the killing of Louis DeBartolo, who was found dead on January 31, 1976.

April 14, 1978
Deceased: John Charles McDonald
Killer: Unknown

John Charles McDonald, forty-two, of 5001 Carriageway, Rolling Meadows, was found shot in the head and neck in an alley behind 446 North Racine Avenue. The seventh professional burglar murdered so far this year, the victim was a codefendant in 1972 with this year's first victim, Bernard F. Ryan, and had been grilled by police after Ryan's death. The victim had prior conviction for attempted burglary in 1966 with George Fedoruk. Police felt the mob might be behind the killings to reassert their control over burglary rackets, lost when Willie "Potatoes" Daddano was imprisoned in 1969.

July 28, 1978
Deceased: James "Jimmy the Bomber" Catuara
Killer: Unknown

James "Jimmy the Bomber" Catuara, seventy-two, of 9600 South Kilbourn, Oak Lawn, was found shot twice in the head, once in the neck and back, facedown near his red Cadillac at the northeast corner of Hubbard and Ogden, Chicago. He had been gunned down around 7:00

AM, by several hit men waiting in a blue van in this remote industrial area. Longtime mob boss on South Side, Catuara, as theory points out, hit a capped string of murders of underlings, including Sam Annerino, Richie Ferraro, and Steve Ostrowsky in alleged takeover of chop shop rackets by Albert Tocco and William Earl Dauber.

September 8, 1978
Deceased: Melvin Young
Killer: Unknown

Melvin Young, forty-two, of Elk Grove Village, was found Friday afternoon shot in the chest in the trunk of his silver '78 Lincoln Continental Mark V parked at O'Hare Airport. He was estimated to have been there several days but not prior to Sunday when the lot was last checked. He recently sold Custom Metal Polishing & Plating Company at 1750 North Campbell, which specialized in customizing cycles. He had a couple of arrests for possession of stolen vehicles.

September 27, 1978
Deceased: Robert Martinez Vaca
Killer: Unknown

Robert Martinez Vaca, forty-six, of unknown address, was found by the co-owner of Pub at 6:28 AM. He was shot several times with a .38 caliber in the back and neck while sitting in the front seat of a stolen car parked between 3:00 and 6:00 AM in a lot next to the Village Pub at 8839 Twenty-second Place, North Riverside. A professional burglar or robber, Vaca's associates included mob cartage thief Anthony Legato, and Illinois Legislative Investigating Commission (ILIC) reported in mid sixties he was Marshall Caifano's driver when Vaca was on juice himself. Federal tapes of James Inendino revealed Vaca was his juice collector and, on Thursday, September 21, was called in for questioning. He was believed killed in order to silence him before he talked as he did for ILIC in the '60s investigation of juice rackets.

1979

March 11, 1979
Deceased: George Nicholas Christofalos, a.k.a. George N. Lardas
Killers: Joey Borsellino, Gerry Scarpelli, Jerry Scalise

George Nicholas Christofalos, forty-one, of Lake Bluff, was shot and killed just after the 4:00 AM closing of his L&L No. 2 Club at Rte 41 and Buckley Road while warming up his '76 Eldorado convertible. He was met in the lot by two men wearing ski masks. One gunman pinned an employee to the door of the club while the other pumped three 12-gauge shotgun blasts through the car window and into his left upper body. The victim had a long record for vice and immigration violations (born in Greece, naturalized Canadian, married American).

He reportedly befriended former CPD captain Mark C. Thanasouras after the latter's release from prison and possibly was former business partner of John D. Lourgos. Thanasouras was shot on July 22, 1977, and Lourgos on April 4, 1977.

May 22, 1979
Deceased: John Anthony Borsellino
Killer: Unknown

John Anthony Borsellino, forty-eight, of 744 Magnolia Circle, Lombard. His body was found in a farmer's field near Frankfort, just west of the Cook/Will County line. He was shot five times in the back of the head with a small-caliber gun. His body was fully clothed with a T-shirt advertising Brown's Bingo Hall at 6060 West Belmont. He had served time for his part in the Spector Freight silver robbery.

June 1, 1979
Deceased: Timothy "Timmy" W. O'Brien
Killer: Unknown

Timothy "Timmy" W. O'Brien, thirty-nine, of 8750 South Merton, Oak Lawn, was owner of Irish Keystone Auto Parts, Bobbins. His body was found in the trunk of his car on Old Western Avenue, Blue

Island, shot in head by a shotgun. He was clothed in black slacks with a black sport shirt pulled up over his head. He was under indictment for receiving stolen property as part of his major chop shop operation. His arrest record for auto theft dated back to 1957.

September 28, 1979
Deceased: Gerald "Ding Dong" V. Carusiello
Killer: Unknown

Gerald "Ding Dong" V. Carusiello, forty-seven, of Melrose Park, was shot seven times in the back at a condo development at 951 North Highway 53, Addison. An armed robber and burglar, he had a record dating back twenty-six years. He had once been chauffeur for Joseph Aiuppa. He was wearing jeans, dark sweatshirt, scarf, and gloves and was carrying a screwdriver, $1,750 in cash, but no identity. He might have been set up by others suggesting a burglar. Two men were seen fleeing the scene in a late-model green Dodge.

1980

July 2, 1980
Deceased: William Earl "Billy" Dauber, Charlotte Dauber
Killers: William "Butch" Petrocelli, Gerry Scarpelli, Frank Calabrese Sr.
LOMBARDO TOO

William, forty-five, and Charlotte, thirty-seven, of Monee Road, Crete, were killed by multiple shotgun and rifle shots fired from a stolen 1978 blue Ford van on Monee-Manhattan Road in rural Will County. Dauber was en route home from a morning court appearance in Joliet. He was also facing federal gun and cocaine charges. Dauber had been a hit man and chop shop enforcer, first for James Catuara and later for Albert Tocco. Charlotte's hit was said to have been intended as well.

November 28, 1980
Deceased: Eleftherios "Nick" Valentzas
Killer: Unknown

Eleftherios "Nick" Valentzas, thirty-four, of 546 East Park, Villa Park, received multiple shotgun and pistol shots while entering a car in the parking lot at 2222 North Harlem, Elmwood Park. Two men wearing dark clothing approached the car and began firing rounds into the chest and head at close range. A man with a limp was observed leaving the scene carrying a shotgun. The victim had operated a Greek coffee house in the 6000 block of Belmont and had been paying $300/month of "street taxes" on gambling game to Donald Scalise, Nick Boulahanis, and Frank Rinella. Money went from them to Bobby Salerno and Phillip "Philly the Fruit" Latorre and then to Butch Petrocelli. The victim was to testify in court for a federal extortion case against the three.

1981

March 14, 1981
Deceased: William Joe "Butch" Petrocelli
Killers: Jim LaPietra; Frank Calabrese Sr.; Nick Calabrese; Frank Santucci

William Joe "Butch" Petrocelli, forty-three, of 342 Forest Ave, Hillside, was found in the backseat of his car parked at 4307 West Twenty-fifth Place with throat cut, hands bound by tape, surgical tape over mouth, and nose and face burned with a lighter fluid. Cause of death was by asphyxiation. He had been reported missing to FBI by his girlfriend. He reportedly had held out $100,000 collected for the family of imprisoned Harry Aleman and defied mob orders to turn over money. He worked for Joseph Ferriola, Aleman's uncle. The victim and Aleman were former partners as hit men, but Butch had risen to oversee activities of bookies at tracks and other high-level Ferriola interests.

May 6, 1981
Deceased: Fiore Forestiere
Killer: Unknown

Fiore Forestiere, fifty-eight, was found shot to death in a van near 8140 O'Connor Drive, River Grove. He was shot five times, once in the head and four times in the chest. He lived in Glen Ellyn. He was an ex-con with a record.

May 18, 1981
Deceased: Sam Faruggia
Killer: Unknown

Sam Faruggia, sixty, of 906 Franklin Street, River Forest, was found stabbed at least five times with the throat cut, wrapped in a rug in a station wagon at 758 North Leclaire. His daughter reported him missing to River Forest Police on May 15 after he failed to arrive at work on Monday morning. He had operated Melody Music, a jukebox firm, and Leyden Acceptance at 3809 West Grand, firms formerly run by Chuckie English.

August 5, 1981
Deceased: Charles F. Monday, a.k.a. Charles Mondzyk
Killer: Unknown

Charles F. Monday, forty-four, was found in the trunk of a car in the 6200 block of West Schubert. He was beaten to death and was missing for thirteen days. Neighbors noticed the car and called police. He worked with Anthony Legato.

August 7, 1981
Deceased: Anthony Legato
Killer: Unknown

Anthony Legato, fifty, of Berwyn, was found in the trunk of a 1975 Ford, wrapped in a blanket. He was previously reported missing for sixteen days. Car was parked at 4759 West George. Legato was reported missing the same day as Monday. They knew each other and had common dealings in drugs.

September 13, 1981
Deceased: Nicholas D'Andrea
Killer: Frank Calabrese Jr.; Nick Calabrese; James Tiarcello

Nicholas D'Andrea, forty-nine, of Chicago Heights, was found murdered in the trunk of a burning car near Crete. He left his home approximately at 2:00 PM, and the car was discovered burning at 9:30 PM the same day. He was suspected to have been involved in arranging the attempted murder of Alfred Pilotto. D'Andrea worked for Albert Tocco and dealt in drugs and gambling.

October 3, 1981
Deceased: Samuel Guzzino
Killer: Unknown

Samuel Guzzino, fifty-one, of Chicago Heights, was found in a ditch in South suburban Beecher, shot in the head and his throat slit. He worked for Albert Tocco. Guzzino played golf with Alfred Pilotto, and it was assumed he had something to do with the attempted murder on him while golfing. It is felt that D'Andrea was tortured to obtain names of those who were to kill Pilotto, the South suburban crime boss, and the death of Guzzino followed.

1982

June 3, 1982
Deceased: Robert Hayden Plummer
Killer: Rocky Infelise

Robert Hayden Plummer, fifty-one, of Lake Forest, was found in the trunk of his late-model Lincoln Continental in a motel parking lot at U.S. 45 and Rte 83 in Mundelein. He was reported missing by his wife on May 23. He was badly decomposed; autopsy indicated he was struck three times on the back of his head with a blunt object and struck once on the left side of his head above the ear. He had been indicted in 1971 as a member of a multi-million-dollar interstate gambling operation.

October 8, 1982
Deceased: Leo "John" Manfredi, a.k.a. Leonard Corfini, John Dubois
Killer: Unknown

Leo "John" Manfredi, sixty-seven, of Cicero, was found in the basement of a closed pizza parlor at 6233 West Roosevelt, Berwyn, shot four times in the head. It is suspected that he was using juice money from loan-sharking without permission to finance drug deals that fell through and could not make payments to the outfit.

1983

January 11, 1983
Deceased: Robert P. Subatich
Killer: Unknown

Robert P. Subatich, forty-four, of Michigan City Road in Calumet City, was found in the trunk of his '81 Lincoln Mark VI in an O'Hare Airport garage, shot once in the head. His car was in the garage since December 27. Subatich was reported missing by his mother on January 4. He was suspected of being involved in cocaine dealing and chop shop operations.

January 20, 1983
Deceased: Allen M. Dorfman
Killers: John Fecarotta, Frank Schweihs

Allen M. Dorfman, sixty, of Deerfield, was shot in the head eight times with a .22-caliber automatic in a parking lot of a hotel in Lincolnwood. He was the owner of Amalgamated Insurance. Agencies

Inc., which handled premiums/claims on millions of dollars of Teamster business, and was former consultant to Central States Pension Fund. He recently was convicted in a federal court in Chicago with Roy Williams, Joey Lombardo, Thomas O'Mailey, and Amos Massa. He was killed awaiting sentencing.

July 14, 1983
Deceased: John Gattuso
Killers: Sam Carlisi, James DiForti

John Gattuso – forty-seven, of 2324 West Taylor, Chicago, and 1721 Sunset Ridge, Glenview – was discovered alongside the body of Jasper Campise, both wrapped in plastic bags in the trunk of Campise's 1981 Volvo Sedan parked in the lot of the Pebblewood condo complex at 55070 Pebblewood Lane, Naperville. Gattuso was stabbed once in the neck and four times in the abdomen. Also, a rope was knotted around his neck indicating that he had been strangled, possibly during a torturing session aimed at learning if he had become an informer. Campise and Gattuso were charged with the bungled attempted murder of mob gambling boss Ken Eto. Gattuso was named by Eto as the triggerman. It is believed that the crime syndicate elders, angered by the failure of Campise and Gattuso to carry out the Eto killing, decided to have the pair slain to prevent their talking. Federal agents' efforts to enlist Campise and Gattuso in the federal witness protection program – although unsuccessful – might have triggered their abductions. The bungled murder try, coupled with the possibility the pair would join Eto as tattlers, provided clear-cut motives for their deaths. Gattuso, who was a Cook County deputy sheriff, had been an operator of syndicate honky-tonk taverns, gay bars, and restaurants. Ernest "Rocco" Infelise, one of the mob's top enforcers and executioners, was listed as a prime suspect in the murder of Campise and Gattuso. Unlike past syndicate murders, no attempt was made to hide the bodies, indicating that the syndicate was "sending a message" to other wayward mob members.

ETO HAD A HOUSE OFF GREENWOOD IN P.RIDGE

July 14, 1983
Deceased: Jasper Campise
Killers: Sam Carlisi, James DiForti

RELATED TO LOVERDE'S

Jasper Campise, sixty-eight, of 1535 Forest, River Forest, was discovered alongside the body of John Gattuso, both wrapped in plastic bags in the trunk of Campise's 1981 Volvo Sedan parked in the lot of the Pebblewood condo complex at 55070 Pebblewood Lane, Naperville. Campise was stabbed five times in the left side of his body. Campise and Gattuso were charged with the bungled attempted murder of mob gambling boss Ken Eto. Eto identified Gattuso as the triggerman. It is believed that the crime syndicate elders, angered by the failure of Campise and Gattuso to carry out the Eto killing, decided to have the pair slain to prevent their talking. Federal agents' efforts to enlist Campise and Gattuso in the federal witness protection program – although unsuccessful – might have triggered their abductions. The bungled murder try, coupled with the possibility the pair would join Eto as tattlers, provided clear-cut motives for their deaths. Campise, a longtime syndicate loan shark operator, was arrested in 1966 for the murder of Dominick "Hunk" Galiano, a syndicate vice operator. Ernest "Rocco" Infelise, one of the mob's top enforcers and executioners, was listed as a prime suspect in the murder of Campise and Gattuso. Unlike some past syndicate murders, no attempt was made to hide the bodies, indicating that the syndicate was "sending a message" to other wayward mob members.

1984

December 16, 1984
Deceased: Anthony V. Crissie
Killer: Unknown

Anthony V. Crissie, forty-nine, of 337 North East River Road, Des Plaines, was discovered by police in the town of Countryside full of bullet holes, one in the chest and three in the back of the head from a .22-caliber pistol equipped with a silencer. He had been deeply enmeshed in underworld affairs for more than a decade as a mob partner and financier of business deals involving organized crime.

Crissie, former director and stockholder of River Grove Bank & Trust Co., ran the Mutual Development Corp. at 10330 Roberts Road, Palos Heights, which financed syndicate business deals. In the late 1970s, he was a partner with then mob gambling boss Ken Eto and hoodlum Sam Sarcinelli in Taco-Si, a Skokie food business. Recently before his death, Crissie had been quizzed by federal agents on his knowledge of underworld money matters. Fear that he would talk could have led to his slaying.

1985

January 10, 1985
Deceased: Leonard "Lennie" Yaras
Killer: Unknown

Leonard Yaras, forty-four, of 4001 West Chase Lane, Lincolnwood, was shot to death while preparing to drive away after visiting the All-American Laundry and Cleaners at 4224 West Division, where he had a financial interest. Yaras was shot eleven times, including four times in the head and neck. The assassination was carried out by four men, two of whom were triggermen. Yaras was president of A-1 Industrial Uniforms, also located in the building at 4224 West Division. He is the son of the late rackets boss David Yaras. Leonard Yaras operated one of the syndicate's most lucrative sports-betting operations in Rogers Park, under the direction of major crime boss Joseph "Joey Nagall" A. Ferriola. Joseph "Joey the Clown" Lombardo, a mob chief about equal to Ferriola in the syndicate hierarchy, had sent two lieutenants to take over Yaras's betting operations. Yaras resisted the Lombardo takeover. The gangland assassination was suspected to be caused by the struggle over the North Side gambling turf.

February 9, 1985
Deceased: Charles "Chuckie" English Killer: Unknown

Charles English, seventy, of 1131 North Lathrop, River Forest, was shot several times with a handgun, once between the eyes, in the parking lot of Horwath's Restaurant at 1850 North Harlem, Elmwood Park. As he was preparing to enter a Cadillac in the parking lot, two men wearing ski masks approached him, one of them firing a handgun. English's police record dates back to 1933 he was *regarded* as the no. 1 lieutenant of Sam Giancana during Giancana's reign as Chicago's syndicate chieftain from 1957-66. At one time, English headed all gambling activity in the Twenty-ninth Ward and operated bookmaking, vending machines, and loan shark operations in Cicero. Following Giancana's reign, English was a top lieutenant of Anthony J. Accardo. In 1976, he was demoted and stripped by the mob of his ownership of a jukebox company and a record company, Lormar Distributing at 2311 North Western, for refusing to set up Giancana for assassination. In a few months prior to his death, English switched his allegiance from Joseph Lombardo to Joseph Ferriola. English could have been a victim of a power struggle between the two mob chiefs.

February 12, 1985
Deceased: Hal Smith
Killers: Rocky Infelise, Bobby Salerno, Louie Marino, Bobby Believa

Hal Smith, forty-eight, of 315 Kenilworth Drive, Prospect Heights, was found murdered in the trunk of his Cadillac Seville left in the parking lot of the Arlington Park Hilton Hotel, Arlington Heights. His body had been badly beaten and his throat slashed. An autopsy showed that Smith died of strangulation, probably with a rope or belt. The postmortem examination also revealed nonfatal slash wounds to the front of Smith's neck, indicating he was tortured before being slain. Smith, a sports-betting kingpin, was described by U.S. Department of Justice officials as the largest independent bookmaker who came to be controlled by the crime syndicate. Possible motives for the murder included that Smith was known to be cooperating with federal agents in a minor investigation of crime syndicate gambling activities in the Chicago area. Also, there was a mob crackdown headed by gambling boss Joseph Ferriola to force independent bookies out of business. Smith had resisted the mob takeover of gambling rackets.

July 26, 1985
Deceased: Patrick "Patsy" Ricciardi
Killer: Unknown

Patrick Ricciardi, fifty-nine, of 5348 North Virginia, was discovered in the trunk of a stolen car that had been towed to a police parking lot. When the owner of the car showed up to claim it, the police noticed something dripping from the car's trunk. Ricciardi was found shot once in the head. Ricciardi, a cousin of the late syndicate chieftain Felix "Milwaukee Phil" Alderisio, had gained stature in the mob after he transformed the shuttered but once respectable Admiral Theater into a profitable X-rated movie house through which the mob reportedly laundered cash from illegal rackets by inflating attendance figures. In addition to being the boss of the crime syndicate's lucrative pornographic movie operations, Ricciardi was considered the key to tracing a cache of cash estimated at more than $5 million entrusted to him by his cousin Alderisio. Suspected of being a federal informant, Ricciardi was a double threat to crime syndicate leaders: he not only knew the intimate workings of the pornographic film business, but he also knew the secret of Alderisio's millions.

1986

January 13, 1986
Deceased: Michael S. Lentini
Killer: Unknown

Michael S. Lentini, age forty-four, of 9110 Grant, was shot three times as he was about to leave for work. He had started the car and turned on the headlights when shots were fired through the car's windows. Lentini was a pressman on the midnight shift at Regensteiner Publishing Enterprises Inc. at 1224 West Van Buren.

January 27, 1986
Deceased: Richard N. DePrizio
Killer: Unknown

Richard N. DePrizio, male, white, age thirty-six, was shot in the head twice. His body was found in a parking lot at 2520 South Wolf Road in Westchester. He was about to be indicted by the federal government for fraud involving city contracts by his construction company, V. N. DePrizio Construction Company. The company went into bankruptcy in 1983; DePrizio owed everybody.

June 22, 1986
Deceased: Anthony J. Spilotro
Killers: Frank Calabrese Sr.; Nick Calabrese; James Marcello; John Fecarotta

Anthony J. Spilotro, forty-eight years of age, was found with his brother Michael buried in a five-foot deep grave in a cornfield at a Northwest Indiana wildlife preserves. They were reported missing on June 14, and the Lincoln they used was found in a lot at the Howard Johnson's Motel at Mannheim and Irving Park Road. Anthony Spilotro was described as the overseer of the Chicago crime syndicate's Las Vegas operations.

June 22, 1986
Deceased: Michael P. Spilotro
Killers: Frank Calabrese Sr.; Nick Calabrese; James Marcello; John Fecarotta

Michael P. Spilotro, forty-two years of age, was found with his brother Anthony buried in a five-foot deep grave in a cornfield at a Northwest Indiana wildlife preserves. They were reported missing on June 14, and the Lincoln they used was found in a lot at the Howard Johnson's Motel at Mannheim and Irving Park Road. Michael was under indictment in Chicago for federal extortion charges. Michael might have been killed only because he was with Anthony.

September 14, 1986
Deceased: John A. Fecarotta
Killers: Nick Calabrese, Frank Calabrese Sr.

John A. Fecarotta, fifty-eight years of age, of 268 Gage Road, Riverside, was shot and killed on September 14, 1986. The body was found lying in the doorway, shot at least four times with a .38-caliber revolver. Fecarotta, a former organizer for a Chicago labor union, had been tied to organized crime.

November 13, 1986
Deceased: Thomas B. McKillip
Killer: Unknown

Thomas B. McKillip, forty-nine years of age, was found shot and stabbed in the back of a 1977 Chevrolet Blazer in Buffalo Grove. He had been shot twice in the back of the head with a small-caliber pistol and stabbed in the chest.

September 23, 1987
Deceased: John Castaldo
Killer: Unknown

The bullet-riddled body of John Castaldo, twenty-eight-year-old owner of two beauty salons in River Forest, was found in a Bellwood alley shortly after he was seen entering a Cadillac with three men inside.

1988

February 18, 1988
Deceased: Joe Gehl
Killer: James Naples

Bookmaker Joe Gehl, age twenty-eight, who couldn't pay a $5,000 gambling debt, was killed by James Naples, thirty-five.

August 14, 1988
Deceased: John E. Pronger
Killer: Unknown

John E. Pronger, sixty-four years of age, was killed by two shots from a .357-caliber Magnum late Sunday or early Monday as he stood in the doorway of his house at 2547 Springhill Drive where he had been living for about a year.

November 22, 1988
Deceased: Philip Goodman
Killer: Unknown

Philip Goodman, a seventy-three-year-old Las Vegas man, a former Chicagoan, suffered massive head injuries in a beating in his room at the Admiral Oasis Motel at 9353 Waukegan Road where his body was found Tuesday by a motel employee.

1990

May 14, 1990
Deceased: James Pellegrino
Killer: Unknown

James Pellegrino – male, white, age thirty-one, of 122 Thomas Court, Mokena, Illinois – was reported missing by his wife on May 14, 1990. The body was found on June 4 in the Des Plaines River at 8901 West Lawrence Avenue by two men canoeing down the Des Plaines River. They observed a tarp caught onto the branch of a tree hanging over the river. They pulled it to shore, looked inside, and discovered the body. They then called the police, and the Sixteenth District responded. The victim was shot once in the back of the head with what is believed to be a .25-caliber slug. His head was in a plastic bag taped closed. His hands and feet were tied with a rope, and he was then wrapped in the tarp, which was taped shut. It is believed to be a falling-out between burglars and drug dealers. Homicide is still under investigation.

July 1, 1990
Deceased: Victor Lazarus Sr.
Killed: Unknown

The body of Lazarus, eighty-eight, who lived in an Evanston retirement hotel, was found Sunday in the trunk of his car at a North Side parking lot. He had been shot twice in the head.

November 6, 1990
Deceased: Edward Pedote
Killed: Unknown

Fence and wholesale jeweler at 5 South Wabash Avenue, Chicago, Illinois, Pedote was found at 1823 South Cicero in Cicero, Illinois, inside a furniture resale store. He had been beaten to death with a table leg and possibly shot in the face with a small-caliber weapon. He left home in Naperville with a large amount of jewelry and about $50,000 in cash. His pockets were empty when the body was found. He had pled guilty six years ago to federal robbery, weapons, and drug charges and was sentenced to five-years' probation

November 5, 1992
Deceased: Sam Taglia
Killer: Allegedly by Albert Vena

Sam Taglia, age fifty (DOB June 30, 1942), was shot twice in the head and had his throat cut. His IR number 29334 showed about forty previous arrests for robbery, burglary, auto theft, and narcotics violations. He had done five years in the penitentiary for six of these offenses in 1967. He had been living with Delia Taglia at 416 Thatcher, unit 2 in River Forest since 1992.

Before that, he was at 1122 West Thirty-second Avenue, Melrose Park. He was found at Thirteenth and Main in the trunk of his auto.

The Fat Lady is Singing

As the saying goes, "It ain't over until the fat lady sings," well she is singing now, and it's over.

I never thought I would see the day when there wouldn't be any enforcement against illegal gambling in Chicago. But that day has arrived; the powers to be in the Chicago Police Department and maybe the mayor's office have disbanded the gambling unit of the Vice Control Section, Organized Crime Division.

When I heard about this I couldn't believe it, there was no way they would close down the Gambling Unit for the simple reason that the outfit controlled gambling operations in Chicago as well as the suburbs. It was their main source of revenue from wire-rooms, handbooks, video poker machines and even the illegal state lottery.

I worked in the Gambling Unit from 1966 to the day I retired as a sergeant in 1992. My main job was busting up wire-rooms in the city as well as the suburbs. We also confiscated hundreds of video poker machines when they appeared in 1979. Then we worked on the numbers game "Policy," which was then turned into the legitimate Illinois State Lottery. But the outfit made bigger payouts on winning numbers on the daily pick 3 and pick 4 drawings so people began playing the illegal state lottery instead of the legitimate one. Policy of course began to fade away. But the Chicago Outfit was making millions from their involvement in illegal gambling, even though we made hundreds of gambling raids every year. But the way things are now they don't have anything to worry about.

A nationwide survey of gambling in these United States was conducted about 40 years ago that showed that we were in the midst of the greatest gambling boom of all time, and that gambling, most of it illegal, was our biggest industry.

At that time about 70% of our adult population-almost 86 million Americans of whom 40 million were men and 46 million were women were gambling the astronomical sum of $500 billion annually on all kinds of gambling. Almost 98% or $490 billion of this amount was wagered illegally; only $10 billion legally.

That $500 billion total made gambling the leading industry in the United States in the amount of money handled 40 years ago. This sum far exceeded the plant manufacture cost of automobiles, trucks, tractors, buses and all other land motor vehicles combined. Note that this $500 billion was not the gambling industry income; it is the annual gambling handle.

There is no way to determine the gambling handle today in the United States with new forms of gambling like the state lotteries, video poker machines, off track betting parlors, casinos, Bolita, baseball and football pools. The most popular betting was on college and pro football and college and pro basketball games. $98% of this type of gambling was bet illegally.

Big-time gambling in America is not controlled by a single group or syndicate, contrary to what ill advised writers, law enforcement agents, legislators and politicians keep saying. Each city, town and hamlet has its own underworld characters that run the local gambling and seldom team up with outside operators. The gambling bosses may know each other and may sometimes do business together, but there is no single group or syndicate that controls gambling throughout the country. Organized crime bosses seldom sign their names to affidavits stating that they own or control the gambling operation.

Gambling is the principal source of income for organized crime. Gambling provides organized crime with the money it needs to flourish which was revealed at the President's Commission on Organized Crime Hearings on gambling in New York, New York June 24 – 26, 1985. I appeared at this hearing as an expert witness on gambling and the Chicago Outfit's involvement in all forms of illegal gambling they controlled in the Chicago area.

The commission was concerned at this hearing about organized crime being able to infiltrate, exploit and profit from legalized gambling in Illinois. I am aware that the Chicago Outfit has been booking bets on the Legal Illinois State lottery. Players of the lottery have been making their daily lottery bets with bookmakers who accept bets as low as a dime on the daily pick 3 or pick 4 lotteries. The outfit also pays better odds. On a $1.00 winning ticket for the pick 3 game the state will pay you $500 where the outfit will pay you $600.

Historically, illegal gambling's largest revenue producer has been: sports bookmaking. Some people are for the legalization of sports gambling, but then other people say that if it were legalized more people would gamble who didn't gamble before. We have to face the fact that there is a tremendous amount of sports betting in this society. The reason you have "Monday Night Football" being so successful is because there is an enormous amount of betting on Monday Night Football. Gambling is part of our national pastime at this point and I don't believe you are going to introduce a lot more people into sports betting if it were to be legalized than we have now. The fact of the matter is anybody who wants to bet on the Super Bowl, who can't find a bookmaker in this society, has to be regarded as mentally retarded.

When I questioned a friend of mine who worked in the Organized Crime Division of the Chicago Police Department about why the gambling unit had been disbanded he told me that the people assigned to that unit were not performing as well as expected. Due to vice detectives retiring and transferring to other units most of the new people assigned to the gambling unit were inexperienced and had no idea of what the job consisted of or how to investigate a gambling case. As a result they were unable to make any gambling raids, let alone get a search warrant.

I was asked to appear on WLS-TV with Investigative Reporter Chuck Goudie to give my opinion as to why the gambling unit had been disbanded. Having worked gambling for 40 years and was formerly assigned to the gambling unit for almost 30 years I told him that I thought that it was a bad idea to disband the unit as illegal gambling was still flourishing and was controlled by organized crime.

Gambling activity is the most serious form of organized crime. This type of activity supplies the financial grease that lubricates the machinery of other operations, such as the importation of narcotics, penetration of legitimate business, corruption of officials and so on. Whenever feasible or necessary, organized crime is not above cheating its gambling public. This may involve bribing athletes, manipulating the winning combination in numbers play, influencing track odds by betting large sums on a given horse at the last minute.

The street bookmaker should be considered a vital part of the total structure of organized crime. A lot of intelligence can be obtained from street bookmakers; he is a member of the Chicago Outfit or pays street taxes to them to operate. From past experience when I began to work on bookmakers I learned that they will lead you to other connections in organized crime and I was able to raid numerous mob gambling operations. Common sense is all it takes to work on gambling. Some people think that some citizen will call up and report mob gambling operations, forget about it. The only place to learn about busting up gambling operations is out in the street.

The latest news on gambling is that on October 13, 2009 the Illinois racing board voted unanimously to license three California companies to take electronic bets from Illinois residents through computers, phones and other mobile devices.

The board estimated about $100 million in unauthorized online horse wagers were made annually in Illinois. Of course a lot of those wagers were made with mob controlled operations.

Robert Thukral, president of Twinspires.Com said his company was looking forward to providing Illinois residents the flexibility of wagering on line, over the phone or on their offline channels including the racetrack and the off-track betting locations in the region.

On second thought maybe the Chicago Police were right getting rid of the gambling unit as long as video poker machines are going to be legit, now we have legal betting on the horses. But then I suggest they figure out a way to legalize sports betting. I know a few mustache Pete's out there that are making a fortune booking football, basketball and baseball. What the hell who cares anyway, it still is a victimless crime. "Yea Right."

I must admit that being a bookmaker was not all it was cracked up to be, there were hills and valleys for the bookmakers that took bets. For example independent bookmakers who had to pay the outfit street taxes to operate were responsible for paying and collecting monies either owed them or winnings they had to pay their customers. One such bookmaker by the name of Ken Meister volunteered the following sad stories that happened to him and his associate Joe "Pooch" Pascucci. I happen to know both of these guys and have had the pleasure of busting up their gambling operations a few times, nothing personal of course.

According to the two bookmakers, they met a player who frequented a tavern (Turners) on Chicago's north side, the player wanted to make some bets on baseball. Of course Ken and Joe told the player they would be happy to accommodate him and gave him their phone number so he could call in his bets. The player proceeded to make 10, $1,000 parlay bets keying the White Sox with 10 other teams. As things turned out the White Sox won but the other 10 teams lost. The player lost $10,000 to Ken and Joe. Arrangements were made to meet so the player could pay off his bets the next week. The player showed up on a motor scooter and confessed that he didn't have any cash

At this point Ken and Joe were very upset with the player but being good citizens they did not believe in violence. A deal was agreed by all concerned that the player would pay Ken and Joe $1,000 a month until his debt was paid. The bad news was that the player was killed in a car accident three weeks later.

Another sad story was in the 1980's at a restaurant called Myron and Phil's in Lincolnwood, Il a bookmaker (Mike Posner) frequented the restaurant on occasion and met Ken and Joe there to talk about some business. Posner told them that he had a small bettor who was a bartender in a tavern called AJ's and that the guy bet between $50 and $100 and Posner didn't want to handle his action because he was to small a bettor and would they be interested in taking his action.

Ken told Posner that he would take the guys bets for the first 5 or 6 weeks of the football season. As things turned out the guy won from $400 to $1,000 a week for the first 5 weeks of the season. But the next week he lost $2500. Ken called the player as usual to meet him to settle up his account. The player then informed Ken that he was busted and didn't have any cash to pay him.

Ken asked the guy if he pushed the money he won up his nose, the player, who was a cocaine addict confessed that yes he did. At that point Ken began slamming his house phone up and down on a table until his wife told him he was nuts and he was ruining the table and the phone.

The last sad story about a bookmaker's dilemma occurred twenty years ago in the area of Cicero and Addison Avenue in Chicago in a tavern. The owner of the tavern was a horse player who owed Joe "Pooch" Pascucci $600 for the week's action.

As Joe arrived at the tavern to collect his winnings the owner was being wheeled out of the tavern on a gurney. Joe rushed up to the Para-Medics like a close relative concerned about the well being of the tavern owner and asked them about the sick man's condition. Joe was told that the man appeared to have suffered a heart attack. Joe is only about 5'2 and walked along side the gurney and without being heard by the para-medics kept asking the heart attack victim where he had put the envelope. Not getting an answer Joe attempted to get in the ambulance like a grieving relative to question the man again. It didn't work and the ambulance left Joe standing on the street in tears without his $600. As far as I know Ken and Joe had some bad luck on occasion but not enough to give up the business, especially now that there won't be anybody looking for them.

U.S. Department of Justice

Federal Bureau of Investigation

In Reply, Please Refer to
File No.

219 South Dearborn #905
Chicago, Illinois 60604
February 18, 1993

Matt Rodriquez
Superintendent of Police
Chicago Police Department
1121 South State Street,
Chicago, Illinois 60605

Re: Gus Alex; Leonard Patrick;
Mario John Rainone;
Nicholas Gio;
James Frederick LaValley;

James William Bollman;
James Frederick LaValley;
Nicholas Gio; et al.

Dear Matt,

        The purpose of this letter is to commend the excellent work of Sergeant Donald Herion, previously assigned to the Gambling Unit, Vice Control Section, Organized Crime Division, Chicago Police Department.

        During the period 1988 through 1991, Sergeant Donald Herion worked closely with Agents of the Chicago Division in developing evidence in connection with a major Organized Crime gambling and extortion ring headed by James William Bollman, James Frederick LaValley, Nicholas Gio, and others.

        Sergeant Herion developed an informant whom he convinced to work with the Chicago office of the Federal Bureau of Investigation (FBI). Through joint operation of this source the subjects involved in the gambling operation and extortion were identified as James William Bollman, an organized crime connected bookmaker, James Frederick LaValley, a Chicago Organized Crime enforcer and collector and his partner Nicholas Gio, and ultimately resulted in the indictment, arrest and convictions of Bollman, LaValley, and Nicholas Gio.

        Further, in a spinoff of this initial investigation, the Chicago office of the FBI, with the assistance of Sergeant Herion also developed a strong racketeering and extortion case against Leonard Patrick, age 79, and Gus Alex, age 76, both of whom had long been targets of both Federal and local investigative agencies and prosecutive authorities for over 50 years. Sergeant Herion conducted a gambling raid on the residence of Leonard Patrick in Chicago which resulted in the seizure of vital evidence later utilized and introduced in Federal court. Sergeant Herion, through his unparalleled experience in conducting gambling and Organized Crime investigations, exhibited single minded determination and aggressive leadership providing investigative support and surveillance assistance which proved of immense value during the course of three separate, but related Organized Crime cases.

        Accordingly, I would like to express my sincere appreciation for the assistance provided by Sergeant Donald Herion who made a significant contribution to the Federal convictions of these Organized Crime mobsters.

Very Sincerely Yours,

William D. Branon
Special Agent in Charge

by: Leone J. Flosi
Supervisory Special Agent

Index

A

Aaron Cohen, 254
Aaron "Obie" Oberlander, 257
Abarbanell, Steve, 253
Abbinanti, Bobby, 253
Abercrombie, Earl S. Jr., 299
Abernathy, Ralph, 71
Abshire, Lydia, 270–71, 315
Accardo, Arthur, 114–16, 214
Accardo, Joseph, 253
Accardo, Tony, 111, 114, 214–15, 279
Adam Resnick, 222, 224–25, 258
Adam Sroki, 259
Addlesman, Earl Omer, 281
Adelman, Jeff, 253
Adler, Arthur, 15–16
Agnes Craft, 254
Aiuppa, Joseph "Joey/Joe," 308
Albate, Anthony, 253
Aleman, Harry, 111, 188, 253, 288, 290, 292, 309
Alesse, Rich, 253
Al-Tones, 63, 66
Al-Tone's, 65–66
Alyea, Raymond, 253
Amari, Anthony, 253
Amato, Frank, 253
Amin, Alia, 253
Andriacchi, Bruno, 253
Angelini, Donald, 97, 144, 253
Angelini, Don "Wizard of Odds," 97–99, 144, 253
Angel-Kaplan Sports News Inc, 97–101
Annenberg, ML "Moe," 87–89
Annerino, Samuel J., 300–301, 306
Antonelli, Carmen, 81–85, 253
Antos, Ronald, 253
Argamaso, Balterzal, 253
Arizona Properties Inc., 78–79, 83–84
Arnieri, Anthony, 253
Arnold, Edward, 253
Arnold, Joseph "Big Joe," 124, 127
Aronson, Paul, 253
Arora

Varavit, 253
Yithya, 253
arraignment, 45, 48–50
arrest procedure, 47, 52
Asher, William, 253
A. Testa, Jess, 259
Atlantic City casinos, 131–34
Attallah, Elias, 253
Aureli, Frank, 253
Azimi, Hussein, 253

B

Badamo, Selana, 253
Bagmell, Mary, 253
Bagwell, Paul, 253
Bailey, Walter, 71
Bajrami, Rosanna, 253
Bak, Edward, 253
Bakes, Ned C., 292
Baldwin, Roger, 253
Balsis, Richard, 253
Balzano, Paul, 253
Bandringa, Sandra, 253
Bandusky, Kenneth, 253
Banea, Richard, 253
Bangelowski, Richard, 253
Bank of Boston, 134
Barbaro, Dominick, 253
Barlas, Thomas, 253
Barnes, John, 237
Barnes, Nelson, 253
Barsella, Bruno, 253
Bartuca, Frank, 254
Basase, Anthony, 254
Basil Stapralis, 259
Basso, Dominick, 254
Basso, Michael, 254
Bates, Brenetta, 254

Battaglia, Patrick, 253
Battle, Jose Miguel Sr., 194, 196
Bausone, Mark, 254
Bell, Delbert, 254
Bellavia, Robert, 254
Bellos, Paul, 254
Belpedio, Louie, 254
Benes, Joseph, 254
Benitivich, Isadore, 254
Berk, Vincent, 254
Berkowitz, Marilyn, 254
Bernstein, Harvey, 254
Bertucci, Phil, 254
Bills, Sam, 254
bingo, 203–4, 206–9, 219
Black Cat, 65–67
blackjack, 104, 106, 138, 200, 219, 222
Blechman, Michael, 254
Blitzstein, Herb, 254
Block, Willie, 89
Bludeau, Peter J., 272
Bolis, Mike, 254
bolita gambling operations, 125–29, 200, 219, 285, 287
Bollman, James, 254
bookmaking, sports, 81, 89, 98–99, 101–2, 143–44, 146–49, 155–58, 164–67, 169, 187–88, 199, 214–15, 219–23, 226–27, 291–92, 316
  Bell Brand Ranches scam, 78–81, 83–85
  Rosebud Restaurant raid, 145–47
Bopo, Frank, 255
Borelli, Ronald, 254
Borsellino, Joe, 254

Borsellino, John Anthony "Joey/Joe," 254, 307
Bosak, Darryl, 254
Boscarino, Angelo John, 277
Bowers, Paul, 254
Bowling, John, 254
bowling alley, 145–46
Bozan, Rose, 254
Braun, Fred, 254
Brennan, Terence, 254
Brigham, George, 254
Britton, Terry, 254
Brown, Albert, 267
Brown, Drew, 28
Brown, Joseph, 254
Brown, Raymond, 254
Bruce, Michael, 99
Buchcanon, Hugh, 254
Buckley, John, 254
Bullock, Bertha Mae, 276
Bura, Frank, 254
Burgmurs, 214
Byron, Daniel, 254

C

Caccamo, Ray, 254
Cain, Richard "Dick," 108–11, 187, 284, 293, 297
Calabrese, Anthony "the Hatchet," 227–28
Calabrese, Frank Sr., 215–16, 227, 293, 296, 303, 308, 319
Calabrese, Nick, 215, 293, 309, 311, 318–19
Calato, Joe, 254
Calcagno, Joseph, 254
Caldarulo, John, 254
Calderone, Mike, 254
Calderone, Ron, 254
Caldrone, Larry, 254
Caliendo, Gabe, 254
Callary, Martin, 254
Calvin Sirkin, 259
Camacho, Jose, 254
Campanelli, John "Haircuts," 254
Campanile, Rocco, 254
Capodice, John, 254
Capone, Al, 87–88, 237, 241, 275, 292
Caponigri, Dan, 254
Capra, Henry, 254
Caracci, Salvatore, 254
Caravelle Motel, 109
Carazzo, Ralph, 127
Carbonari, Ralph, 254
Cardascio, Frank, 254
Carlisi, Sam "Wings," 227, 313
Carlson, Chris, 254
Carmody, John, 254
Carracci, John "Beef," 254
Carroll, Bryan, 235, 239, 242
Carroll, Chuck, 254
Carsello, Andrew, 254
Carter, Larry, 254
Carusiello, Gerald "Ding Dong," 308
Caruso, George, 254
Caruso, Morris "Mutt," 254
Carvotta, Anthony, 254
Casa, Frank, 254
Cascone, Wayne, 285, 287
casino, 131–33, 224
Castaldo, John, 319
Castelbuono, Anthony, 133–34
Cataudella, Nick, 254
Catizone, Anthony, 254
Catizone, Richard, 254

Catuara, James "Jimmy the Bomber," 254, 295, 301, 305
Catuara, James "the Bomber," 254
Cazzato, Arthur, 254
C. Calabrese, Anthony, 227
C. DeBlasio, Raymond, 255
Cecola, Dale, 254
Cecola, Terry, 254
Centrone, Leonard, 278
Cerone, James, 254
Cerva, Bobby, 254
Cesari, Vito, 254
Cesario, Frank, 254
Cesario, Sam "Sambo," 283
Chaconis, John, 254
Chase, Harry, 254
Cherim, Jay, 254
Chiaramonti, Anthony "Tony the Hatch," 226–28
Chicago Dungeon, 186, 188–90
Chicago Mob, 104, 108, 126, 147, 226, 232, 237, 290. *See also* Chicago Outfit
Chicago Outfit, 15, 104, 108–9, 111, 113, 115, 126–28, 137, 144, 148, 177, 199–200, 226–27, 237, 262, 312–15
  North Side, 66, 126, 128, 200, 315
  South Side, 85, 97, 214, 226–27, 283, 306
  West Side, 15, 128, 177, 268
Chicago Police Department, 17, 29, 65, 99, 108–9, 137, 156, 163, 239, 250, 281, 297
  Organized Crime Division, 73, 322, 324
Chierici, Geoffrey, 254

Chindamanee, Vuthana, 254
Chokler, Ben, 254
chop shop racket, 299
Christensen, Morris, 254
Christian Bale, 235–36, 242–44
Christifano, Richard, 254
Christofalos, George Nicholas, 307
Chud, Michael, 254
Cialoni, John, 254
Cilella, Judge, 29–30
Cilella (judge), 29–30
Cimitili, John, 254
Cioe, Arthur, 254
Cipriano, Anthony, 254
Citibank, 197
CoCo, Charlie, 254
Cogan, John, 29
Columbus, George, 207, 254
Combs, Roy, 254
Conner, Karen, 254
Connolly, Mathew, 254
Cook County Sheriff's Office, 148, 179, 181, 213, 219, 222
  Vice Control Division, 197
Cooper, Robert, 227–28
Corbin, Van, 279
Corngold, Joe, 254
Corporation, 194–99
Corriero, Rosario, 254, 283
Corriero, Ross, 254
Cortina, Dominick, 199, 254
Cortina, Dominic "Large," 144, 199, 254
Cosentino, Henry J., 296, 305
Cotton, Vernon, 254
Cowan, Arthur "Boodie," 281
Coy, Edward, 254
Cozzo, Jimmy, 207, 297, 305

Cozzo, Phil, 207, 254
Cozzo, Vincent, 254
Credit Suisse, 134
Crimaldi, Chuckie, 16–17
Crispino, Charles C., 279
Crissie, Anthony V., 314
Crowley, Wilbert F., 114
Culhane, Thomas, 254
Cummings, Homer, 238

D

Daddano, Willie "Potatoes," 110–11, 113–14, 305
Daily Racing Form, 87
Daley, Richard J., 26, 75, 109
Dana, Alex, 147
D'Andrea, Nicholas, 311
D'Andrea, Phil, 241–42
Dauber, Charlotte, 308
Dauber, William Earl "Billy," 308
Deak, Nicholas, 135
Deak-Perera, 134–35
DeBartolo, Louis, 293, 305
DeCanio, Louis, 254
DeCore, Anthony, 254
DeFrank, Marshall, 255
DeGraff, Jay, 254
DeGrazia, Richard, 254
Delaurentis, Sal "Solly D," 254
DelBlasio, Frank, 255
DeLegge, Frank Jr., 292
Del Genio, Ralph, 264–65
Del Guidice, Vincent, 255
DelPilar, Ray, 125
Demke, Charles, 255
Demma, Woody, 255
Demos, George, 255
Dennis, James, 255

Department of Agriculture, 197
Department of Justice, 127, 132, 238, 316
Depp, Johnny, 235–36, 241–42, 244
DePrizio, Richard N., 318
DeRose, Edward, 255
DeSantis, Richie, 255
DeSanto, Carmen, 255
Desilvestro, Renato, 255
DeStefano, Mario, 16–17
DeStefano, Michael, 16
DeStefano, Sam, 15–18, 114, 255, 275, 284
DeStefano, Sam "Mad Sam," 15–17, 114, 255, 275, 284
Devilin, Gregg, 255
Devine, Jeffrey, 255
DeVito, James, 255
DeVivo, Carlo, 289
Dewitt, Charles, 255
Diamond, Loren, 255
Dichiarinte, Anthony "Tony D," 286
DiConstanzo, Joe, 255
DiCostanzo, Frank, 255
DiDomenico, William, 255
DiFazio, Donald "Captain D," 226
DiFilippo, John, 255
DiFronzo, John "No Nose," 147, 255
DiGiacomo, Biagio, 120–23
Dillinger, John, 54, 56, 235, 238–43
Dillinger Squad, 239
DiMeo, Louis, 268, 275
Dionisio, Antonio, 255
DiPasquale, Phil, 156, 213, 215

DiVarco, Joe, 255
Dixon, Benny, 255
Doherty, John, 255
Don, Herbert, 255
Donkel, Richard, 255
Donner, Leonard, 255
Donnie Brasco, 236
Dore, John, 255
Dorfman, Allen M., 126, 312
Dote, Anthony, 255
Dote, Carl, 255
Doyle, Harry, 255
Drug Enforcement Administration, 132–33, 197
Ducato, Robert, 255
Ducek, Robert, 255

E

Ehredt, Jeffrey, 255
Elam, Nick, 255
Eldorado, Anthony, 255
Ellano, Vince, 255
Ellison, Carol, 255
Emody, Alfred, 255
Eng, Joe, 255
Engalls, Richard, 255
Engel, Richard, 255
Englehart, Mike, 255
English, Charles "Chuckie," 268, 290, 310, 315
Enright, Dennis, 255
Erwin, James, 295
Esposito, Frank, 255
Eto, Ken "the Jap," 255
Eto, Ken "Tokyo Joe," 124–29, 137, 200, 313–14

F

Factor, Jake "the Barber," 236–37
Falbo, Frank, 255
Faruggia, Sam, 310
Fatigato, Anthony, 255
Faulk, Shelby, 264, 283
Fazio, Gary, 255
FBI (Federal Bureau of Investigation), 17, 72–73, 102, 110, 121–22, 125, 127, 140, 144, 158, 171–74, 195, 199, 213–14, 231, 235–38
Fecarotta, John A., 284, 312, 318–19
Fehl, Harry, 255
Ferraro, Richard, 298–99, 301, 306
Ferriola, Joseph "Joe Nagall," 122, 303, 309, 315–16
Fiala, Allen, 255
Fields, Fredrick, 255
Filippi, Leo Frank, 301
Finck, Ed, 255
Finn, Charles, 255
Fitzgerald, James, 255
Fitzpatrick, Kevin, 255
Fitzpatrick, Patrick, 255
Flakus, John, 255
Flemming, Larry, 255
Florio, Dominic, 255
Flowers, Paul, 255
Foley, Thomas, 255
Foreman, Jack, 255
Foreman, Joel, 255
Foreman, Leo S., 15, 17, 275, 284
Forestiere, Fiore, 310
Forrest, Clarence A., 278
Frachella, Thomas, 255

Francis, Thomas, 255
Frank (dope dealer), 63
Frankian, Chuck, 255
Fraser, Joseph, 255
Frawley, Linda, 255
Frazin, Sidney, 273, 310
Freeman, Edward, 255
Friduss, Carol, 255
friend of ours, 121
Frieri, Anthony, 255
Frisch, Frank, 255
Froustis, Michail, 255
Fuertsch, Michael, 255
Fundukian, Moore, 255
Funicella, Wesley, 280

G

Gabriel, John, 255
Galan, Augie, 255
Galanos, Nick, 255, 291
Galanos, Nick "Keg," 255
Galluppi, Albert, 149, 255
Gancarz, Dennis, 255
Garafolo, Charles, 255
Garcia, Steven Robert, 115, 302, 304
Garrett, Evelyn, 255
Garrison, Robert, 255
Gasperini, Danny, 255
Gattuso, John, 124–25, 128, 200, 313–14
G. Bicker, E., 254
Geers, Bernard, 255
Gehl, Joe, 319
Geisler, Steve, 255
Gelber, Julius, 255
Geller, Morton, 255
Gene Del Guidice, 254

General News Bureau, 87–88
Gentile, Joseph, 267
Gernardo, Angelo, 255
Giancana, Salvatore "Sam/Momo," 15–16, 97, 110–11, 113–14, 285, 290, 316
Gianforte, Joseph, 255
Gianforte, Sam, 255
Giannone, Anthony, 255
Gianopoulas, James, 255
Gibe, Charles, 255
Gibe, Russ, 255
Giemzik, Patrick, 255
Gilbert, Dan "Tubbo," 236–37
Gio, Nick, 255
Giorango, Anthony, 255
Giorango, Mike, 255
Giuffrida, Gaetano, 133–34
Glickman, Jerry, 255
Glickman, Joel, 255
Goldberg, Marvin, 255
Golden Nugget case, 133–35
Goldman, Sherman, 255
Gonzales, Guillermo, 255
Gonzalez (bolita gambling boss), 128
Goodman, Ken, 255
Gora, Richard, 255
Gordon, Danny, 255
Gordon, Kenneth, 274
Gorniak, Edward, 158, 255
Goto, Tadamasa, 140–41
Goulakos, Frank, 291
Grafner, Peter, 255
Grand Palace Bingo Hall, 204, 206–8
Gratice, Michael, 256
Greco, Arthur, 256
Greene, John, 256

Grieco, Joseph, 127
Guerrero, Guillerino Rivera, 197–98
Guerrieri, Lavergne, 256
Gus "Slim" Alex, 256
Gutierrez, Eugene, 256
Guzaldo, Cosmo, 256
Guzaldo, Phil, 256
Guzaldo, Tony, 256
Guzman, Villegas, 256
Guzzino, Samuel, 311

H

Haggerty, Paul, 293
Hai Than, Phan, 256
Halperin, Richard, 256
Hamilton, John, 239–42
Hamilton, Joseph, 256
Hamilton, Red, 240, 242
Hamm, William, 237
Hanauer, Larry, 256
handbook, 164, 249, 268, 273
Hannah, Robert T., 280
Hanrahan, Jim, 148, 169, 171
Hansen, James, 256
Hansen, Richard, 256
Harder, Robert W., 288
Haro, Rudolfo, 256
Harris, Howard, 256
Harris, Jack, 256
Harrison, Eddie Mae, 277, 309
Hartman, James, 256
Haute, Terre, 98
Heishman, John, 256
Hellwig, Mark, 256
Hendrich, Mathew, 256
Hennigan, John, 269
Herion, Don

Chicago Police Department vice detective, 65, 109, 163
Cook County Sheriff's Vice Detection Unit director, 213, 219, 222
Public Enemies technical advisor, 235
Herman, Paul, 256
Hermann, Clarence, 256
Hertogs, Bobby, 115
Hertogs, Robert A., 305
Hett, Thomas, 106
Hezinger, John, 256
Hilberger, Lawrence, 256
Hillenbrandt, Robert, 256
Hillesheim, Conrad, 256
Hoffman, Robert, 256
Holiday, Adolph, 256
Hollendonner, Mark, 256
Hoover (FBI director), 72, 236–38
Horn, Willie, 277
Horrell, Thomas, 256
Hospodar, Steve, 256
Howard, Lamont, 256
Howard Miller, 78–79, 81
Hucek, Joanne, 256
Humes, Scott, 256

I

Icanbar, Jack, 256
Ignoffo, Ronald, 256
Illinois Bell, 80, 82, 93, 102, 207
Imparato, Angelo, 256
Indiana State Prison, 56, 240
  disciplinary rules, 59
Inendino, James, 256, 288, 306

Inendino, James "Jimmy I," 157, 188, 228
Infelise
  Ernest "Rocco/Rocky," 22, 104, 106, 119, 256, 311, 313–14, 316
  Ernest "Rocky," 256
Inserra, Vince, 174
Inserro, Vincent "Saint," 128
Internal Revenue Service, 133, 197–98
Ivanoff, George, 256

Jasper Campise, 124–25, 128, 200, 254, 313–14
Jerome, Frank, 256
J. McGovern, Richard, 257
J. McGuire, William, 256
Johnson, Everette, 256
Johnson, Leo, 272
Johnson, Robert, 256
Jones, Mathew, 256
Joss, Darrin, 256
Joyce, Michael, 265
juice loan. *See* loan-sharking

J

Jackson, David, 256
Jackson, Walter, 256
Jackson, William "Action," 266, 268
Jacobowsky, Thomas, 256
Jacobs, Harris, 256
Jacobs, Jake, 256
Jacobs, James, 256
Jacobs, Michael, 256
Jacobson, Burt, 256
Jacobson, William, 256
Jaffe, Ronald, 256
Jahoda, William, 104–6
Jans, Murry, 256
Japanese National Police, 139–40
Jaroki, Sam, 256
Jarrett, Ronald J. Jr., 215–16, 256
Jarrett, Ronald W. Sr., 213–15, 217, 226, 293–94
Jarrett Jr., Ronnie, 256
Jarrett Sr., Ronnie, 256
Jarzembowski, Dan, 256
Jasinski, Steven, 158, 256

K

Kabukicho, 140
Kacor, Raymond, 256
Kahn, Irv, 256
Kajiyama, Susumu, 139–40
Kansas City Massacre, 238
Kaplan, William, 97–99
Kasperek, John, 256
Kassmier, David, 256
Kasten, Harold, 256
Katsis, Nick, 256
Katz, Bernard, 256
Kaye, Alan, 256
Kaye, Sanford, 256
Kelly, Frank, 82–85
Kelly, Kevin, 256
Kerrott, Thomas, 256
Kervin, Martin, 256
Kevil, William, 256
Kica, Joseph, 256
Kilpatrick, John A., 266
King, Martin Luther Jr., 71–73
King, Maurice "Peanut," 132–33
Klosowski, Phil, 256
Klotz, Morris, 256

Kobylarz, John, 256
Kocoras, Charles, 158
Kondilis, Jim, 148–49
Kopple, Louis, 256
Kopulos, Dave, 256
Kossar, James, 256
Kozik, Robert, 256
Kreznor, William, 256
Kucala, Lenny, 256
Kwate, Herbert, 272, 316

L

La Cosa Nostra, 121, 194–95
LaCrosse, Daniel, 256
LaMantia, Santo, 256
Lanacki, Donald, 256
Lang, Alan, 256
Langer, Brian, 256
Lansky, Meyer, 88, 194
LaPietra, Angelo, 85, 293–95
LaPietra, Angelo "the Hook," 85, 128, 214, 293–95
LaPlaca, John, 256
LaPorte, Frank, 279, 304
Lardino, John, 256
Laurie, George, 256
Laurie, Jerry, 256
LaValley, Jimmy, 256
Lawler, William, 256
Laws, Rose, 105, 256
Leader, David, 180, 256
Leaney, Leo, 256
Leavitt, Jerome, 256
Lederer, Lawrence, 256
LeDonne, Michael, 256
Lee, Theodore, 256
Legato, Anthony, 306, 310
Lehman, Mark, 256

Leman, William, 256
Leno, Tore, 256
Lentini, Michael S., 317
Lenza, Donald, 256
Lenza, Gerry, 256
LePore, James, 256
Lesniak, Jeff, 257
Levinson, Harvey, 214
Levy, Mark, 257
Lewis, Benjamin, 273
Lewis, Robert "Bobby," 257
Liberatore, Mario, 274
Likas, Bobby, 257
Lingle, Alfred "Jake," 88
Liss, Walter, 257
Litberg, Morris, 262–63
Lloyd, Wayne "Rico," 146–47, 221
loan-sharking, 15–16, 127, 138–39, 157, 188, 227, 263, 265, 282–84, 293, 296–97, 306, 312, 314, 316
Lobash, Robert, 257
Locallo, Vic, 257
LoCoco, Nick, 256
Lombardo, Joe "the Clown," 257, 277, 288
Lombardo, Joseph "Joey the Clown," 125, 288, 313, 315
London, Sam, 257
Long, David, 257
Long, Willie, 46
Lopez, Eugenio "James Crizell," 128
Lorraine Motel, 71, 73
Lourgos, John D., 297, 307
Loverdi, James, 257
Loverdi, Michael, 257
Loy Clark, 254

Lubansky, Steve, 257
Lubertozzi, Dan, 257
Luffman, Eugene "Yudi," 257
Lynch, Jack, 87–88
Lyons, Terance, 257

M

Macatek, Steven, 257
Mackey, Thomas, 257
Mader, Gerald, 257
Mafia, 27, 119–23, 134, 137–38, 186, 194–95, 228
   initiation rites, 119
Maggio, Anthony, 257
Maggio, Donald, 257
Maggio, Nick, 257
Maggio, Orlando, 257
Magliano, Ron, 257
Makas, Sygmunt, 257
Makley, Charles, 240–41
Maltese (mobster), 106
Manfredi, Leo "John," 312
Mangiamele, Robert, 257
Mann, John, 257
Mann, Michael, 235–36, 241–42
Manzella, John, 257
Manzella, Louis, 257
Marasso, Frank, 257
Marcello, Samuel J. Sr., 285–87
Marco D'Amico, 147, 178, 254
Marcus, Leon, 113–14
Marino, Louie, 257, 316
Markese, Nick, 257
Marks, Marvin, 257
Marlborough diamond theft, 230, 241
Marshall, Roy, 257
Marusarz, John, 257

Marusarz, Patrick J., 296, 305
Mason, Legg, 133
Massucci, Ralph, 257
Matelli, Nick, 257
Matriciano, Thomas, 257
Matroci, Louis, 257
Mattioli, Dave, 257
Maurogeanes, James, 257
Mavrogeames, James, 257
Mazzuca, Joe, 257
McAvoy, Donald, 257
McCandless, Thomas, 257
McCarron (coroner), 27
McCarthy, Matt, 257
McCarthy, Thomas, 298, 307
McCormick, Kevin, 257
McDonald, John Charles, 115, 305
McGlennon, David, 257
McKillip, Thomas B., 319
McKinley, Brian, 257
McNally, Edward J., 262–63, 277
McVey, David, 257
Mecca, Anthony, 257
mechanic, 104–6
Meister, Dan, 257
Meister, Ken, 257, 325
Melchert, Michael, 257
Melchior, William, 257
Melchiore, William, 257
Mendell, John, 115, 214–15, 302–4
Mendola, Guy Jr., 110, 276
Messino, Willie, 257
Metrick, Barry, 257
Michals, George, 257
Michelon, Ron, 257
Micus, Walter, 126
Milice, Robert, 257

Miller, Harvey, 257
Miller, Robert, 257
Miller, Walter, 238
Milos, Terrence, 257
Minarczyk, James, 257
Minaugh, Patrick, 257
Minkus, Sam, 98, 170, 257
Miraglia, James "Rocco/Roscoe," 271
Miranda rights, 45–46
Moccio, James, 257
Monday, Charles F., 310
money laundering, 131–32, 134, 141, 197–98
Monte, 125, 200
Monteleone, August, 257
Monteleone, John "Johnny Apes," 216, 227, 303
Moody, Ben, 257
More, Ronald, 257
More, Scott, 257
Moretti, Sal, 113–14
Moretti, Vincent, 113–15, 302–4
Morici, James, 257
Morici, Joseph, 257
Morsovillo, Dan, 257
Moschiano, Anthony, 275
Moskal, Stan, 257
Moy, Harvey, 257
Mulberg, Charles, 257
Murphy, Gerald, 257
Murphy, James, 257
Murray, Wilbur, 257

N

Najman, Robert, 149

narcotics trafficking, 131–32, 163, 197, 199, 250, 264–65, 275–76, 299, 312, 321
heroin trafficking, 132–34
Nardiello, Anthony, 257
National Guard, 74–75
National Publications in Chicago, 98
National Publications of Miami, 98
Nationwide News Service, 89
Navarro, Terry, 223
Naverro, Joseph, 257
Navigato, Thomas, 257
Nemirow, Henry, 257
New Deal, 238
N. Frpstis, Peter, 255
Nicholas, James, 106–7, 257
Nicholas, James "Jimmy," 104–7
Nicoletti, Charles "Chuck," 297
Nitti, Frank, 88, 237, 241
Nitti, Nick, 257
Nitz, James, 257
Nolan, James, 257
Nolfe, Anthony, 257
Nolfe, Steve, 257
Noorullah, Sultian, 257
Norton, Jim, 148–49, 171, 189, 248–50, 259
Norton, Michael, 229, 248–51
Norton, Mike, 248–51
Norton, Mitchell, 257
Nuttler, Max, 257

O

Oakes, Linda, 257
O'Brien, John, 257
O'Dell, Brett, 257

offtrack betting
  Chicago City operations, 87, 145, 163–64, 199
  New York City operations, 181, 199
O'Flynn, Kevin, 257
Ogilvie, Richard, 109–10
Ognibene, Joseph, 26–27
Oliva, Gary, 257
Oliver, Jack, 257
Oliver, James, 257
Olson, James, 257
omertà, 121
Orange Blossom jewelry store robbery, 215
organized crime, 87, 98, 121, 131, 135, 139, 141, 158, 168, 194, 198–99, 214, 253, 314, 319
Orlando, Anthony, 257
Orlando, Thomas, 257
Orozco, Eduardo, 134–35
Orsi, John, 257
Oshansky, Ben, 101, 257
Ostrowsky, Steven H., 295, 306
Otto, Jerry, 257
Our Lady of the Angels arson, 25–26, 28–30

P

Pace, Joseph, 257
Pacini, James, 257
Pacynski, Errol, 258
Padone (mob victim), 128–29
Pagounis, Billy, 258
Palaggi, James A., 301
Paloian, Emmett, 14, 155–58, 256
Paloian, Gregory "Emmett," 155, 256
Paloian, Gregory Emmett, 155–58
Palumbo, Lenny, 186–87
Panico, Anthony, 258
Panovich, James, 258
Papelli, Louie, 258
Park, Melrose, 145, 149, 178, 268–69, 278–79, 289–90, 292–93, 297, 308, 321
parlay-card gambling, 98, 167, 169–70, 173–74
Parrilli, Charles, 258
Parrilli, Louie, 258
Parrillo, August, 258
Parrillo, Paul, 258
Pascqual, Noli, 258
Pascucci, Joe, 258
Pasinski, Edward, 258
Pasinski, Eugene, 258
Patrick, Lenny, 89, 258
Pawlowski, Joseph, 258
Payton, Elvin, 250
Peara, George, 258
Pecucci, Frank, 64
Pedraza, Robert, 258
Pellegrino, James, 320
Pellicore (monsignor), 26–27
Pepitone, Joseph, 258
Perlman, Sheldon, 258
Perozzi, Tony, 258
Perrone, Frank, 258
Peters, Bob, 25–26, 28, 238
Peterson, Leroy, 258
Petrocelli
  Butch, 157, 188, 228, 290, 292, 298, 300, 303, 308–9

William "Butch," 157, 228, 258, 290, 292, 298, 300, 303, 308
William Joe "Butch," 157, 188, 228, 290, 298, 303, 309
Petronella, Anthony, 258
Pettit, Larry, 258
Phanthamaly, Proxay, 258
Philadelphia Inquirer, 88
Phillips, Jack, 258
Pierce (South Side mobster), 97, 283
Pierpont, Harry "Pete," 240–41
Pignato, Michael, 258
Pikarski, Richard, 258
Pilotto, Arthur, 258
Pinedo, Roman, 258
Pinto, Anthony, 258
Pinto, Bruce, 258
Piro, Frank, 258
Pitt, Maureen, 258
Plummer, Robert Hayden, 311
poker gambling, 104, 219
Polcheri, Ben, 258
policy racket, 137
Polino, Ray, 258
Polito, Joseph F., 280, 319
Ponti, Robert, 258
Ponzio, Anthony P., 278, 289
Poonbunker, Prakarn, 258
Pope, Albert, 258
Portnoy, Marshall, 258
Posner, Bernard "PP," 258
Powers, John Arthur, 262–63
Powers, Robert, 258
Pozsgay, Donald, 258
P. Paclke, Daniel, 257
Pratico, Louis, 279
Prestigacomo, Bernie, 258
Prestigacomo, Michael, 258

Preston, Donald, 258
Price, George, 258
Prignano, James, 258
Prio, Ross, 128, 137
prison, survival, 54
Provenzano, Mark, 258
Prushnick, Glenn, 258
Psiminas, Nick, 258
Public Enemies, 235–36, 238–40, 242, 244
Puerto Rican lottery, 128, 197–98, 200
Pufahl, Larry, 258
Puhl, David, 258
Puntillo, John, 258
Punzalan, Renaldo, 258
Purvis, Melvin, 235–37

Q

Quinn (Chicago fire chief), 75

R

Rabin, Henry, 258
Rachel, Arthur "the Brain," 230
Radtke, John, 258
Raganese, Michael, 271
Ragen, James, 87–89
Rainone, Mario, 258
Ranola, Sam, 258
Rantis, Socrates "Sam," 285–87
Rattaglia, Patrick, 258
Ray, James Earl, 72–73
Rediger, Ernest, 258
Reich, Gary, 258
Reichel, Paul, 258
Reid, John, 29–30
Reid, Susan, 258
Renno, Donald R., 115, 302–4

Resnick, Adam, 219–25, 258
Rhodes, Walter, 258
Ricciardi, Patrick "Patsy," 317
Riccio, Roger, 145, 149, 220, 258
Riccio, Roger "the Dodger," 143–46, 148–50, 220, 258
Richardson, Jacquelin, 258
Richardson, Rueben, 258
Rigan, Kenneth, 258
riot, Chicago, 74
   Robert Hall incident, 74–75
Rivera, Sam, 296
Roberson, James, 258
Roberts, Willard, 258
Robinson, Ed, 258
Robinson, Eddie, 128, 258
Rocco, Joseph, 258
Rodich, Jimmy, 258
Roebuck, Thomas, 258
Roemer, Bill, 174
Rogala, John, 258
Rogers, William, 258
Roman, Elmer, 258
Roman, Miguel, 258
Rosado, Beatrice, 250–51
Rose, Harry, 258
Rosenberg, Alan R., 281
Rosengard, Joseph, 258
Rosengard, Julius, 258
Rosenthal, Frank "Lefty," 98–99
Rossi, Louis, 258
Rothenbaum, Leslie, 258
Rotondo, Michael, 258
Rovelli, Salvatore, 119–20
Rudd, Darnell, 258
Russell, James, 258
Russell, Thomas, 258
Russell, Tim, 258
Russo (mobster), 122

Ruzich, Steven, 258
Ryan, Bernard F., 115, 302, 304–5
Rydz, Abraham, 196
Ryndak, Bruno, 258

S

Saladino, Frank, 215, 293–94, 303
Salerno, Robert, 258
Saletko, Morris, 300
Saletta, Frank, 258
Salvatore Gibbelina, 255
Sammarco, James, 258
Sampson, Clyde, 258
Santos, Melvin, 258
Saracco, Ben, 258
Saracco, James, 258
Saracco, Paulie, 119–20
Saraceno, Chris, 258
Saraceno, Natale, 258
Sarillo, Joe, 258
Sarillo, Joseph, 258
Sarno, Mike, 258
Saulter, Jean, 258
Saulters, Jean, 258
Savides, Chris, 258
Savides, Dino, 258
Scala, John, 258
Scalise, Jerry "One-Armed," 230–32
Scanlon, Jack, 258
Scavo, Philip, 270
Scavo, Phillip, 270–71
Schiersz, Ray, 258
Schimick, Tom, 258
Schneider, Howard, 258
Schneider, John R., 299

Schutte, Francis, 258
Scotland Yard, 72, 230–32
Scottie, Dan, 259
Seaberg, Darla, 259
Securities and Exchange Surveillance Commission (Japan), 139
Sedan, Volvo, 313–14
Segretti, Jeff, 259
Segretti, Michael, 259
Semla, James, 259
Senn, Phyllis, 259
Serritella, Chris, 259
Settino, Charles, 259
Shabas, Norman, 259
Shallow, Gerald, 108–9
Shamest, Al, 259
Shanley, William, 239
Shapiro, Moe, 259
Sheahan, Mike, 148, 179, 213
Sheehan, Mike, 179
Sheehan, Pat, 259
Sheehan, Phil, 259
Sheldon, Terry, 259
Sheppard, Carl, 259
shill, 104
Shoes (Jim Norton's store partner), 249
Silva, Joseph, 259
Simmons, Arthur, 259
Simone, William, 285–87
Sinclair Oil Company, 67–68
Singleton (John Dillinger's robbery accomplice), 54
Sinople, Louis, 259
Sitarski, Tom, 259
Skar, Manny, 277, 318
Skoka, Joseph, 259
Sloan, Thomas, 259

Sluyk, Gerrit, 259
Smith, Donald, 259
Smith, Hal, 145, 259, 316
Smith, L. C., 263
Smith, Michael, 259
Smith, Renee, 259
S. Mrozek, Bradley, 258
Sneyd, Ramon George. *See* Ray, James Earl
Solano, Vince, 124–25, 128, 200
Soleau, Mike, 259
Solone, Ralph, 259
Sommer, George, 259
Sommes, Greg, 259
Sorrentino, Alex, 273
Soupas, Steve, 259
Soverino, Frank, 259
Spano, Paul, 259
Spellman, John, 82–84
Spencer, Ray, 259
Speranza, Ernest, 259
Sperka, Edward, 259
Spilotro, Anthony, 259, 318
Spilotro, Anthony J. *See* Spilotro, Tony
Spilotro, Michael P., 318
Spilotro, Tony, 16–18, 115, 214, 271–72, 275, 277, 284, 288, 318
Spilotro, Victor, 259
Spina, Chris, 259
Sroki, Adam, 259
Starvos, Alex, 259
State's Attorney's Office, 80, 82, 99–100, 169
  Regan, Tom, 144
  Ward, Daniel P., 29
Stavropoulos
  Demitri "Jim," 259

Demitri "Jimmy," 149, 220–21, 259, 295, 301
Stella, Ronald, 259
Stellato, Anthony, 259
Stellman, Marvin, 259
Stellwagen, Dina, 259
Sterling, Tex, 259
Stluka, Vicky, 259
Stokes, Willie, 259
Stone, William, 259
Storino, Peter, 259
Strada, Robert, 259
Strange, Charles, 259
Strange, Willie, 259
Strocchia, Ralph, 157, 259
Subatich, Robert P., 312
Sugarman, Leslie, 171–74
Sugarman, Lester, 259
Suggs, Hayward, 259
Sullivan, Lang, 259
Sullivan, Pat, 259
Sullivan, Thomas, 259
Sum, Thomas, 259
Swanson, Donald. *See* Renno, Donald R.
Swider, James, 259
Szany, Robert, 259
Szyc, Richard, 259

T

Taglia, Sam, 321
Takenaka, Masahisa, 138
Talerico, Mike, 259
Taradash, Arnold, 259
Tarala, Edward, 259
Tarala, Greg, 259
Teinbelle, George, 259
Tennes, Mont, 87
Tenuta, Louie, 259
Tenuta, William, 259
Teske, Larry, 259
Testa, Albert "Transom," 268
Testa, Jesse, 259
Thanasouras, Mark C., 300
Theo, Joseph Frank, 298
Thomas, Ted, 259
Tito, Anthony, 259
Tom, Ray, 125
Tominello, Ray, 259
Tonelli, Mario "Motts," 203–6, 208–10
Torello, James "Turk," 284, 293–94
Torello, John, 259
Touhy, Roger, 237–38
Trafficante, Santo, 194–95
traffic tickets, 19–21, 24
Tragas, George, 18, 63–65
Tragas, Louis "Louie," 62–69
Trapp, Linda, 259
Tripp, Linda, 259
Trobiani, Alfonso, 259
Trobiani, Ralph, 259
Troiani, Alfred, 259
Trotta, Carmen, 282
Truppo, Bobby, 259
Tucker, Forrest, 79, 83, 85
Tumlin, Paul, 259
Turano, Antonio, 134
Turgeon, Arthur, 259
Turzitti, Anthony, 145

U

undercover methods, 163
FBI surveillance, 174

parlay-card investigation,
    167–71, 173–74
things not to do, 173
video poker machines
    investigation, 176, 178, 180,
    215
wirerooms investigation,
    164–65, 167
Urbanetti, Carl, 259
Urso, Frank, 259

V

Vaca, Robert Martinez, 306
Valente, Dino J., 304
Valente, Gerald J., 270
Valentzas, Eleftherios "Nick," 309
Van Houghton, Robert, 259
Vanloon, Randy, 259
Van Meter, Homer, 56, 235, 238, 240
Van Wilzenburg, Adam, 259
Vasukri, Vathanasombat, 259
Vaughm, Anthony, 259
Vaughn, Tony, 188, 190
Veesart, Ted, 259
Vegas, Las, 91, 115, 132, 214, 224, 301, 303
Vehla, Paul, 259
Venetucci, Donald, 259
Vente, Peter, 259
Verlick, Anthony, 98, 170–73, 259
Vermeyen, Lane, 259
Vermeyens, Fred, 259
Vertucci, Joseph, 259
video poker machine gambling,
    176–82, 185, 322–23, 325
Villerreal, James, 295–96

Vine, Irving, 274
Vivirito, August "Gus," 269
Vodvarka, Albert, 259
Vogue Printing, 172, 174
Volanti, Henry, 270, 272
Volpentesta, Joe, 259
Vuletich, Daniel, 259

W

Wakita, Mitsuri, 278
Wakuta, Mitsuri, 278
Wallach, Robert, 259
Wally (Herion's partner), 78–84
Walsh, James, 259
Wasik, James, 259
Wasz, Bruce, 259
Weber, Thomas, 259
Weis, Adolph, 259
Wheatly, William, 259
Wheatly Jr., William, 259
Whirity, John, 260
White, Andrew, 260
White, Charles William, 276
Whitfield, David, 260
Wicker, Paul, 260
William J. McCarthy, 271–72
Williams (judge), 54
Williams, Joan, 277
Williams, Judge, 54
Williams, Orion, 287
Wilson, Donald, 260
Wilson, Robert, 260
Wilson, Tom, 260
Wiltse, Carl, 265
Wing, Joe, 260
Wingertner, Robert, 260
Winkler, Warren, 260
Wise, Robert, 49

Wisniewski, John, 260
Witsman, Bill, 110
Wojcik, Jerry, 260
Wren, Donald, 260
Wright, Jerry, 260
W. Stein, Kurt, 259
Wysocki, Stanley, 260

Y

yakuza, 137–41
   child pornography, 139–40
   Ichiwa-kai, 139
   methamphetamine trade, 141
   Yamaguchi-gumi, 138–40
Yale, Jesse, 180, 260
Yama, James, 260
Yaras, Davey, 89
Yaras, Leonard, 315
Yario, Frank, 260
Yario, James, 260
Yavitz, William, 260
Yoeun, Son, 260
Young, Kelvin, 306
Young, Melvin, 306

Z

Zagorski, Lottie, 260
Zamora, Oscar, 260
Zamora, Victor, 260
Zanon, William, 260
Zel Olken, 257
003, 221–22
Zidek, David, 260
Zindell, Jim, 260
Zitzer, Tom, 260
Zivilich, Paul, 260
Zizzo, Thomas, 260
Zucker, Glen, 260
Zymantas, August, 260

Made in the USA
Columbia, SC
04 January 2020